"You don't have to listen to the people who tell you you've got to leave an indelible mark on this planet or you've got to change the world. It's something that you are already doing by just living life. So, you know, don't get tricked by your ego. Leave it behind and just live a good and wholesome life. "

Cricketer Kumar Sangakkara

PUBLISHED BY
SRI SERENDIPITY PUBLISHING
WORLDWIDE
65 Leyn Baan Street, Galle Fort,
Sri Lanka
Tel: +94 776838659 or email
julietcoombe@yahoo.com.au

First published by
Sri Serendipity Publishing
in Sri Lanka

ISBN 978-955-0000-005

Around The Galle Fort in 80
Lives
By Juliet Coombe

Words copyright
Sri Serendipity Publishing House
(Juliet Coombe)

Photographic copyright
Sri Serendipity Publishing House
(Juliet Coombe, Izzy Ashton,
Atheeq Ifthikar Mahuroof, Dr.
Janaka Ruben,
Stephen LaBrooy,
Dominic Sansoni,
John Churchill, Carly Minsky,
Mohamed Musfir, Galle Fort
Hotel photo library, and Robert
Sedgley drawing page 305)

Research
From
2005 - 2015

AUTHOR OF THE BOOK	Juliet Coombe
RESEARCH AND ADDITIONAL WRITING	Izzy Ashton
PROOFING	Mr. Keeler and Izzy Ashton
DESIGN	Kavinda Dhammika, designerkavinda@gmail.com
LAYOUTS	Kavinda Dhammika
TRANSLATOR & ASSISTANT RESEARCHER	Aslam Anver
PRINTED BY	Nethu Print Solution, Niroshan Fernando
MAP DESIGNED BY	Juliet Coombe and Kavinda Dhammika and Overseen by the Galle Heritage Foundation
COVER FRONT AND BACK BY ARTIST	Asia H.

Although the authors and Sri Serendipity Publishing House try to make the information as accurate as possible up to the point of going to press. We accept no responsibility for any loss, injury or inconvenience sustained by anyone using this book. In the case of the Fort Jumper characters we do not recommend anyone under any circumstances having a go.

Since writing the first edition of Around The Galle Fort in 80 Lives during the height of the civil war, Juliet has set up a full time publishing house based out of Galle Fort. For more information on this and other titles go to www.sriserendipity.com. If you have any interesting historical or personal stories about the ancient citadel do please drop Juliet a line for the next edition julietcoombe@yahoo.com.au.

The author feels that travellers are beginning to want to discover the depths of a place, its society and complex traditions, rather than just skim the surface. She hopes this exciting new edition of the book will persuade those coming to Galle Fort for a day to linger a little longer and meet some of the characters that make it such a special place.

Sri Lanka has been occupied by the Portuguese, Dutch and English, which has resulted in a rich language with different ways of spelling names and everyday items. We have tried to be as accurate and consistent as possible. Please let us know for future editions if we have failed at any point in the book to achieve this. N.B. All our references are from the time when Galle Fort was Tarshish and are from King Solomon's ancient dictionary, when life was simpler and how you spelt something didn't really matter.

This book is dedicated to His Honour Judge Coombe & Juliet's two Fort sons, Amzar and Samad, and all the inhabitants of Galle Fort for their time and support with this book.

Contents

DIVE INTO ASIA'S MOST EXCITING LIVING SEA FORT, FLAG ROCK

80 Lives doesn't sound like much. How do you capture the smells, the shadows, the sounds, and the changing faces of a four-hundred-year-old marvel, with such a small gathering? You shall soon see.

If the stories are to be believed, and there is no reason to doubt them, yours truly was potty-trained in the Galle Fort. At 15 Parawa Street, to be precise, under the kind supervision of Aunty Moninna Goonawardana and her husband Ranjit, who both featured in the last volume of Juliet's wonderful labour of love, passion, curiosity and mild insanity.

Like with the previous edition, this one comes with a keen eye for a brilliant image, an eager ear for a good story and a shrewd sense of history, one that engages with the past, while celebrating the carnival that is the present.

Galle Fort has enjoyed a visible renaissance over the past ten years and Juliet has chronicled it lovingly. In this volume we have a charming parade of eccentrics, goat ladies, astrologers, gentlemen abroad, jumpers, treasure hunters, cave men, crooners, lighthouse keepers and soldiers. Juliet's camera catches the light bouncing off poster shops, antique houses, monkeys, craftspeople, cricket games and witch doctors. There are tales of love, ghost stories and legal thrillers here. And plenty of room for glorious food shots.

Since mastering the use of my bowels, I have then crawled onto the ramparts, tumbled by the lighthouse and scuffed my knees on the Fort's paved streets. My family returned every year and there were always new places to play and new people to play with. These days I travel the Fort on bike or pushing a pram, and it still works its magic on me.

It is on these journeys that 80 Lives feels like more than you think. If you lay 80 Lives back to back (at three lives a century), it'll take you to the beginning of Lanka's history, with a prince landing on a shore. It'll remind you of how many have landed on the shores close to the Fort. Of how many left their traces here. Of how many decided to stay.

And it's then that you realize that the Fort is more than a sum of its parts or of its pasts. It is more than its many places of worship, its quirks of architecture, its strange characters and its quaint cul-de-sacs.

It is living and it is breathing, and will continue to evolve and shed its skin. And likewise these books will continue to grow. They will keep a living breathing account of the Fort, its changing face and all the people who share it. They will preserve moments and stories that will grow with the telling. They will tell us that the Fort belongs to everyone and that everyone may be touched by it.

Thanks for all the hard work Juliet. May there be many more lives and many more stories to come.

'Shehan Karunatilaka is a Sri Lankan writer most notable for his book *Chinaman: The Legend of Pradeep Mathew* which won many awards.'

Parakrama
Dahanayake
Galle Heritage
Foundation
Chairman
Galle Heritage
Centre for
visitors to the
Fort, Baladaksha
Mawatha, Galle
&
No. 212 1/1
Wakwella Road
Galle
www.galleheritage.
gov.lk
Tel: 0777721547

Asia's most exciting sea Fort is at the crossroads of massive commercial changes and the greatest challenge today is to maintain its rich history while also trying to keep the original Fort people in situ. But to survive Galle Heritage Foundation recognises that livelihoods need to be created, though not at the expense of the heritage of the buildings. The Chairman of The Galle Heritage Foundation, Parakrama Dahanayake says we have to think of how the Galle Fort fits into the country and the world: "Some people in our society are trying to use heritage to divide people, as can be seen particularly in the Northern and Eastern Provinces, where the old monuments are being claimed by some to belong to Buddhists and others to Tamils. What I want is to use heritage to unite people and bring about lasting peace, because what you want them to understand is, Galle Fort is not just the heritage of the people of Galle, it's a shared heritage for all of us. Of course it's a very diverse country with diverse cultures, diverse religions, people with different beliefs but that does not mean that we should be divided. On the contrary the heritage has come about by embracing diversity, and these diversities should be seen as a uniting factor, as this is how the common heritage has been enriched."

The Galle Heritage Foundation is passionate about making everyone understand the value of keeping the living heritage alive, demonstrating this through exhibitions at the Maritime Museum and discussions within the community on the importance of the various architectures and keeping them intact, as this is where the real value of the buildings lie. "All over the world they have this conflict between heritage management and people who want to improve their livelihoods and quality of life. One way of doing this is by using heritage as a draw for tourism, and this is where we have to strike a balance. It's useless having the heritage site unless it is going to benefit the people living there, otherwise there will come a time when people do not want to maintain their part of it." The Chairman says, "It's a shift but it's a good development because you can't just isolate a heritage site and keep it time locked. It's called a living site and thus change is inevitable. It is directly linked to the lives of the people so that is why we are promoting the homestay initiative as much as possible so people won't sell their properties. Keep your properties but convert some of the property, some rooms, and use it for tourism. Even if you want to have a souvenir or jewellery shop in part of the building it's ok, unless it harms the heritage structure."

"The project restoring 55 historic houses in Galle Fort has social, cultural, and religious aspects. One of the most serious architectural changes done to the Dutch period houses was the

This is the historic dungeon museum with a model of a Dutch soldier telling an African slave how to build the historic walls

bricking up of the colonnaded verandas during the last century, a practice formerly adopted by the Muslim majority in the Fort' (it is not so much because they were Muslims but because they were desert dwellers). Some foreign sociologists inquired as to why we told them to open up those facades, as it's wrong to tell them to change that which is against their culture. We never forced them to do that though for ventilation purposes, it's better to open the verandas up. The practice probably originated from desert living where it is sensible to stop the sand blowing into the buildings. If you look at the original countries of many that have moved to the Fort, there may be practical reasons why certain things were done to buildings but these might not be appropriate when they come to a place like Sri Lanka."

"The project was ground breaking for the whole of Sri Lanka as it was the first time that private owners in a heritage site or elsewhere were helped to maintain their historic homes specifically through a project funded by foreign grants. Even in Kandy the private owners had to do the restoration entirely from their own pockets."

"My vision for the Galle Fort is for it to continue to possess its essential quietness, its essential flavour. The essential quality of the site should be there and should not be harmed by ill thought out changes. "Your suggestion to build a period boat, a model of 'Avondster', to take tourists around the Galle area to get a better idea of how merchant sea life really was, is good as activities with the sea and with the history of Galle's ancient harbour are key to enlarging the range of things people can do here."

"It is important not to constrain ourselves with the technical issues of heritage management: we should always look at the broader picture. Of primary importance is unity and peace in the country. Everybody's efforts should be focused in that direction and then we will have a long term heritage that we can be proud of."

INTRODUCTION TO
GALLE FORT

11

This gate stands at the entrance of one of the Fort's original ammunition storage areas

"Before our trading posts, our plundering, our tall ships created this port and this town, there was nothing here but a large village of acrobatic coconut pickers, fishermen tossed high in the spray, cinnamon peddlers governed by a Dutch pastor who wore a wig and no doubt treated himself with mercury"
Nicolas Bouvier
"The Scorpion-Fish"
Stayed at 22 Hospital Street, Galle Fort

Galle Fort – two words synonymous with the sheer gall and absolute force it takes to usher in with gravitas the gravity of their meaning – pronounce it proper or be caught between a rock and a hard place and what with rising ramparts walls all around there ain't really a place you can run, except maybe to one of the secret beaches that nestle along the perimeters of a street once known as Indigo. Enter the old fortress built out of breathing corals as the black tunnel gate opens up into a gash of bellowing air, with distended creepers riding pillion on giant Banyan trees hobnobbing with an ancient merchant caste.

A strange choreography can always be detected here, with the musical call to prayer emanating from the mosque or the temple's sound system merging with the toots of ice cream vendors' bicycle horns and other hot and spicy snacks and pickle vendors plying the sonorities of their trade as the Indian Ocean thunders and whooshes by, barfing on the black rocks its named after.

Its history as a series of huge spice storehouses, a secure vantage point of military importance, is buoyed by its lofty, grandiose colonial architecture and precariously narrow streets filled at night with an exceedingly large number of closely fitted, harrowing houses reminiscent of a B-movie backlot from the days of German Expressionism, and past the army camps - a reminder of dues paid in blood to the nation, on to the spooky lament of the white cathedral that is the Dutch Reformed church, Galle Fort, all of which awakens within one that which is primal in man, the desire to explore the many faces of its dungeons and crypts, lairs and corridors, before delving into the dark placenta of black magic replete with chicken blood and cow heads buried in back gardens from sacrifices made for one's first born, and come back from the murky depths with a brightly tentacled octopus slobbering all over your hand.

Reinventing itself over the centuries, even decades and sometimes even daily seems to be second nature to Galle Fort and the joie de vivre of the inhabitants, the young and the old, the natives and the foreigners, is seen in gusto in the modern shop designs, the medley of restaurants and the joyous flights of fancy found in the new boutique hotels and the splendid Dutch Hospital complex.

Around the Fort in 80 Lives, a decade on from when the first book was researched will take you into the ever changing living history of this exciting sea-faring maritime Fort and its people, who have experienced in ten years the world's worst tsunami, the tail end of Asia's longest civil war and now peace and the assorted issues that revolve around the increasing commercialisation of this incredible UNESCO Heritage listed citadel. The book allows you to meet some of the special people that make

"The Fort is 400 years old and over those centuries has been under the command of the Portuguese, the Dutch (VOC), the British and now finally the Sri Lankans themselves. Evidence of each of these nationalities can be seen in both the architecture of the Fort and the legacies that were left behind"

The lighthouse was built by the British in 1938

"As a result of the 2004 tsunami, 230,000 people in 14 different countries lost their lives. No one within the Fort's walls was killed"

up this four hundred year old Fort- a unique environ that was once the capital of the Southern Province and the country's main gateway to the world.

The history of old Galle Fort is a tempestuous one and despite numerous invasions, different colonial rulers, the 2004 Boxing Day tsunami and a Tamil Tiger attack on the naval base across the bay in 2006, it remains totally intact and is considered one of the world's greatest examples of 17th Century colonial fortification.

Some say it's protected by the tomb of a Muslim saint on the beach just outside the Fort walls on the Indian Ocean side by the army camp, which miraculously purifies salty seawater and turns it into pure drinking water. Others claim that King Solomon left behind the key to the universe, which acts as a totem against all evil and then there are the magical sea rocks that surround the Fort walls, which the locals say are bewitched, protecting it from the unpredictable sea, acting as breakers against the waves so that people can swim all year round in the waters directly around the Fort walls.

This tree is the 'wig Banyan:' it looks like a woman's long wig

"Amazingly during the 30 year long Civil War, the Fort was never attacked although the Sea Tigers (part of the Tamil Tigers), disguising themselves as fishermen, attacked the Maritime Base in the Galle harbour in 2006."

As you walk from the Galle main town bus stand, past the world famous Galle international cricket stadium, fishermen will try to sell you tuna, butter fish or the catch of the day, and then the noise of bartering vanishes as you walk through the archway of the old gate, made of shells taken from a ship's ballast, coral and clay, into this tiny citadel of around two thousand people. It is a place where you will find everything from a treasure hunter to time locked historical houses. Like all cities there is a naughty boy whose exploits are legendary and an expert diver called Noor who harnesses giant octopus as well as a lad that uncovers bounty from four hundred year old shipwrecks, a mischievous travelling ginger tea seller and a hundred gem merchants and wickedly talented chutney makers whose produce used to stop sailors from getting scurvy. There is the house that was a pigsty, which supplied the rich Dutch merchants with pork, one that was a horse's stable, and houses that had milking parlours in their tiny backyards. It is a place in which the mosque trustee and the Buddhist monk have regular telephone conversations and where all religions live in harmony

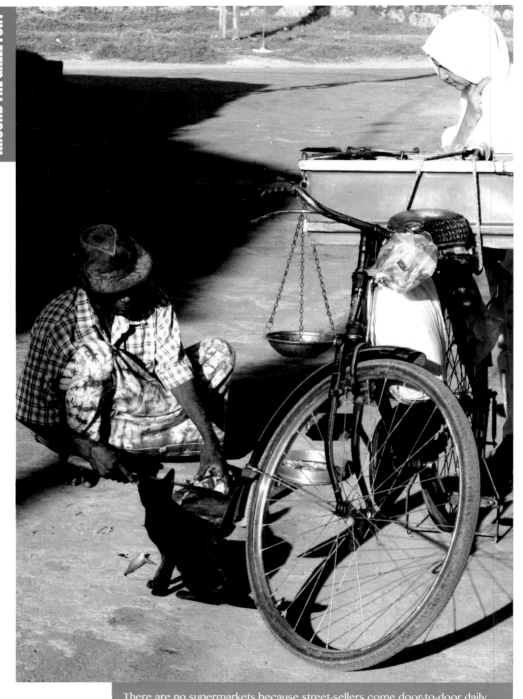

There are no supermarkets because street-sellers come door-to-door daily

despite the fact that just outside the walls there are from time to time religious uprisings and ethnic unrest.

As you wander and get lost in the maze of backstreets, old men will accompany you and talk proudly about the various theories of Galle's true origins, stories that you can enjoy hotly debating over sweet cups of fresh ginger or mint tea. Fazal on Leyn Baan Street at the Royal Dutch Café with a little encouragement will show you his historical collection of china plates and his album of photographs showing what happened on the day the tsunami hit the Fort and Galle New Town. Fazal loves to share information handed down over seven generations through his family and each time you go to his café you will find out a little bit more about the Fort. Wherever you wander someone will have a story to tell about the area - such as the Fort as the legendary city of Tarshish of biblical times and the place where King Solomon, the first foreigner to arrive in Sri Lanka, obtained chests full of gems and spices to woo the Queen of Sheba.

Some of the Muslims will debate this point saying that the Moors have been trading for thousands of years in these waters, and then there are those who say the Portuguese were the first foreigners to come to Galle and build this enigmatic Fort of war known in colonial times as the 'Black Fort' in order to protect this ancient trading port in the middle of the world. Parts of these walls can still be seen in Law Court Square by the Maritime Museum. In the National Museum by the Amangalla Hotel on Church Street you will discover the official line on the matter, which describes how the first recorded ship arrived accidentally under Captain Lourenco de Almedia in 1505, when his boat was driven off course from the Maldives and had to take shelter in Galle's harbour. Legend has it that on arriving the Portuguese heard a cock crow from a rock (cock is galo in Portuguese) and as a result named this new port Galo. The other theory is that Galle means stones in Singhalese and the Fort is indeed

"It has been suggested that Galle was the ancient seaport of Tarshish from which King Solomon is said to have bought spices, gems, peacock feathers and other treasures"

19

surrounded by treacherous rocks. Recognizing Sri Lanka's central trading position, the Portuguese invaders built a Fort to protect the harbour. The Dutch later destroyed this structure with the exception of Zwart Bastion. The truth lies somewhere between the official and the unofficial history.

Merchants for centuries have come from all over the world to trade with Sri Lanka and many of them dazzled by the island's magnificent beauty decided to settle in Galle. These gem, gold and silver traders came from Portugal, Morocco, Arabia, Malaysia, China and Southern India, each leaving their mark, which you can see both in the current mix of people living in the Fort, the food and through the artifacts on show in the National Museum on Church Street and in the historical archives in Colombo.

"Lourenco de Almedia was originally sent by his father to explore the Maldives, to establish alliances and to form trade relations. He of course did much more than that"

The three rooms in the National Museum are full of exquisite colonial swords, tortoise shell fans, intricate ivory relics and hand carved wooden jewellery boxes. At the entrance a map explains the layout of the area covering the five main streets that include Rope Walk 'Leyn Baan' and Lighthouse Street 'Zeeburg Street', illustrating how little has changed since 1640 when Dutch traders forced the Portuguese out and built the current hundred acres Galle Fort, which in 1988 became a UNESCO World Heritage-listed site.

The only subsequent changes that were made were by the British who completely took over in 1815 and remained in power until Sri Lanka gained Independence in February 1948. The British only made small architectural alterations to the Fort's existing structure firstly adding a second entrance gate in 1887 to help with the congestion (now known as the Main Gate), the Clock Tower overlooking the cricket ground in 1888, the iconic white, still functioning Lighthouse on the south side of the Fort built in 1938, and white picket fencing to the porches. In addition they added a British Coat of Arms over the entrances of the Old

Sculptures of the Portuguese conquerors of the Fort

"Jayawardene & Sangakkara set a world record against South Africa in 2006 when they scored a partnership of 624 runs. They both now own houses in the Fort"

Dutch Gate and created lovely rose gardens that can still be seen in a number of private houses' colonnaded courtyards along Pedlar Street. Writer, E. Jackson summed the place up by saying "the peculiar style of houses, the overhanging trees...the balmy and delicious atmosphere...tend to throw an air of novelty and romance around."

Today you can find people from all over the world living in the ancient citadel walls including legendary cricketers, Mahela Jayawardene and Kumar Sangakkara. This living historical city is not only safe,

The Fort offers many an experience, like having a 2 metre long python draped around your neck

"The Fort is majority Muslim but is also home to many Buddhists, Roman Catholics, Hindus, Christians and one Burgher family, a peaceful city where they can all happily co-exist"

but also a great example of how Muslims happily run businesses alongside Buddhists, Roman Catholics, Tamils and in many cases have mixed religious marriages. Here at least it is believed that all religions are one and should live harmoniously and peacefully together.

As you continue on through the Fort's backstreets you will come across random cows, meandering monitor lizards, naughty purple leaf monkeys and street sellers on rickety old bikes selling bright sunflower yellow

23

coconuts to drink, the ubiquitous rice and curry served in earthenware pots, fish sellers, the lottery guy and sari seller. If you wait long enough everything you need to stock a house with will pass by in front of you from handmade household goods created from woven bamboo to exotic tropical fruit and vegetable carts, which go daily from house to house. If the heat gets too much you can always stop at one of the many family run street cafés like Punto on Pedlar Street or restaurants like Elita on Hospital Street with great views of the harbour and try the national dish of hoppers, a sort of squashed pancake made from fermented palm sap or sip on a cool glass of seasonal fresh fruit juice.

"A cousin R.L. Brohier, wrote a few months after Nesta's passing at the N.O.H (now the Amangalla): "For a very long time to come, in its corridors and rooms and in the quiet well-laid garden, that presence of a gracious lady, Nesta Ephraums Brohier, will linger."

Amangalla Hotel, originally built to be the Dutch governor's residence was previously the site of the world famous New Oriental Hotel. An enchanting place to escape the heat, here fans whirr as young honeymoon couples sit sipping champagne on the main veranda overlooking the ramparts, bankers debate Sri Lanka's investment potential, politicians schmooze, and NGOs nut out plans to save the world whilst staff will happily talk about the history of the Fort. It's an eclectic mix just like the hotel itself. The hotel's name comes from aman, or "peace" in Sanskrit, and 'galla', the Sinhalese name for the town of Galle. In 2004, the Aman hotel group returned the place to its former glory, retaining the hotel's walls and original polished teak floorboards. The Zaal – the Great Dutch Hall with its chandeliers and plush furnishings is not only the main fine dining area but also a meeting place for writers, movers and shakers and future world leaders.

Next door to this elegant Aman hotel on the corner of Church and Middle Street is the eccentric Old Dutch Reformed Church originally built in 1755. Inside, the floor of the church is a stunning mosaic of original paved Dutch tombstones adorned with a regal coat of arms and the occasional skull and crossbones. The friendly

The President, Mahinda Rajapaksa comes to Galle for many reasons, one of which is to meet with his horoscope reader

"The Post Office building has also been the British Commissariat Store and the Dutch Administrators & Assistants quarters"

caretaker will happily take you round on a fifteen-minute tour of the graveyard and church, including pointing out the catacombs where the poor used to get buried.

To find out more about the area pop into the library on the same road built in 1832, and if you have any postcards needing to be sent then nothing is more fun than Asia's oldest post office next door. The old guys will happily package things up in brown paper and hand stamp your mail whilst eating rice and curry or if it's the monsoon season they will amuse you by juggling buckets to catch the rain coming through the historic tiled roof.

As the temperature starts to drop you will see locals leaving their houses and heading off to the ramparts, the circular Fort walls, to enjoy short eats on their daily strolls in the cool of the late afternoon sea breeze. Here they exchange gossip, play cricket, sell Dutch style lace work, hand carved wooden troops of elephants and magic boxes to hide your valuables in. They also come to sit on the original walls made from corals, lime and mud to watch

The rampart walls come alive at sunset

up to four of the world's seven different types of turtles appearing around 5pm opposite the Buddhist temple on Rampart Street.

"Marine turtles have been roaming the world's oceans for about 190 million years. Today four out of the seven species that remain regularly visit Sri Lanka's beaches to nest"

These turtles escaped the hatcheries broken during the Boxing Day tsunami and have subsequently made the Fort their new home. Another highlight is watching the crazy Rasta village boys' freestyle jump thirty-five feet from Flag Rock at Lighthouse Bastion into the sea often with only four feet of water and inches away from a series of lethal rocks. Here you can enjoy some fresh fruit from Flag Rock market and find a seat in the cool of the trees, as there is nothing more relaxing than looking out at the azure crystal clear Indian Ocean and views of the surrounding headlands. Andrew Carnegie said in 1879 "there is no prettier sea shore in the world, nor more beautiful surf." Just after the sun sets you will hear the daily lilting sounds of the mosque calling the Muslim community to prayer. Old men and small boys will scurry past to get to the prayer hall in time for evening prayers. You can't miss them in their white kurtha traditional Islamic dress and woven head caps used to keep their hair firmly in place. During Ramadan the city seems to fall asleep for a month while fasting takes place from dawn to dusk reminding everyone rich and poor alike of the importance of water and what it is like to be poor. During this time donations are made to the surrounding villages and the fast is broken nightly with dates from Mecca and a thick porridge.

A lovely way to finish off a day of exploring this ancient citadel is to head back into the old quarter and spend an hour or so at the Historical Mansion on Leyn Baan Street, which gives a fascinating insight into the history of the area. In the main courtyard you can watch a local woman demonstrating the intricacies of Portuguese and Dutch style lace making and an old man recreating the ancient art of gem polishing.

"'I am quite sure there is no more picturesque a sight than the fishermen drawing in their nets...while the beach is alive with women and children in bright colours anxiously watching the result'
Andrew Carnegie"

Afterwards you can wander freely through the mansion and enjoy several rooms packed with an eccentric colonial collection of artifacts including a newspaper cutting of Queen Elizabeth's visit in 1954, and many items found from shipwrecks. In the end room there is a detailed display of raw gemstones. Looking at the glittering draws of sparkling sapphires and moonstones I can see why the Muslim traders, when they first came to Sri Lanka dubbed the island "serendib - island of jewels". From that came the word serendipity - the art of making joyous discoveries and nowhere is this truer than in time locked Galle Fort. So go on, walk in through the tunneled 17th Century Dutch gate and immerse yourself in the fascinating lives that exist within its ancient walls. Some of you may never want to leave and indeed many never will. All journeys end somewhere, yet for some the endings to their stories actually come with new beginnings, fresh starts or uprooting from one street to the next or even rekindling one's burning interests and reawakening to

The Meeran Mosque was built in 1904

Every street is named after a part of the Fort's history, legacies from the colonial period

what is one's own. People whether they are fugitives by choice or are restless seekers seem in most cases to find an oasis of resplendent calm in the safety of Galle Fort's ancient walls, and yet it is difficult to pinpoint whether it is in fact the long stretches of solitude one can revel in while walking the precarious ledges of the ramparts beneath the moon or if it is the raucous chatter of daytime with the verve of the children playing outside.

Or is it the friendly reassurance one gleans from the sight of the Fort elders ambling about their ways with poise and aging grace? The Galle Fort is its own world and never has and never will care too much for that which happens outside the walls. It is self-sufficient and even its most hardened inhabitants who hail from all walks of life seem to embody the conviction that Galle Fort is all that really matters, and walking out catching that last glimpse through the cricket ground entrance gate one feels like one has walked through the annals of a nation's glory, all the more enriched from the experience of a city, that to many people may look like a heart with its many bastions acting as veins or the womb canal path in which all of us wish to return into a world of safety and comfort, something most of the world has long since forgotten.

Here the tap of the typewriter is as important as a spoon turning in a cup of spice tea either to drink or tell your fortune. For anyone fortunate enough to visit this place remember one thing: you will never forget the bewitching effect it will have on you.

"You could say that this island has been given over to magic since the day it rose out of the sea"
Nicolas Bouvier "The Scorpion-Fish"

"Galle Fort is a city of five streets, one cricket ground, one clock tower, one lighthouse, more jewellery shops than restaurants and countless numbers of fascinating people just waiting to tell their stories"

31

History of the Fort:

Galle Fort was first built by the Portuguese in 1588 but was fortified by the Dutch during the 17th century from 1649 onwards.

UNESCO was founded on 4th November 1946 and its main goal is "to contribute to the building of peace, the eradication of poverty, sustainable development and intercultural dialogue through education, the sciences, culture, communication and information.

The Fort became a UNESCO World Heritage Site in 1988 on account of its unique exposition of "an urban ensemble, which illustrates the interaction of European architecture and South Asian traditions from the 16th to the 19th centuries.

The Amangalla Hotel was the first one built in the Fort. It was originally built in 1684 to house the Dutch governor and his staff. It was then converted into a hotel and named as the New Oriental Hotel in 1863, catering to European passengers travelling between Europe and Galle Fort in the 19th century.

The official name of the Fort, used by UNESCO, is Old Town of Galle.

The Galle International Cricket ground was originally built as a racecourse in 1876. It was only declared as a cricket stadium in 1927, hosting its first first-class match on 29th February 1984, with the first test match held on 3rd June 1998.

HISTORIC FAMILIES

35

Galle Fort's Taj Mahal

The Amangalla Hotel Formally The New Oriental Hotel
10 Church Street
0912233388

It is as Ernest Hemingway puts it in The Snows of Kilimanjaro – "as wide as all the world, great, high and unbelievably white in the tropical sun of the South." The influence of Batavia or modern day Indonesia, which was a Dutch stronghold, permeates the architecture. The New Oriental Hotel's chequered past, is a wild one as its earliest patrons were boorish dipsomaniacs in the form of soldiers and sailors, who even managed to incite an unruly mob to riot in the hotel's bar where infamous mano-a-mano fights have been aplenty.

Yet the romance of the place is in its quietude, in the heavy wooden Dutch furniture and finishes where, if a voice rises above a whisper, the tiny cobwebs would shudder, and along the tunnel-like corridors that lead from ultra glamorous rooms to pint sized courtyards and thence to the back garden that is walled and the abundance of foliage, trees and open doorways that contain mysteries in an array of boxes, trunks, all gathering legends.

Number Ten, Church Street, Galle Fort has had an amazing history reading through the archives, which has taken it from a garrison for Dutch soldiers in 1684 to the first hotel in Sri Lanka in 1863 to a luxurious, boutique

Nesta celebrating her 90th birthday with Rainey.

Like Havana in Cuba, Galle Fort has many classic cars due to the 100% tax that makes everyone look after their old bangers.

establishment that is considered very much a home away from home for the rich and the discerning. It is older even than the Grand Oriental Hotel in the capital Colombo, thus making the name 'new' somewhat misleading. In fact it is the longest continuously run hotel in Asia. The first documented photo of the hotel is from 1866, and another photo in the library archive album shows the hotel 54 years later, still a beacon of elegance in 1920 and one of the great dames of Asia that everyone should visit at least once in their lives.

Nesta Brohier nee Ephramus ran The New Oriental Hotel practically all her life and her family did so too for two generations before that. In the Amangalla library there is a small museum in honour of her as well as a plaque in the church above her pew. The whole Ephramus family is buried in the Dutch Reformed churchyard across the road, which can be seen from the Amangalla Hotel and Olivia, the woman who beautifully restored the historic building and was the opening manager, comments "they still keep an eye on us." In February 2003 when the Aman group closed the New Oriental Hotel, it had become so run-down that the only thing that you could order was a

"The librarian Nora Roberts' words are as true today as they were in the 1930s, 'Daily, thousands of workers and school children pour in at the two Fort gates. In the evening when the offices and schools are closed, kindly ghosts move up and down in the quiet Galle Fort Town – and over the harbour, under a moon, whisper of the past on Ravana's Hills.'"

"Rainey still owns the garden house near the pool they built together and if he is away do try to book it through the hotel as many honeymoon couples tell me that you can feel the power of love envelope you from the moment you walk through the cottage door."

Lion beer, a lime soda or alternatively be taken on a tour around the garden for 100 rupees (less than a US dollar). Mr. Zecha, Olivia's boss and the founder of the Aman Group knew Nesta personally and so from the beginning it was vital to him to keep the hotel as much as possible like The New Oriental with the original doors, floors and much of the furniture being repaired and kept in place. The Amangalla as it is now called retains all the grandeur in service of an old colonial house rather than a typically posh hotel.

Looking through the historic album in the wonderful hotel library you will find an image of Nesta celebrating her 90th birthday on the 7th May 1995 with Rainey, who was over forty years younger than her. Here you can see them, holding hands and various records in the comments book show that she was still very much an influential and charismatic character in the hotel even at that ripe old age. She kept two Dalmatian dogs, also

The Amangalla is right next door to the Dutch Reformed Church

"Room 25, where the death of the living haunts, the memories of the dead linger, and the knick-knacks of shared lives and articulated moments, create a presence, an aura of sorts that is ad-infinitum."

shown in the photograph from her 90th birthday. This is further confirmed by talking to Rainy about his former friendship with one of the great hotel dames of Asia.

By 1981, the hotel's attractive feature was its 'old world charm', as mentioned in various guest comments from this year, whilst another comment from the same year describes the hotel as 'a compliment to the strong woman who expects to go to heaven'. Guests were surprisingly sentimental about their time at the hotel, one even writing that year that, 'the other part of my heart is still here when I am gone'. In 1982 one guest credited Nesta Brohier with the comment 'Mrs Brohier deserves an architect's degree. HONORIS CAUSA.'

By 1993, the hotel was somewhat rundown after the increasing problems that the terrible civil war had brought to the country as low occupancy made it difficult to keep up with new world standards. One angry guest described it as 'Fawlty towers in Sri Lanka' whilst another was more charmed, writing 'this hotel is old but not falling down. Let us hope it is here 300 more years.' Guests were still sentimental about what the hotel represented, one writing 'my family used to visit the New Oriental Hotel in the 'old days'. Stories of the place permeated my childhood'.

An old tourist brochure describes the hotel:
'The New Oriental Hotel has the character that comes from age and use… our rooms were huge; but the servant's morning bow was a thing of grace and the keys with which we locked our rooms were of the vintage kind that Captain Kidd could well have used in his treasure chests'.

"The hotel observes with its many big Dutch mirrors, a view that is only opposed by the gigantic tree outside, and how its inhabitants over the years would have glimpsed the passing of time, in the violent tides spitting out their white foam as high as the ramparts, reveling in the pathos of follies and the ecstasies of luxury."

An insight into Nesta's management of the hotel can be found from her handwritten lists, lettered a) b) c)… under the titles:
'What have we got',
'What we need to do' (e.g. 'clean and clean and clean')
'People not likely to be interested in coming to the hotel' (e.g. 'loud spoken, noisy people')
'Type of people we want and who are likely to come to us' (e.g. 'Western middle and upper class. Certain business people')

Evidence from a letter addressed to Nesta from a friend, and from a news' clipping of the obituary section shows that Nesta's brother, Roderick, died tragically in 1983. Nesta had cared for him since he was a little boy, since he was handicapped and blind, giving a wonderful insight into her generous nature and spirit. Her life was never easy, losing her husband and both her children and managing in those days a huge operation almost single handedly.

The hotel was finally bought by the Aman group and received a loving restoration, reopening in 2004, 9 days before the tsunami hit the island in the world's biggest ever natural disaster. It now has 31 rooms, comprising of suites and chambers. The pool has moved to where the horses and carriages were, and there is a fancy spa where the hotel shops used to be. The library houses a collection of books, old photographs, photo albums and comments' books from the days of the New Oriental Hotel making it compulsive reading when surrounded by the big elephant bones guarding the main seating area.

I asked Rainey, her long term English debonair friend, what she was really like and he said she was a coquette to the end, zipping up her dresses the wrong way round as this was much more comfortable. When I pushed a little more and I asked about the forty-year age difference, Rainey gave me the biggest smile "only the two of us really know what happened, and now one of us is dead and the other isn't telling."

"Though it went through a phase of being known as 'Faulty Towers in Sri Lanka' the Amangalla is now safely established as one of the island's finest hotels."

An old travel brochure inviting international visitors to Galle

The Black Prince

Ibrahim Jewellers
Safa Ibrahim
47 Church Street
0912234253

Through a set of smaller glass doors you find yourself in Safa's lair on Church Street and as the lights flicker on, the glittering gems reveal themselves, creating a bespangled wallpaper that you can't tear your eyes away from.

Safa is a third generation jeweller, telling me that his family's business "is one of the oldest jewellers in Ceylon." They started in 1909, when his grandfather set up a shop in Colombo. They did fantastically well but in 1978, with his father at the helm of the business, the shop burnt down, an electrical fault that destroyed everything they owned "except the old English Chubb's safe!" A family heirloom, the deep burgundy safe now sits in the wall of the Church Street store, a reminder of the hardship that befell the family and the determination it took to rebuild an empire. In a sense the sturdy safe is a reflection of the kind of resilient and persevering genes that Safa carries in his blood.

After this disastrous event, they had no choice but to return to the family home within the Fort walls where "my father's bedroom turned into a jewellery shop!" It is through the tenacity with which one faces adversity that one's ultimate triumph is decided. It was from this shop that Safa's father had to start from scratch, eventually succeeding in making it one of the most renowned jewellers of sapphires in Sri Lanka. Safa tells me that when his father was in business in 1980, a one-carat sapphire would have cost 2,000 rupees (less than $20US). Today the exact same stone will cost you 20,000 rupees (around $200US) as the price of sapphires continues to increase, from year to year. But Safa says "our sapphires are the best in the world because we have the best lustre in the world." His sapphires sparkle like no one else's.

It is sapphires in their every colour that Safa uses to adorn the majority of his most popular jewellery. His most recent design is beautiful in its simplicity. Small individual gold bands with a single coloured sapphire set on top,

One of Safa's famous sapphire encrusted gold rings

stacking rings that give each customer the ability to create their own collection. The gold he uses is always eighteen carats, only the best and it's his thicker gold rings set with many multi-coloured sapphires that, he tells me, are the most popular with the Western customers: "they sell like hotcakes!"

Another more delicate gold multi-linked ring is adorned with several tiny diamonds. It is the Middle Eastern clients who want "diamonds, diamonds, diamonds," with many requesting exact replicas of Princess Diana's and now Kate Middleton's infamous engagement ring. Safa caters for everyone's needs, a firm believer in the mantra "the customer is always right" but he also spends time perfecting unusual skills, like a hammering effect that creates the most incredible ridged effect on his rings, from his workshop on Leyn Baan Street.

The workshop is concealed behind a big wooden door, high-tech fingerprint technology hiding this maze from the outside world. Through door after door you can see magicians at work, some melting, some polishing and some putting the final touches on the works of art. Many of the pieces currently being made are customised, which Safa says makes up about 50% of the business he generates. But it is Safa himself who prides himself on his

"The 400-carat blue sapphire, known as the 'Blue Belle', which adorns the British crown is from Sri Lanka."

"The British Imperial Crown features a giant oval-cut spinel (previously thought to be a ruby), which is known as the 'Black Prince.'"

ability to make exactly what people want, designing all the jewellery you see in the shop. He has been working with a French jeweller for the past thirty-five years, always learning and perfecting his skills.

But even the best sometimes make mistakes! Safa pulls out a chunky, gold linked necklace, different coloured and shaped semi-precious stones hanging from it, a reminder that Sri Lanka does not only specialise in precious stones but in the semi-precious variety too. This piece, however, has never sold, a complete "miscalculation" on his part. He is in fact "about to melt it!" It is easy to imagine the spectre of his father hovering about somewhere in the premises, not quite appreciating this travesty of a necklace but the son seems to have learned from his father.

Apart from this necklace, "everything sells", as Safa knows exactly what to create, to appeal to each individual who wanders into his shop. As he says, "Ceylon is the land of the gems" and his little corner of that land is currently home to the largest blue sapphire Safa has ever owned, a stone that is tucked away inside his indestructible safe. His eyes sparkle like the stone itself as he holds it up to the light, the colour constantly changing, flickering from rich azure to paler cobalt to deep indigo. He knows that he would have no trouble selling it but the problem is that

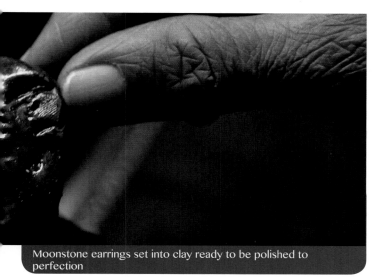

Moonstone earrings set into clay ready to be polished to perfection

"if I sell it, it'll be difficult to replace." And who knows, he says, James Bond may come back in a film titled 'Sapphires are Forever'.

As irreplaceable as this gem is so too is Safa himself. Having worked in the business for thirty-four years now, Safa has created an incredible collection of unique masterpieces. But while the prices have changed and people on his street have come and gone, Safa remains the same, still producing jewellery that pushes the boundaries. The sheer number of hours, cocksure hands and squinting eyes that go into creating world class jewellery is indeed something that seems to be embedded in Safa's work ethic and ethos which explains why innovation doesn't have to be estranged from quality. His most recent design is a flexible ring, the metal bending open accommodates arthritis-ridden fingers, also great for women when they put on weight during pregnancy as they can change its size, allowing for everyone to acquire a bit of Ibrahim magic. Safa like his sapphires will dazzle you with his knowledge of the industry, one in which he hopes his family will continue to develop and expand.

"Sri Lanka is home to 40 out of the (roughly) 85 different varieties of gems."

The Last Goat Lady

Sooriya Markar
38 Leyn Baan

'Gone are the days/when my heart was young and gay' recites Sooriya Markar, with a mischievous twinkle in her eye. 'I made that up!' she says, proudly, proving that, quite to the contrary of her short poem, she's still in possession of all her youthful creativity. In her late 70's, Sooriya has an incredible faculty for remembering details of the British colonial era she grew up in. She even talks knowledgably about the Dutch building the Fort, eventually admitting the obvious: that she wasn't actually there to see it. 'The Dutch made the Fort very excellently' she explains, referencing the devastating tsunami 'they built a wall so that it wouldn't be washed away'. Amongst the things she credits them for, she clearly attributes the Dutch incredible foresight.

Her fondness for colonial times extends even more strongly to the British rule. As she reclines in an armchair, looking out from her saffron-coloured house onto bustling Leyn Baan Street, she loves nothing more than to rattle off English nursery rhymes and Christian hymns, of the type that wouldn't be amiss in a British public school. She is wistful for the times gone-by when English was taught as a first language and Sinhalese as a second language in Sri Lankan schools.

Sooriya can no longer recall exactly how long her ancestral home has been in her family, which goes to show that it must have been a very long time. She was born there, below the high wooden ceilings through which sunlight streams in between the slats. The house retains many of the original Dutch features, most strikingly, the tall wooden doors still marking the entrances. The house has fallen somewhat into disarray, with Sooriya's many pet cats, goats and chickens scrambling over broken furniture and scuttling along discoloured limestone walls. 'The goats have no names... the cats are all called Kitty Cat' she laughs. She is keen to point out the old drainage system built right into the walls, and the old well in the garden,

Sooriya's house is one of the last in the Fort that still has goats as both pets and for their meat and milk.

which she will no longer visit for fear of being knocked out by a falling coconut. A giant jackfruit tree is as far as she will venture into the courtyard; in season she will pick the fruit to eat.

Sooriya has been witness to many changes over her years in Galle Fort, and is glad to see that tourists now flock here to discover its rich history. She has seen British troops marching 'Negroes' down the streets of the Fort during the Second World War, chained up with their mouths padlocked. 'They had to chain the Negroes because they'd pounce on little children; they ate human liver' she whispers, but admits 'I never saw them eat human flesh…I don't know if that's true or false.'

Sooriya speaks just as casually about the time Queen Elizabeth II visited Sri Lanka in 1954. 'I went to Colombo to see the Queen. I gave her my bouquet of flowers' she says, as if this is perfectly commonplace for a teenage girl from a small Fort community. She's proud to embody all the virtues of the Colonial era, and to this day she's still enamoured with the British Royal family. She's even decided to name the three new kittens scampering around her feet 'George', 'Anne' and 'Mary'.

"Goats are very intelligent and curious animals. Their inquisitive nature is exemplified in their constant desire to explore and investigate anything unfamiliar which they come across, a bit like their owner herself!"

47

King of Chill

The Dairy King
Ice Cream Parlour
Mr. T. Nassim
69A Church Street
0773912779

Dairy King stands out in more ways than one in a Fort made of buildings composed of coral and mud, some that hark back to the seventeenth century, others from the British colonial heyday when art deco was all the rage. Dairy King's façade in bright flossy pink and powder blue, sweeps out of the line of old historic houses with an elegant bay window, which is classic Deco with a difference. The colours were intended (like the name of the shop) to be a play on the American brand of ice-cream Dairy Queen, which has red and blue as its colours. Mr. T. Nassim was quite clear that he wasn't going to be going into a matriarchal monarchy though—it was a case of being a King or nothing!

His family's ice-creams are legendary and even more varied and imaginative during the tourist season when he and his wife, the ice cream maker, experiment with exotic and unusual flavours (chilli is next on their list) than during the quiet season when there is no market for the more experimental ones like bright pink bubble gum. The ice-cream is still made every day fresh by his wife and not stored indefinitely, in fact he has to stop his children eating whatever remains at the end of the day as it is simply so good that the stuff vanishes into thin air. This magical secret ice-cream mix is made at his family home behind the shop using only milk and real cream in the traditional way; this is a man who does things correctly and he says you can really taste the difference between real chocolate and home made vanilla.

Mr. T. Nassim is part of one of the oldest Fort families who originally lived in Middle Street before he was married, in a magnificent Galle Heritage restored house which is believed to have been the Dutch Governor's residence. The walls in the 28, Middle Street house (which has been in the family for several generations) are over a metre thick and constructed not from modern bricks but hunks of clay, coral and ballast shells from trading ships, used to prevent the ships from tipping over on the way to pick up spices from Galle.

Children flock to the Dairy King's palace to enjoy a variety of flavours

Although his father, two of his uncles, his grandfather and numerous other relatives made their living as lawyers and served with distinction (several became Judges) it was also a part-time hobby for the family to pursue a gentlemen's jewellery business. The reason for this occupation becoming a "hobby" was in part a response to the Muslim tradition of not putting money in the bank to collect interest but rather investing and accruing one's money by other means such as holding onto valuable stones hidden in secret boxes. The family abandoned their business following the tsunami as they felt that the industry had gone into decline. He fears the commercial edge that is taking over the town and the way in which old families have retreated to live in the back of their homes in order to sell goods on the street-front is sad as it destroys the look of these wonderful historic streets.

"Galle should be a place to be happy and relax." So you can enjoy his cinnamon that will improve your memory, crunchy cashew giving you energy to keep on walking, coconut good for the skin and mint ice cream, along with the chocolate range that are just so naughty but nice…so go on treat yourselves, well at least until his children have learnt the art of lock picking.

"Mr T. Nassim can remember the days when it was possible to play cricket in the street and when all the houses were occupied throughout the year and not just when their foreign or rich owners came to visit."

The Heritage Café

61 Pedlar Street
(Barista Café
53 Lighthouse
Street)
Email:
theheritagecafe@
hotmail.com
091 224 6668
077 6973218

The British colonial red letterbox sets the scene for the gargantuan colonial façade of The Heritage Café that straddles both Pedlar and Lighthouse Street replete with imposing columns and original courtyard, considering the volatile horizon in pensive calm, solid and stoic, concealing the boundless ever changing energy and innervations of different generations and the various uses the building has provided for over the centuries.

Manhal the owner of The Heritage Café explains with immense pride over a fish platter fit for a king that this is the only sea fortress of its kind, proud of its living history and families that in some cases have been around as long as the walls. Here in the four hundred year old Fort you see Fort children with satchels heading out to school early morning, street peddlers plying their trade daily, and the Army running past them keeping up with a rigorous routine reinforcing why they are one of the best in the world. This is in dynamic contrast to other Forts around Asia, which are for the most part merely empty museums.

Manhal, always with a story to tell about the past and the biggest twinkly smile thinks his family has been living on Pedlar Street for around ten generations or more. On the wall of The Heritage Café courtyard he shows me a birth certificate from 1899, revealing that a boy called Henry Montagu was born in the building on the 24th of March at 53, Lighthouse Street, Galle Fort, Ceylon. The Montagu's were a British family that came only a few months ago as tourists to visit the Café in search of their family tree. The birth certificate revealed the other side of the family – where one Lady Burrows late Antonito formerly De Vos was there. De Vos is an old Dutch family who are still very much part of the Fort, with veteran Ashley De Vos another Burgher who is a top architect well known to the area, but whether the grand dame is a direct relation or not is yet to be proven.

The Heritage Cafe's unbeatable and irresistible prawn cocktail

"The Heritage Café is famous for its avocado and cascading lagoon prawn cocktail, with the green avocado offset with the grated orange carrot, tomato and swirls of red onion mix."

Manhal's actual family, not withstanding his business, has lived for generations at 75, Pedlar Street, where the family who were at one time famous jewellers of the Bombay Taj Mahal made jewellery for the royal family of India. Moving into all types of businesses over the centuries including from hospitality and different merchant trades, the family has had a long term love affair with the place and Manhal says "When I was small my home at No. 75 was always a lively place before the 30 year civil war, where we entertained people from all parts of the world, while bicycle rickshaws wheeled their way past our veranda daily, some carrying stately guests and others peddling wares to sell from house to house. Those were the days when crime was non-existent and the Fort felt like one big open house."

"They pride themselves on being child friendly, a setting created by Manhal's wife Huzaifah, who once had a Montessori school in the Fort and knows how important it is for a mother to enjoy her food while the little ones play safely."

The building itself is open with a row of arches and columns allowing you to enjoy the rock/coral garden with sweet smelling Araliya, Frangipani and ferns in old copper rice pots that gives one a sense of the medieval period and of the Fort's heyday, when ox carts rattled along the streets, and fishermen sold the latest catch of the day from boxes on the back of their rickety Singer bikes swimming in panniers straight from the sea.

Being in the centre of the Fort you can hear in the open courtyard both the chanting of the mosque with the call to prayers five times a day, mixed in with the music of the Buddhist temple and the twittering of birds which include peacocks and the cheeky purple leaf monkeys that know where all the best places to eat in town are.

I discover that the old bakery was situated here until 2004 and used the well water to mix the dough, and

Though the food will delight, the stories will astound

"Manhal plans to open the first vegetarian restaurant in Galle Fort at 75, Pedlar Street to give his one time family home a new lease of life, interestingly food with an Indian twist harking back to his ancestral roots."

today this is one of only a handful of historic Dutch wells left in the Fort. The entrance between the Barista coffee shop and the restaurant still has a lucky horseshoe over the door reflecting the original stables in the Fort and the belief in the power of magic of which an upside down horseshoe is still considered to be the bringer of good luck. Part of the magic of the restaurant is Manhal's stories. "I often think of myself and Shafeek who owns the kade, the grocery shop opposite my house playing marbles and carrom." Looking around it does not take much to understand why the Fort is Manhal's life and through his life at The Heritage Café you will learn about the real life of this awe inspiring seafaring port while tucking into a platter of fresh fish straight from the sea.

A Spoonful of History

Mumtaz Rumi
84 Leyn Baan
0779658354

When you eat Mumtaz Rumi's homemade chutney in the heart of the old Fort, you can practically taste the history of Sri Lanka in a spoonful. A talent that has been passed down four generations, this chutney has been the family recipe for over a hundred years. Mumtaz learnt her skills in the best way one can learn: from watching her family and practising for many years before she took over the business herself. Chutney, if you like, was her inheritance, one she has cherished greatly. They are a Galle Fort family that has lived at 84 Leyn Baan Street for many generations. The small, unassuming kitchen of that house has produced some of the island's best chutney, although keeping the recipe the same with so many ingredients can at times be challenging.

The eighteen ingredients that include, amongst others, dried fish and dates from Mecca, which go into making the chutney, are printed on the label. But even though there is no ancient family secret there, she tells me that it is the particular timing, quantity and quality of her work that makes the chutney into something special and totally unique. As her husband points out, "Anyone can do any job." But it is only when the profession is passed down through a bloodline that people can create something truly extraordinary through their passion and love of cooking. And, after tasting the chutney, I would tend to agree with them. Sweet but with the perfect amount of spice, perfect with both a rice and curry or your early morning hopper, you can almost taste every ingredient, if you just concentrate hard enough.

Her chutney is popular with the locals and tourists alike. It is sold in a few supermarkets around the area, with a lot of foreigners buying it to take back home with them so they can savour the holiday long after it's over. This is a fact that Mumtaz is very proud to tell me. The reality that chutney made by one lady in her kitchen can go all over the world is pretty astounding, when you think of her buyers who range from the English to the Chinese. They have ideas to

Mumtaz Rumi's self-designed label has all 18 ingredients printed on it

expand from just chutney but at the moment there is not enough time, her husband says. Instead they have a little clothing business on the side called Salwar Kameze that sells traditional ladies' clothes. But it is the chutney that is Mumtaz's passion and that, with the help of her husband, she has made into a business to be celebrated.

The new chutney label uses each of their own initials and those of their sons to create a completely unique branding. It is a legacy, left behind for the sons who, she hopes, will follow in her footsteps. As for now, her exceptional assistant remains her husband, although he is quick to tell me that it is all Mumtaz, who makes the chutney what it is.

The high arched doorway, 24 inch coral walls and traditional tiles of 84 Leyn Baan Street are now home to another generation of pattering feet, Mumtaz having grown up in the house that she now brings her own sons up in hopes that they will also do the same. Having been a Fort family for so many years, the house and its inhabitants have seen many changes. They tell me that most of the original families from the street are gone because of a change in livelihood or finances. But the house at 84 Leyn Baan Street has not changed at all. Even though shops and restaurants have come and gone from Galle Fort, new businesses have been created and new people have arrived, Mumtaz's cauldron is still bubbling away and will for generations to come.

"Chutney dates back to 500 BC and is usually grouped into sweet or hot forms; both types contain spices, including chilli and yet the other ingredients vary on where it is made in the world."

A Rose Amongst The Thorns

Beach Haven
Guesthouse
Sita Wijenayake
25 Lighthouse
Street
0912234663

Family photos cover every surface and a happy goldfish swims around in his bowl as Mrs Wijenayake, clad in brightly coloured garments directly reflective of her personality, greets me warmly. A sharp eyed woman with a character that belies her eighty-two years, Sita, as she is known to her friends, begins to tell me how she was once "the rose amongst the thorns" when in 1983, she became the first female councillor in Galle Fort. She grins as she remembers a guest of hers at Beach Haven on Lighthouse Street, outraged that she hadn't revealed who she was! Sita just looks bemused and says well "that was nothing to tell."

She has travelled the world to visit her children and various friends but always returns to her favourite country, Sri Lanka. As a child she travelled her colourful country because of her father's job as a stationmaster, attending schools in most of the major cities. It was only when she married that Sita returned to the magical Fort. Soon after, Sita was given the idea for a guesthouse by three American boys, who needed a safe and legal place to stay. They suggested that she transform her beautiful house into a place for travellers to bed down and she couldn't think of a reason not to. So in 1968, Beach Haven was opened for business.

Not content with just being the first in this category, Sita decided she wanted to go into politics and so became a town councillor. She was not one to just run for the desk job, but fought for the things she believed in and achieved more than many councillors will ever manage to. As one male friend said to her, "you are a woman, a damn nuisance!" She believed so passionately in cleaning up the Fort that it is fair to say, if it were not for her, the streets would not be enjoyable to walk down. She is extremely happy that her actions assisted in creating a Fort to be proud of, a Fort "that smells great!" She is a woman who has always looked out for others, never categorising people on account of their religion or nationality rather looking out for qualities her Buddhism celebrates, like integrity.

The upstairs veranda at Beach Haven is the perfect place to relax

Her selflessness and honest nature is probably one of the reasons why, in 1994, some Dutch friends of hers decided to set up a foundation in her name, the SITA foundation. It enables wealthier people to help send a poor child to school and every month Sita makes sure the children write a letter to their donors. Keeping this bond between child and sponsor is the reason why the foundation is only going from strength to strength. Sita is not one to take any prisoners and if a letter isn't good enough she lets the child know! Every child gets special treatment and a head start in life that they would not have otherwise got. Sita always helps others less fortunate.

Now eighty-two, Sita has finally accepted that enough is enough. Retiring from politics in the late 1990s, Sita's daughter now runs the guesthouse, under the watchful eye of her omnipresent mother. The only thing that seems to annoy her is the fact that nowadays "When I go out everyone stops and talks to me. So now, I just don't go out!" Her door is always open though. Sita is not ready to hang up her socialising hat just yet especially living in a place like Galle Fort, which, she says, is just "like a family." When I ask her what the Fort means to her, it is the only time in the conversation that I have rendered her momentarily speechless. After a moment with a little shake of her head she simply gives me a wise look and says, "it is something you can't explain."

"Doctors from all over the world pick Beach Haven as their base for medical electives"

The Oldest Man

Ahmad Hussein Ismail
45A Church Street
0777902200

'I am a very old man!' Mr Ahmad Hussein Ismail shouts happily, in response to the question 'how are you?' At age 91, he speaks perfect English and is a keen conversationalist, but is quite deaf. Every day after breakfast he takes a seat on the porch of his humble house on Middle Street, his clear blue eyes watching the world pass by, noticing that this view has changed only a little over the past 90 years. 'All the houses were very big back then' he says 'and we didn't have phones.'

The porch on which Mr Ismail spends his days is all that can be seen of the old Dutch house from the street. It is quiet where he sits and he is calm and contented, set apart from the busy household that can be seen in glimpses through the flapping curtain behind which people bustle and children patter. He is a bachelor, having been a sick man for much of his life, but there is no trace of regret in him; he clearly enjoys the peace his childlessness has warranted him in his old age.

Mr Ismail has plenty of time to reflect on his childhood spent in Galle Fort during the British rule, which he calls 'the Christian era'. He credits the British as kind rulers, and remembers a time during which British sports such as cricket and football had yet to become widespread in Sri Lanka, when social activity began at 5am on the ramparts, crowded with people chatting, a time at which exercise consisted only of running around and around the Fort. He is surprisingly nostalgic for the wartime, when many foreign troops appeared in Galle Fort, remembering it as a time of unique cross-cultural sharing and integration. He has fond memories of this experience, since, despite not sharing a common language, British, Japanese, Ceylonese, American and Italian people thoroughly enjoyed each other's company.

The Oldest Man belongs to a long line of gem-merchants, originally from Morocco, who settled in Galle Fort. His father worked for the famous OLM Marcan Markar gem

The oldest man in Galle Fort's humble house on Church Street

"'They are the survivors of a commercial caste which traded in citronella and indigo before the port silted up, and brought them into dire financial straits and inactivity' by *The Scorpion-Fish* by Nicolas Bouvier."

business, whilst he himself took up jobs in various small jewellery firms. He is the revered authority of the old Fort families, being, quite literally, the Elder of the community. He feels that Galle Fort is a uniquely special place, since people of all different cultures and religions live together, and have historically attended religious celebrations together, so as to ensure there was communal unity. 'The Fort is a place for everyone to unite' he says, proudly. The only thing he is more proud of, it seems, is his age, which he says might even be 98.

Trustee of the Mosque

Rauf Authad
37 Rampart Street
0912380566

Rauf Authad is proud of his role and heritage as the Trustee of the Mosque in Galle Fort, but emphasises that this is not his professional qualification. He speaks nine languages and is the fifth generation of gem merchants from Galle Fort, and the third generation to take up the position of the Trustee.

His father spent a significant amount of time in Vietnam, running a jewellery shop, only returning permanently to the Fort during the Vietnamese-American war. But Mr Authad is himself an essential member of the Galle

Once a fortnight the Meeran Mosque holds women's prayers at which there are between 60-100 women of the Fort.

"If all the Qur'ans in the world were destroyed, the Arabic would still remain thanks to the millions of Muslims, called 'hafiz' or 'guardians' who have memorized the text letter for letter from beginning to end."

Fort Muslim community, having been appointed by this community to his 6th term as the Trustee of the Mosque.

The Mosque is unique in many ways, largely a consequence of its serving Muslim travellers as well as locals. One such feature catering to tourist devotees is its female section. In most parts of the world, Muslim women tend to pray at home, whilst men attend the Mosque for daily and weekly prayers. As Mr Authad explains, prayer space is segregated by gender because there is a risk that the personal cleanliness required for prayer will be nullified if a man touches a woman who is not an immediate member of his family.

However, once a fortnight, the Mosque holds women's prayers, which are exclusively organised, recited and attended entirely by women. Her husband further explains that women are discouraged from attending the Mosque whilst men are praying because their presence would cause too many disturbances and distractions for the men.

> "'Islam' means 'surrender' or 'submission' and the root of the word comes from the word 'salam' which means 'peace.'"

The community may be segregated along gender lines, but there is no separation in religious practice between the two Muslim sects that live, pray and feast alongside each other in Galle Fort. There are always two trustees of the Mosque: one from the Shazuliya sect and the other from the Cadirya sect, which differ in their interpretation of the Prophet Mohamed's teachings. Members of both sects can go to the Arabic College in the Fort to discuss issues of interpretation, translation and clarification of the holy text.

Rauf Authad is proud to be the sole possessor of an old photograph showing the original site of the Mosque, when it was a small personal prayer house built by a lady named Kadheeja. He relates that the site of the Mosque is on land reclaimed from the sea by the Portuguese when they built their Black Fort. The land remained empty during the period in which the Fort was renovated by the Dutch, but was eventually used by the military as horse barracks. Kadheeja, the ultimate owner of the land, originally owned a fruit stall where she lived outside Galle Fort in Magalle, but found her business and security compromised during the Second World War and so sent a request to the chief of the army asking to buy land inside the Fort. When her request was granted, she became the first civilian, and the first Muslim, to live inside the Fort's walls. The small Mosque she built served only the husbands of her two

The first civilian and the first Muslim to live inside the Fort's walls was a women called Kadheeja.

> "Rauf sees the Muslim community of the Fort as a shining example to the rest of Sri Lanka and the world."

daughters, but soon Muslims began buying property inside the Fort, and the original Mosque had to be rebuilt to cater for the growing community. The cement wall surrounding the Mosque is dated by a plaque put up in 1938, and the new Mosque was built by a man from Weligama, affectionately known as Nondi (Sinhalese for 'lame'), who also built the Pooruwa Mosque in the United States.

Even more so than the Mosque's fascinating history, the Trustee is also proud of the unique Muslim community which constitutes an essential part of the cross-cultural interaction that characterises Galle Fort. In addition to the famous wealthy Muslim families that have made names for themselves in Galle Fort, Rauf judges the most important feature of the community to be its peaceful and constructive coexistence with Buddhists and Hindus, at whose festivals the Muslims often participate. In this sense, he sees the Muslim community of the Fort as a shining example to the rest of the Island, and the world.

Disaster's Miracle

Sally Sainambu,
Zaharana &
Shazana
2/7 New Lane II
0776559168

As Sally Sainambu glances at her daughter Zaharana, you can see that the story I'm about to be told is one that is engraved within their minds, an event that they will never be able to forget. There are three generations of women within this room who have all been directly and extraordinarily affected by the tsunami that happened on Boxing Day in 2004. It was a day that the entire world remembers due to it being the largest natural disaster to ever occur, but for this particular family on New Lane II, their lives were never the same again. The bond between these women is unlike any I've seen, an unspoken knowledge of what has passed and of the impact that it had on their family.

It was an unforgettable day for both good reasons and bad, a day that left many families incomplete but actually, in the end, completed theirs. For, amidst all the horror and pain of that day, a blessing was bestowed on them in the form of Zaharana's daughter Shazana, a beautiful young Arabic girl whose smile lights up the entire room. It was on the morning of the tsunami that Zaharana felt the first pangs of labour. Sally took her to the local hospital in Mahamodera and then headed home to make some lunch, not thinking that that would be the last time she saw her daughter for two days. When Zaharana saw the wall of water coming towards her, she knew for the sake of her unborn baby that she had to flee. In her haste to escape she slipped into a drain that had been left open. Struggling to free herself, she felt a strong set of hands pulling her up, releasing her from the trap. On she ran, eventually ending up at the Karapitiya Hospital where a passing nurse, on seeing Zaharana's situation, led her aside and safely delivered the baby.

In the midst of all the chaos, a new life was born. Shazana was a beacon of hope, a miracle tsunami baby that her family did not think could have possibly survived. Zaharana's husband spent all afternoon struggling through nine feet of muddy swirling water, swimming past bodies

Three generations of this miracle family live at 2/7 New Lane II

and cars until eventually he stumbled across his wife and his new baby daughter. It was at this time that Sally was working at the Amangalla hotel in the Fort and, as she tells me, they did more than their bit on this awful day. Upon seeing the desperate plight of many people, the owner of the hotel opened the doors to the citadel, feeding and giving beds to those in need.

The behaviour of people opening up their homes, giving everything they had was remarkable. Friends gave them a pram and the local foreigners sent top doctors to check that both mother and baby were in good health. Of course once the incredible story got out about the legendary tsunami baby, there was a lot of press who wanted to speak to the family. Sally dealt with them in the most courteous and respectful way, telling them all that they wanted to know, all the while protecting her family from the ferocious glare of the media. She is a matriarch you wouldn't want to mess with, an independent woman who, up until five years ago, was still out working all day every day to provide for her family.

But, she says, her working days are over. For now, it is time to spend her days with her family and thank God that they survived when a quarter of a million people across the Indian Ocean died. She says it was God who protected her family that day and for that she is forever grateful.

"When the animals go to higher ground, the sea water bubbles like bubble bath and then recedes to the horizon, emptying the sea of all its water is a warning to get to higher ground."

Frozen in Time

Retired Prison Officer
W. R. Gunesekara
22 Hospital Street 0779848326

The old white shutters creak as they open, sunlight pouring in and falling on the wooden desk, still in the exact same position it has been for decades. You can almost see the ghost of Nicolas Bouvier seated, feverishly delirious, writing letters that years later became The Scorpion Fish, the only distractions the birds in the trees and the odd stray cat jumping from roof to roof. Number 22 Hospital Street within the ancient citadel that is Galle Fort is where Mr Bouvier experienced the dark side of the Fort, staying there for six months in the 1950s. The house and devil dancing that took place at midnight across the road made such an impression on him that it features heavily in the book. When you stand in the room where he stayed during those turbulent months, you can feel the real life drama behind his writing: "The room costs one rupee a day. The sun costs nothing: it lights up the room, strolls across the wall."

This magical place is the home of W.R. Gunesekara, a retired prison officer and the owner of one of the first boarding houses in the Fort, a home for Mr Bouvier during his time there. A prison officer is not the profession you would have guessed for Mr Gunesekara when you first encounter his smiling, friendly face, his twinkling, mischievous eyes only adding to a character who you most certainly would not mind spending an afternoon with. He worked in the prison for thirty-three years, telling me he loved what he did. If he hadn't loved it then he would definitely not have lasted that long!

The family is proud of their novel guest they once had, a flicker of sadness passing over Mr Gunesekara's face when he tells me that he never returned. Mr Bouvier was not very well during his stay in Sri Lanka but he was a good, kind man who went about his business with no disturbance caused, Mr Gunesekara tells me. As you walk through the shady entrance hall and push back the curtain that leads you to the courtyard, you can see what it was that Mr Bouvier fell in love with here. His room

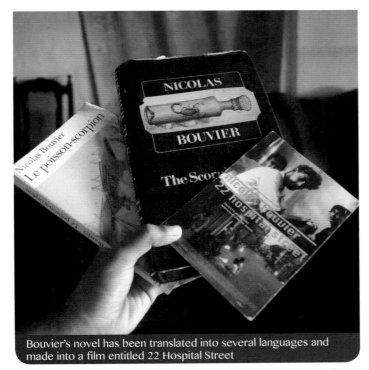

Bouvier's novel has been translated into several languages and made into a film entitled 22 Hospital Street

"'The morning, rich with expectations, was lighter than a bubble. To all its suggestions, my answer was: yes.' The Scorpion-Fish."

overlooked the large central courtyard, an architectural feature that harks back to when the Dutch ruled the Fort.

The house is no longer a boarding house but a home and that's the way the family wants it to stay. They say that they get many people, mainly Swiss and French tourists who track them down on Facebook requesting a visit, though it is Mr Gunesekara's daughter who informs me of this, social media being something that Mr Gunesekara has not quite mastered yet. Many people do visit the house still, wanting to see if there is some truth behind Mr Bouvier's exquisitely dark descriptions. And I can tell you that there most certainly is, right down to the particular features of Hospital Street and the unique Fort itself: "But here, a superabundant nature decorates at the same time as it wears away: festoons of salt wink under the windows, mother-of-pearl and coral grow in the volutes of leprons stucco, light flatters the rinds of rotten fruit and shellfish creep into the smallest whorls of architecture."

A Heroic Joker

Hameen Magdon
Ismail
52 Church Street
0912234575

"How old are you Hameen?" a young boy shouts as he passes by number 52 Church Street. After a brief pause, Hameen's wrinkled, sagacious face breaks into a smile as he replies with "I'm only 52!" This may be just a slight exaggeration on Hameen's part (his daughter Fathuma reveals that he is in fact in the grand old and incredibly impressive age of 92) but this kind of jest rings true of his nature as one of Galle Fort's greatest jokers, who at another time claimed to be as old as the ancient citadel's old gate.

Indeed the youngsters of the Fort remember walking past Hameen's house on their way back from school or on their way to one of the infamous rampart cricket matches and getting the shock of their life as a loud horn was blown in their direction. Upon looking in the direction of the noise, all the children would see would be Hameen, looking up and down the street as if to determine the source of the sound, horn nowhere to be seen.

Hameen is one of Galle Fort's greatest assets, greeted affectionately by every single person who passes by his house where he now lives with his family, having previously run a jewellery and gem shop in Trincomalee. His daughter Fathuma tells me that the part of her father's life that he is most proud of is his eight-year service in the Army during the Second World War against Germany and remembers how the RAF were stationed in what is now the Galle Fort Hotel throughout World War II. Hameen was himself stationed in Italy for the years he was fighting during this devastating international conflict, leaving Sri Lanka at the mere age of 18 to fight a battle whose consequences changed the face of world history.

Hameen played his part just as so many had done before him but it becomes apparent that his bravery must have exceeded others around him as Fathuma reveals that, during his service, he was in fact awarded several Army medals, which now reside with his son in Australia. Though the medals may not be there, his valiant legacy

The old entrance to the Galle Fort

"Hameen is a joker, a youthful spirit who, it is clear, even at the grand old age of 92, will never really grow up."

lives on within his children who were all born and bred in Galle Fort, in his wife's house on Church Street that they call home.

So if you ever happen to wander along this stretch of road just stop and say hello to the old hero who sits dressed in a colourful sarong outside his house, watching the world go by. But beware, you never know what practical joke Hameen might be planning next.

A Lifelong Allegiance

President of the YMBA Associa-tion
Sarath Dias
Lighthouse Street 0912234616

A few steps up from the street and in through a set of small wooden doors, you pass a noticeboard covered in fading bits of paper, advertising the events of the week to come, a little shop selling Sri Lankan trinkets and an old fashioned ice cream machine. Past secret offices, a billiard room, a canteen and a wooden newspaper stand, you will find yourself in Galle Fort's very own Young Men's Buddhist Association. A place where people can seek shelter, play snooker or simply just eat a cheap meal. And seated in one of these said offices, surrounded by old photos of the Association's previous Presidents and their staff, is Sarath Dias, the twenty-eighth president of the YMBA.

This year marks Sarath's twenty-fourth year in charge, having tried to hand over the position to another but constantly being coaxed back. The trouble is, he tells me, that no one wants him to go! Greatly respected by the people of the Fort, he has dedicated his own life to the bettering of others'. The association relies on the support and donations of local people, however big or small. Those who want to help can make a difference. Sarath has proven that all it takes is a lot of hard work and several years of devoted work. Since he started at the YMBA, the number of buildings they own and

The YMBA offers a refuge for those seeking it, every daily paper available for your enjoyment is free of charge.

work out of has increased from two to an amazing sixteen buildings, all of which are used to provide support for those in need.

First and foremost his work has a religious purpose, offering people a chance to hear visiting monks speak and even providing rooms to rent on the first floor of the Lighthouse Street building. He also has a strong belief in social work, providing, amongst other things houses for elders, a disabled girls school and a home for the blind. Sarath has a vision for the future, a day care and Montessori school that caters for around forty children nurturing the talent of tomorrow.

The YMBA is only going from strength to strength and this is all thanks to one man. Sarath is a selfless figure, a shining example to the rest of the Fort, upholding a belief that he is running his association in a "very special place." It is safe to say that Sarath is a man with a big heart and a generous spirit, a man who adopts and executes Buddhist principles within every single aspect of his life.

"Sarath Dias is the twenty-eighth President of the YMBA and has been for twenty-four years."

Majesty in the Blood

The Thassim
Family
28 Middle Street
0912222109

As you enter through the huge arched gabled doorway of 28 Middle Street with remnants of coloured glass, one is immediately struck by the depths of history from top to bottom, pillar to slab, from the thick old coral walls and the deep-rooted beams. Old photos stand on top of antique chests of drawers and a slight breeze disturbs the otherwise still air. Once home to the Dutch East Indian Company now the house is a physical history book of the Thassim family through the generations. Fathima Riyasa Nassim sits proudly in her chair, the matriarch of this incredible family, still exuding some of the grandness that the house so inspires.

Grandeur, it seems, is not only embedded within her house but runs through her veins. A descendent of the Macan Markar family, their grandfather having lived at Sea View on the ramparts, they are one of the most revered families still left in the Fort. Fathima arrived on Middle Street when she was six years old, attending Southlands School, just opposite her house. She was the only girl with two brothers, one of whom was born in the very house she still occupies today. She remembers the street when it was full of Dutch Burghers, many who left in the 1970s, and when presents were bought and given and birthdays celebrated with the entire street. Fathima looks wistful as she recalls her own childhood on this charmed street. Her past and her family's history are in the very walls of the house, still very much remaining a part of their lives.

A certain Ahmed Hussein Macan Markar took on the impossible task of writing down the history of the family, resulting in a dusty, old tome that holds the secrets of Fathima's past. Her father, Mohammed Thassim was a gem trader, a merchant who worked in both Colombo and Galle. He was a famous trader, even selling one of the largest cat's eyes in the world. He travelled across the world and it was only a few months ago that an Englishman and his family appeared on the doorstep of 28 Middle Street, much to the great excitement of the family. He announced

Three children from the younger generation of the interminable Thassim family

that he had been friends with a young Mohammed and proceeded to present black and white photographs of the two of them together. There is both great joy and sadness in Fathima's eyes as she pulls out the photos to show me. Many of her relations have now left the Fort, leaving behind a history that not many remember. But she is adamant that she will always stay.

She tells me that there is a Muslim saint buried in the ramparts that surround the Fort, providing an invisible protection over everyone within it. This is a belief that Fathima holds strongly within her, as the Fort rapidly changes around her since the civil war ended in May 2009. One of the greatest changes, she has noticed, is that more people are building swimming pools. When I ask if she has any plans of the same kind, she chuckles and gives me a firm shake of the head! The multicultural community of the Fort is a reality that Fathima only celebrates. She is clear though that the Fort will only remain as great as it once was if everyone is "friendly" to one another. That is the quality that it makes her happy to see. And she, without a doubt, exemplifies it in every way.

"Macan Markar was the founder of the Gem and Jewellery establishment in 1860 at the New Oriental Hotel. Not only did he sell one of the largest cat's eyes in the world but four Royal family members visited his shop; King Edward VII in 1875, King George V in 1901, King Edward VIII in 1922, and Queen Elizabeth II in 1954."

A Unified Diversity

Shanthini
Mahadeva
66 Leyn Baan
0915625227

"You can break a whole stick but you can't break a whole bunch," is an attitude that is fundamental to the unique nature of Galle Fort and one that Shanthini Mahadeva feels is the reason why her Jaffna Tamil family have lived in the Fort for four generations. Her male relations have all been bankers at Commercial Bank, formerly Mercantile Bank, and even her sister Jayanthi is continuing the tradition.

Shanthini tells me that they are very simple, humble folk who pride themselves on the fact that they have the common touch. Everything in life, they believe, takes place because of God's will and Shanthini is philosophical as she lays down her thesis for life: "There is only one religion, the religion of love. There is only one caste, the caste of humanity and there is only one language, the language of love." For her, in her own life, the most important aspect of it is to act out of love, something she says the Fort inhabitants excel at.

Even during the civil war, Shanthini says that their family was not affected because of the kindness shown by their neighbours towards them whether they were Sinhalese, Muslim, Buddhist or Christian. Everyone looked out for everyone and Shanthini says it is because of this that "when we enter through the Galle Fort entrance, we are entering our home.

Four generations of Jaffna Tamils live at 66, Leyn Baan Street

As Jaffna Tamils we feel very secure. We are not strangers." Indeed her extended family is extremely cosmopolitan in the way that they lead and have led their lives with many living overseas and others having married into prestigious Sinhalese families. For example their father's uncle, Mr. C. Sadhananthan married the former Governor General of Sri Lanka, Sir Oliver Gunathilake's daughter, Sheila, uniting two very different families with no concern or even thought for their different beliefs.

Shanthini says that the main concern for her is to help people physically, financially and emotionally just as their family have done for the last four generations, regardless of caste, creed and nationality. Their house is a multicultural hotspot, people of all shapes and sizes, colours and race being welcome in their snug dining room. The house itself is a 300 year old historical haven, its high ceilings harking back to colonial times. A chest of drawers standing in the corner of the bedroom demonstrates the family's open-mindedness as a portrait of Lord Buddha sits next to a cross in front of a small Hindu figure. Shanthini and her sister are extremely proud of their own and the Fort's heritage, something Shanthini also demonstrates through her position on the Executive Committee of the Galle Fort library.

"If you connect yourself to the divine, you can achieve permanent happiness. Money will not give you peace of mind. You earn people and not money in your life. We are all different sweets, but ultimately all made from the same sugar."

The Story Teller Of Galle Fort

The Royal Dutch Cafe
Fazal
72 Leyn Baan
0771774949

"It was a terrible time....there was much bloodshed and terrible things were done. In trying to overthrow the government the military movement was indiscriminate in its violence. Bodies burned in the streets and people were tied to lamp-posts and shot in the forehead…it was terrible."

Fazal runs a hand through his long greying locks and then calmly reaches forward to take a sip of his tea. In that instant as I attempt to take in the full horror that he speaks of with such calm in his slow, measured tones I realise that these stories have a certain power and potency because they still lie within the realms of living memory. Here is a man talking about the bloody years of 1983-2009 during which the chimera of civil war tore the soul and body of Sri Lanka into bloody rags which are only gradually being sewn back together in times of peace. One of the incidents leading up to the civil war involves the JVP's 1972 campaign which saw students attempt to overthrow the government and much bloodshed on both sides. In Fazal there is a link to Sri Lanka's embittered and bloody past and also to the long cultural traditions of an ancient Fort filled with love, life and rampant diversity.

As the pair of us drink tea on the veranda, whilst the rain outside drives every sane person to find shelter and pours in torrents out of gutter ends, I see again the sign for the Royal Dutch Café propped against this veranda that is alive with plants and filled with a collection of objects that bewilder the eye. This sign proclaims the legendary nature of this café—"The best tea in town!". This may seem like an exaggeration until the drink arrives in its glass cup and saucer steaming gently and exuding such an aroma of ginger that it can fill a Western mind with images of warm winters by a fireside and yuletide treats sitting in the snow. Upon the gently steaming surface of this cup float several slivers of ginger root which momentarily distract the eye from its work in examining the incredible collection of objects that cover the room. Like a snapshot of the Arab

Fazal not only has the most incredible collection of ancient objects but he also makes the best tea in town!

trader's house in Kipling's Kim there are a huge number of fascinating objects hanging from the ceiling from antique glass lamps stained with age to the cloth lamps studded with tiny mirrors which are there to add atmosphere to this restaurant. Though there may be pictures of an English picnic on the place mat and one of the paintings on the wall depicts a classic European fruit basket one struggles to find anything in this fascinating home which is not connected to the deep history and culture of Galle Fort.

Despite the fascinating setting I have been informed in advance that the beating heart of interest in this café is to be found in the tales and stories of the man who stands stately and proud in the entrance to the veranda. There is a semi-regal mien to this tall man. His sharp black trousers and strong leather belt tell you that he is proud of his appearance and as he pads softly barefoot across the veranda to lead me to a seat one is in the care of a gentleman who delights in the pleasure of his guests. Yet Fazal's greatest skill is not in serving customers but in regaling them with stories of the past that he can pull from time immemorial to the modern era as he brushes his top lip with one outstretched finger or else locks his long fingers together and muses.

"Tea is a source of antioxidants but for Fazal it is a drink that is accompanied by stories of another era."

"The objects found within Fazal's lair range from antique glass lamps to cloth covered mirrored lamps to miniature replicas of war-time guns."

Fazal's ancestors came from Morocco seven generations ago (other Moroccans have been trading in these waters for almost a thousand years) and with pride Fazal gestures to the front room crammed with sequined clothes to tell me that this was where he was born, into a family of jewellers and clothes-sellers. His unique use of spices in curries show the impact of his Moroccan past but he insists that he relies on milk and oil from the coconut in the Sri Lankan style to moisten his food rather than the oil relied upon in India and Pakistan (he believes this technique makes the dish too greasy). Fazal insists spice is there for flavour and not for heat alone although when asked what his own favourite level of heat is he chuckles and adds "Spicy!".

Fazal has lived all of his life in this house and Fort and in his mind there are tales of Adam and Eve who he insists lived here in Eden and were the father and mother of mankind who lived not in a world of countries but in one land for all. He believes Satan will often come between man and a woman but whilst respecting the ancient traditions of the Sinhalese such as devil dancing and mask

The story teller enjoying the nightlife on Leyn Baan Street at the first house to be restored by the Galle Heritage Foundation.

"Fazal's ancestors originally came from Morocco, seven generations ago. Fazal himself was born in the house on Leyn Baan Street that is now the Royal Dutch Cafe."

wearing he is firm in his own beliefs. When speaking of the Hindu family opposite who hang limes and chillies with strange masks from their door to prevent evil entering he says that he cannot believe that such things can keep evil out as evil and sorrow pervade the home of every man. Fazal himself would be afraid to put such a thing in his window as he believes it would keep the angels away. He is reluctant to drive evil away as he believes that sorrow cannot be kept out of a house, but believes that in keeping a house open one accepts happiness and joy also. His belief in the penetrating power of sorrow can be linked to the horror he has known and he shakes his head as he speaks of the tsunami saying that nature's power is impossible to resist. Perhaps it is due to his having such a vast experience of pain and life within the confines of his mind that Fazal discards the words of scientists who claim our ancestry lies in apes and monkeys—these men are too arrogant and cannot persuade Fazal that their version of the truth is credible. As I take a seat he crosses the street to exchange words with a peddler bringing the fresh vegetable produce for the shop on his hand-drawn

As the board on the wall states, literally and metaphorically the best spice tea in town

"Fazal tells tales of his life all over the world, including those about his time working in Saudi Arabia, where he learned to speak both Hindi and Urdu."

cart and throughout our conversation Fazal raises hands in acknowledgement, greeting anyone who passes in the street; here is a creature of the Fort. When asking about the shisha that sits upon the veranda edge I receive a wicked smile and he chuckles recalling the days some forty years ago when every family in the Fort used to have one though they were not made from glass and china as the one that sits before us now but rather bamboo. These "gudac" used to be smoked by every woman between 50 and 70 who made their own flavours that were varied according to their own preferences—there were no banana or pineapple flavours then he scoffs. There has been much change in the Fort since Fazal first arrived and he fears too much change may alter the historic nature of the place. A particular bugbear of his is people erecting shutters to block out their windows in order to observe the latest style. In his opinion such a style deadens the atmosphere of the town by shutting people into their homes and is merely a response to a short-term trend that will anyhow be subject to change in a few short years.

This is a man who has travelled and who has lived. Upon one wall hangs a tapestry depicting Mecca and when I ask Fazal if this is merely a curio he bought locally he launches enthusiastically into tales of his time in Saudi Arabia working for an oil company where he learned to speak Hindi and Urdu, and to cook with the spices of the desert. His travels have taken him far and wide and from the deep archive of his memory he can spout forth on lands across Asia including India and Pakistan. There are few breaks to his stories save when he feels the need to draw inspiration from a languid draw on a cigarette that droops from his long fingers or during a brief interlude when he darts into the depths of his shop to evict a rather disgruntled cat.

This ease and calm demonstrates how, despite his wide travels and the horror that he has seen Fazal remains devoted to his birthplace and the quiet Fort in which it sits. He says that the clean, unpolluted, tranquil and peaceful pace of life in Galle is more in tune with the makeup of his being than the fast-paced way of life in Colombo and other large cities both in Sri Lanka and abroad. Whenever he leaves the Fort his thoughts dwell here he explains and when he leaves Galle for too long his heart draws him back. He is keen for his children and grandchildren to stay here and to preserve and continue the traditional life which he evidently relishes. When I come to leave he bows his head and I wonder whether I or any other guest he meets that day will have aroused his interest sufficiently to merit being added to the catalogue of characters that revolve about his extraordinary mind to be released back into the world as his moods dictate.

"Fazal fears that there might, in the future, be too much change occuring within the Fort that could alter the historic nature of the ancient citadel."

Veiled in Mystery

Mrs Yesreen Iflal
80 Lighthouse
Street
071 4300445
jewelgem@sltnet.lk

"I was born here. I feel this is home. I can't fit anywhere else."

Mrs Yesreen is a charming Muslim mother and entrepreneur. The family home dates from the 17th century Dutch Period and the lacy, mastery evident in the latticework of the carved wooden shutters, attached with delicate brass butterfly hinges, reveals the precise, elaborate craftsmanship of the period.

Mrs Yesreen's family have lived in the Fort for five generations with many of them being traders in gems and textiles. Her great-grandfather lived in a grand bungalow called Didi's Watte, near Hirimbura Junction, which was formerly an exiled Maldivian King's residence. Her other great-grandfather, Sultan Marikar, was a tea planter in the 19th century and afterwards bought several tea, rubber and coconut estates around the country. A stout copper pot (or thamba hatti) that was used for cooking rice for large functions is still in use, its great lid stained faintly with verdigris. Elegant gilt Arabic letters set in black hang in a glass frame taking centre stage above the couch - a verse from the Koran for protection, picked up on one of the family's trips to Mecca.

Her grandfather on her mother's side was the Maldivian agent for Galle because at that time there was no High Commission in Colombo. His position involved recording every Maldivian trader who came into the harbour. They came into Galle during the months of June and July, as there was no way of making a living in the Maldives during these months. They arrived in dhonis, a traditional type of dug-out canoe used for fishing, which were laden with crates of dried fish and dieyahakuru, or tuna sauce, which is still a delicacy among the older Fort population. Her grandfather, who could speak Dhivehi (Maldivian), was in charge of giving traders permission to come ashore and of granting them emergency passports.

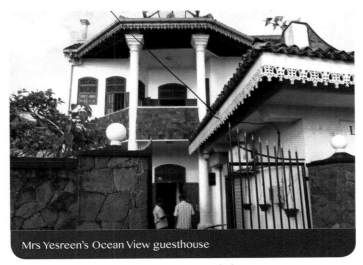

Mrs Yesreen's Ocean View guesthouse

They were required to stay at 80 Lighthouse Street, sometimes for months, so their business could be conducted under supervision. Mrs Yesreen's father remembers that once the Maldivians had run out of their dried fish stock, they would disappear into the kitchen, lock the doors, and not allow anyone entrance until their secret recipe sent its delicious aroma all through the house. Mrs Yesreen admits however to sneaking secret spoonfuls of the dieyahakuru kept in barrels in the larder.

She feels sorry for the children of today who have no time to play due to the highly competitive nature of education nowadays. She is a former teacher, at a school in Galle and in the Open University, she knows how indispensable education is, as is having a good level of English.

The traditional role of Muslim women is to look after the children, support the work of the husband, see to the education of the children and the wellbeing of the house. She has now taken up a role in her husband's jewellery business handling international transactions. They have a factory in Weligama that employs thirty-five workers and a smaller factory at home. She enjoys designing, "I move the stones around, placing diamonds. When I think it's ready I ask my husband what he thinks, if he says yes, it's good, we produce it."

"Mrs Yesreen runs Ocean View one of the most successful guesthouses in the Galle Fort, and she believes travellers love it for the excellent food and spectacular historical views."

An Inescapable Heritage

Sithy Fathima
Samsadeen Kuhafa
62 Lighthouse
Street   0912223417

The ornate wooden carved panel that sits above the door of 62 Lighthouse Street is only the tip of the antique laden iceberg that is Mrs Sithy Fathima Samsadeen Kuhafa's house. As she sits in a rich ebony chair next to her daughter Zainab, her hands neatly folded in her lap, she tells me the story of the incredible décor, a relic of the Dutch rule and a reminder of the previous lives lived under this roof. With an entrance hall paved with dark red and yellow patterned tiles brought from India and elaborate Singaporean wooden screens that separate room from room, the Dutch left a legacy that Sithy is proud to show off.

And show off she can as her grandfather was a member of the royal family of Galle Fort, the Macan Markars and a strong allegiance to the clan is evident when Sithy begins to talk of her family. Born and bred in the Fort, Sithy's father A.L.M. Mohamad was the Director of the Macan Markar jewellery shop in Colombo. He was a diligent worker and a close friend of the family, trusted above others to be sent to Egypt to conduct the family's business there. The house that Sithy currently resides in is still owned by the Macan Markar family, their name living on through the lives of those who knew them.

Sithy regards the Macan Markars with the utmost respect, telling me about the charitable work the family still carries out today. They have helped give homes and food to those in desperate need and they still to this day run the Arabic College that is such an integral part of Fort life. Sithy says that their behaviour is exemplary of their Islamic religion, which stipulates that no family is better than another. Regardless of wealth or position in society, they are all the same, a feeling that sadly Sithy believes has been slightly lost as the Fort begins to modernise, saying, "it's not like those days anymore."

Sithy herself however is very much a woman of the world having travelled to London, England in the 1970s to work

The entrance to the house still boasts the original wooden carvings

"Sithy spent the 1970s working in London at the department store Selfridges. Ironically she ended up in the tea section!"

with her husband in the famous Selfridges department store. Their Sri Lankan heritage was ever present, as her husband ended up working in the tea section of the store, selling various products, the majority of which had come from their homeland. Sithy tells me that she has been all over the world, living a life she has loved. But she knew she would always come back to the Fort. Her family's history is a part of her and it lives on within the house on Lighthouse Street and in the stories that will be re-told for generations.

Time Locked Trinket

Historical
Mansion
Kamal Hussain
31-39 Leyn Baan
0912234114

"New things you can replace. Old things are irreplaceable." Such is the mentality that has formed the basis of the empire that is now the Historical Mansion, right through from the inventor of the museum, Mr Hussain senior, who has passed the museum onto his eldest son Kamal who now runs it, along with the arcade, gem making workshop in the central courtyard and the fabulous antiques gallery with filigree jewellery that is hundreds of years old. Newness is not important to Kamal, he simply wants to preserve what his father collected so that future generations can understand and appreciate the lives that were lived without electricity hence the notches in the walls for candles and if you wanted water you had to draw it from the central courtyard well.

The building on Leyn Baan Street was just a ruin when old Mr Hussain bought it in 1985 and it wasn't until 1992 when none other than President Premadasa himself opened the historic Dutch museum. The Dutch well that stands in the open courtyard is one of the few things that Mr Hussain didn't have to alter, it being one of the oldest and still functioning wells within the Fort. Kamal's father was originally a gem merchant who collected antiques simply as a hobby. But he decided to set up the museum as a service to the country, a monument that could live forever, preserving his beloved collection and giving one a valuable snapshot of how we used to live our lives.

You enter into this time capsule through an old wooden doorframe with a typical Dutch style gable, underneath a gloriously colourful stained glass window to find yourself in a cool entrance hall framed by enormous white colonial archways. The museum has a specific route which you can follow round the building beginning with an array of ceramic plates, past an old gramophone complete with an interesting selection of records and even a small glass bottle labelled 'Tsunami Sand, 2004' forever preserved as a reminder of what the country experienced on that terrible day. A lace maker and an old gem cutter sit side by side,

This well is one of the oldest and still functioning wells in the Fort

"The VOC slab is the oldest object in the museum - they found it when they were re-constructing the old Dutch well in the courtyard."

displaying the talents that are so infamous around this area of Sri Lanka.

Kamal's favourite part of the museum, however, is the old Sri Lankan kitchen at the back of the building, perfectly preserved the way it would have been many centuries ago, complete with an arched stone oven and small clay pots, the likes of which Kamal tells me, he wouldn't have even found in his granny's house!

That is the beauty of the Historical Mansion. Within it everyone can find something that reminds them of their history or even learn something about it that they never

"In the museum, the Mansion has currency from over 100 countries: they have a 5 and a 10 rupee note from when the British ruled Sri Lanka. Today they are worth about 50,000 and 100,000 rupees respectively."

knew before. The museum houses only three donations, everything else having been purchased by either Kamal or his father over many years. The donations are incredibly varied and were made by local people living in the area, finding objects that they believed would be of more worth in a museum than in their homes. There is a cobra-skin handbag that belonged to an Army Colonel's mother, a small chair given by the Macan Markar family and a silver sword that was the property of an old Navy Officer. Everything else, Kamal tells me, has been bought by them because they recognised the rarity of some pieces, for example an old Dutch wine pot that would've been used to serve the kings, now sits proudly in a tall glass case. There is no way that Kamal would ever sell anything that is on display in the museum. No matter whoever the buyer

A laminated newspaper shows details and black and white photographs of Queen Elizabeth's tour of Sri Lanka in 1954.

"In the Historical Mansions one can learn about the history of gems. Alexandrite is the most expensive stone they have with the largest one they've ever had being 12 carats. They also once had a blue sapphire that was 38 carats."

may be or whatever they offer, Kamal's answer is always a no. Money for him is not what the Mansion is about; it is one of the only free museums in South Asia. Kamal embodies an attitude that was instilled in him by his father, a man he saw "courageously" rise from nothing to the creation of a business empire. The family are one of the few who have nearly all still remained within the Fort and when I remark that that is quite unusual nowadays, Kamal just smiles proudly: "There are 7 siblings and my father calls us the lucky 7 and none of us ever want to leave the Fort."

Knights in Arabia

Arabic College
Student
Abdul Kaher,
60 Church Street

Arabic words fly out over the sea, as a group of young white-robed figures on the ramparts at 2 o'clock in the morning, gaze up towards the starry sky with a senior bearded man, pointing, gesturing and explaining the importance of the stars. These are the constellations, which their ancestors would have used to navigate their way to the island of Serendib from the Arab world thousands of years ago. On further investigation the insomniac observer will discover that these are students from the Arabic College on Church Street, receiving their practical monthly astrological education.

Astrology is clearly a popular element of their schooling as the boys make twinkling gestures with their hands, when they explain what these night time tuition sessions' involve. M.S.M. Rila explains that the Prophet, Muhammed said that the Muslim calendar should be determined by the state of the moon. "There are no specific days; they have to be predicted by the moon." Knowledge of star signs is also important because they can be used to determine the direction of Mecca, so that they face the right way in prayers. They can also reveal auspicious times to hold certain events or to do specific work.

The Arabic College on Church Street currently has sixty students, but on average this ranges between fifty to sixty-five students from all around the country. It was established in 1892 and has gained the reputation of being the best Arabic institution in Sri Lanka. The Principal is greatly respected within the community and Muslims come to seek answers from him regarding religious matters.

Student Abdul Kaher came to the Fort from his home in Galle after he had completed and passed his O'Levels, aged 17. The College aims to give an all round education, not only studying Islam and

The Arabic college on Church Street normally houses between 50-65 students.

"Astrology, in its broadest sense, is a search for the meaning in the sky, based on the belief in a link between astronomical phenomena and events in the human world."

its teaching but also the standard classes studied at every school in the country. All classes are conducted in Arabic but in their free time the students speak Sinhalese or Tamil. As well as learning the Koran by heart, hafiz, and special knowledge, aalim, the students learn to respect and follow the religion carefully. When they leave the College after seven years they are fully educated in Muslim religion and law. The main subjects that they study are religion; languages-Arabic, Tamil and English; logic; law and grammar. The boys proudly reveal that the Fort College is the best place to study Arabic grammar in the country, as well as the best place for stargazing in the world. There have been many star pupils including Abdul Gayoom who is the Former President of the Maldives.

If they pass their final exams they are given the chance to study further in Egypt. After an interview at the Egyptian Embassy in Colombo they should get a visa,

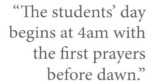

"The students' day begins at 4am with the first prayers before dawn."

which allows them to study there for a few years. After graduating, Abdul wants to do a course on the Shariah and Aquida law, though where he will go to, only time will tell.

The daily routine at the College is very structured with the pupils waking up at four and having first prayers before dawn. After this they drink a special tea before reciting the Koran for twenty minutes. At 6 am they wash before a 5-minute assembly at 7.10. Studies follow until 11.30 when there is a second prayer. After lunch the boys have a thirty-minute rest before having Arabic, English and Tamil classes. They have the rest of the afternoon free until the early evening when they have to fully recite what they learnt in the morning. For Abdul, his dream would be to come back and teach at the College, a position that he would be honoured to uphold in such a place as Galle Fort and an institution such as the Arabic College.

This is the Arabic students halls of residence. The founder of the college was Fathima Aneesa, a member of the Macan Markar family, who still patronises and covers all the costs of the institution.

"The Arabic College was established in 1892 as a place of excellence, which it continues to achieve through funding from the original patrons the Macan Markar family"

Islam is a religion that has pre-figured and pre-determined modern history. The College's ancient syllabus and shelter from the harsh outside world may seem delightfully romantic to some. In the late afternoon, the students can be seen sitting in the large, open windows high up in the Arabic College buildings, or perhaps in the early morning stopping to watch a monitor lizard drinking out of a pool of rainwater on the Fort walls before disappearing into their study building. This whitewashed former post office with its heavy frontal latticing is the entrance to another world, one that you can pass by every day without really knowing the secret of why these people first came to Sri Lanka. They were in search of something, not just gems and spices, but some greater spiritual enrichment.

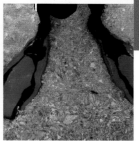

FORT
PEDDLERS

An All-Weather Seller

Coconut, Drinks &
Hat Seller
D. Gamageababynona
Opposite the clock
tower in the car park
0773871113

As the sun beats down ferociously on your back, from across the haze you spot a line of bright fire orange coconuts, hanging in the shade of gigantic green leaves, seemingly a mirage to your delirious eyes. This is no mirage but simply D. Gamageababynona, a small weather-beaten old lady with a twinkle in her eye, standing just out of sight behind her wares. She tells me that coconuts were the obvious things to choose to sell, appealing to tourists and locals alike and leaving her with a nice profit at the end of the day! Behind the row of coconuts is a small blue hut, from which she also sells drinks, snacks and a few straw hats, which she says, on a hot day like this sells almost as well as the coconuts.

Mrs Gamageababynona has been working in this spot for three years, starting the business to support her family. The first shop was in Habaraduwa but it was destroyed in the tsunami, after which the government reclaimed the land, leaving no chance of re-building. So having never lived in the Fort, she decided to come and work inside its walls, joining her son who already worked in the minister's house behind where she now sells from. And so the blue hut in the car park appeared, the ideal spot to pick up a coconut before you head onto the ramparts to watch the cricket or if you are simply driving past and in need of refreshment.

Mrs Gamageababynona sells two different types of coconut from her stall, the most common one being the bright fiery orange variety called 'gon thambili' and the younger green variety known as 'Kurumba'. Coconut water has always been used by ancient medicine but ever since the Western doctors caught onto its restorative powers, it has grown in popularity. It has many health benefits, a few of which are that it soothes internal discomfort and also hydrates you much faster than pure water. Many also splash some onto their face as it has been said to help maintain a youthful complexion. Mrs Gamageababynona is, in reality, selling liquid gold, its pricelessness only realised by the few who know of its powers.

The most beneficial quality of a coconut is that it soothes internal discomfort, hydrating you faster than pure water.

"While coconuts cost about 50 rupees (25 English pence), in London the same amount sells for £5 or 1000 rupees a carton!"

Mrs Gamageababynona harnessed the power of the coconut and has used it to earn a living for her family. She enjoys working within the walls, as the Fort has only been getting cleaner and more beautiful over the last few years. And she says she can't complain. During the season she can sell between 20,000 and 30,000 rupees worth of coconuts! She despises the rain as it ruins her business and the hats and makes a cooling drink no longer so appealing when you are drenched to the skin. But she has even thought of that possibility, serving tea and coffee from inside the little blue shelter. She is a woman who thinks of every eventuality, supporting her family whilst doing a job that she loves. With that, she is off, chatting to the next customer while they choose which coconut to buy, her dancing smile never leaving her face.

The Serenader of Galle Fort

Chaminda
Wherever the wind takes him...can be found outside the YMBA

The lighthouse is a beacon of special significance for Galle's resident music-man. It was here that he learnt to play guitar, by the rampart's 'singing wall' – a local spot for burgeoning young musicians. It was also the place he passed one of the final evenings with the love of his life. 'There are some songs I can't sing', Chaminda explains 'they make me too sad'. The Fort serenader is a sensitive soul. Often found in the billiards room of the YMBA, this one-time national billiards competitor has a personal story of love and loss as poetic as the songs with which he captivates audiences across the country.

Chaminda and his twin brother were born in Galle Fort, and both started singing at a very young age. They inherited this talent from both their parents. Their father worked in a tea factory on Donsite Estate, but had a passion for music and would often perform songs publicly, whilst their mother would reserve her melancholy, tuneful voice to sing lullabies to her children at night. Chaminda sees his musical abilities as a gift from God, since they have saved him from punishments at school, where monks took favour on the naughty boy with a sweetly innocent voice, and, more importantly, his gift has given him hope in the depths of despair, when he realised that through his music he would always have something to contribute to the world.

As is the curse of romantics everywhere, Chaminda's heavy heart has dominated and directed his life at every stage. Even his musical career is characterised by his two great love affairs. He decided to throw himself into learning guitar from his brother's friend, after being rejected by the Head Prefect of Galle Muslim Ladies' College for not being an appropriately well-behaved suitor. After school he struggled to make ends meet and it was not until, at age 22, when he found himself featured in a modern-day Cinderella love-story that he was inspired to realise his potential as a singer.

Through music, Chaminda knows he will always have something to contribute to the world.

Chaminda's Cinderella came in the form of an orphaned Catholic Sri Lankan teenager named Asha, forced to work as a servant for his friend's family in Italy. Chaminda, whilst visiting this friend, would play guitar for her every evening, and soon realised she had a beautiful singing voice. The pair fell in love over a course of wistful nights spent singing together, and eloped back to Colombo, where they were married. But marital bliss eluded the young couple, who moved to Galle, spent their last 3,000 rupees on a new denim skirt for Asha to wear, then suffered with no money, no support, and broken promises from friends and employers. After 6 months together, Asha disappeared, leaving Chaminda in a state of devastation, perpetually searching for his wife for the next 19 years.

Against all expectations, Asha suddenly re-entered Chaminda's life in 2013, after he had already made a name for himself as a local musician, seeking him out at the local roti shop in Galle Fort. They passed an idyllic three months together whilst she lived in a villa next door to the YMBA, and spent their days walking around the ramparts arm-in-arm, exploring Galle's old streets, and singing songs together, re-living their own love-story. Chaminda's emotions rise to his eyes as he explains that the only souvenir he has from this time is a silver bangle she bought

"Chaminda is under the curse of romantics everywhere, his heart dominating and dictating his life at every stage, none more so than through his music and songs."

99

"Chaminda believes that his life can be summed up in one line of musical lyrics: 'I always have to come back because my roots are here.' The Fort is his home and, despite the despair he has felt at points, he can never stay away for long."

him, which he wears everyday. Fate, it seems, was not kind to Chaminda, since Asha eventually left Galle Fort, filling the music-man with sorrow once again.

It's clear that Chaminda projects the breadth and depth of his emotional experience through his songs. He's performed at cafes, hotels, and weddings all over the country, drawing unexpected feelings out of his audiences wherever he goes. He recalls the time he sang his favourite song, Lionel Richie's 'Hello' to a young couple in the Refresh restaurant in Hikkaduwa, and the lady was suddenly so overwhelmed with sadness that her lover paid Chaminda 1,000 rupees to stop singing. Chaminda takes pride in rehearsing all his new material at the YMBA, and tried out a Sinhalese song there before performing at a foreigner's wedding in Unawatuna. When asked to dedicate a song to the groom's mother, he poured all he had into this song, and was bemused to notice his efforts had been so effective that the woman had been weeping throughout, despite the happy occasion. He doesn't really understand why his music touches people, but, he says

The historic walls have inspired many love songs, and the Fort many a romantic liaison.

'music is a global language', and will only sing songs he believes have hidden meanings or important messages, such as John Lennon's 'Imagine'. Audience favourites include 'Annie's Song' and 'House of the Rising Sun', whilst John Denver's 'Leaving on a Jet Plane' practically sings itself for him, since his audience never fails to accompany him in the chorus.

Chaminda is drawn to Galle Fort, despite the bittersweet nostalgia of his lost love being contained in its streets. He admits, referencing a song lyric, 'I always have to come back because my roots are here', and explains that he loves to spend time walking the ramparts, 'sharing sadness with the sea'. Galle's serenader knows his career as a musician has saved him from despair on numerous occasions, as it allows him to connect with other people by giving them something of the love story he hides in his soul. His religion is music, he says, and watching him perform, it's easy to understand why.

"Chaminda doesn't really understand why his music touches people but, he says that 'Music is a global language.'"

101

Monkey Business

Chinca the Monkey
&
J.Gamini
Opposite the
Amangalla Hotel

Across the road from the oldest hotel in Sri Lanka the Amangalla situated in old Galle Fort, J. Gamini sits cross-legged, waving at passers-by, gesturing at the tiny monkey prancing around him, with assurances of 'Come! She never bites! Never bites!' Trusting tourists be warned – Chinca, the 4 month old domesticated monkey, does in fact have an appetite for human fingers and earlobes, but her baby teeth do little more than affectionately nibble at hands that stroke her, as J. Gamini laughingly continues his now defunct chant of 'Never bites, never bites!' She's a playful thing, and clearly very attached to her owner, who keeps her tied to a long rope, only to avoid the risk of her being hurt by angry shop keepers or passing vehicles. 'She always comes back' he proudly boasts, 'In my house she runs free in the trees, always returning to have tea with me'.

Mr Gamini primarily makes a living from curious tourists who like to rough-and-tumble with baby Chinca climbing all over them, and enjoy the mesmerising snake-charming he performs with the cobra he keeps in a wicker basket, named, appropriately, 'Cobra'. Unlike many peddlers, he demands no money from tourists who stop to watch or take photos. 'If you like it, you give what you like' he explains, remarkably humble and understanding for a man who depends on these tourist donations for his livelihood and most importantly to feed his adorable monkey. He has to spend much of his earnings on food for both pets: bananas, pineapples, mangoes and grapes for little Chinca and eggs and meat for Cobra.

Chinca will be with him for life, and Gamini treats her just like an energetic baby, in turn cradling and scolding her as she fluctuates between sweetly adorable and a wild nuisance. Cobra, on the other hand, takes a new persona every 50 days, since snakes cannot be kept for longer than this before needing to be released back to the jungle near his home. Snake charming using a flute is magical to watch as the cobra unwinds from the wicker basket and dances while hissing into the air.

Chinca, at four months old, is still very much a baby, playfully dancing around her owner on the walls by the Church Street bell tower

The life of an animal charmer is certainly not free from issue, and keeping up with a baby monkey and a dozing snake can take its toll. As soon as Mr Gamini turns his back on Chinca to speak to tourists or rummage through his bag of fruit, the cheeky monkey grabs his wooden snake-charming flute, and in a matter of seconds has gnawed its mouthpiece until it is beyond use. In this way, Gamini has gone through countless instruments in the past 4 months; his frustration is quelled only by the innocent and lovable face of Chinca smiling, staring back at him fixedly, before pouncing on his head to gently nibble his ear, his face contorted in an expression of what can only be affection and joy. Chinca then lies down on her back so that those passing by can rub her fluffy tummy, something she loves when she is not doing acrobatics off the four hundred year old coral and shell walls.

Chinca and Mr Gamini are now a part of the eclectic mix of people who work and play within the Fort walls so make a point of stopping to play with this cheeky little monkey.

"Come, she never bites! Never bites! J Gamini assures passers-by as they stoop to stroke the naughty monkey."

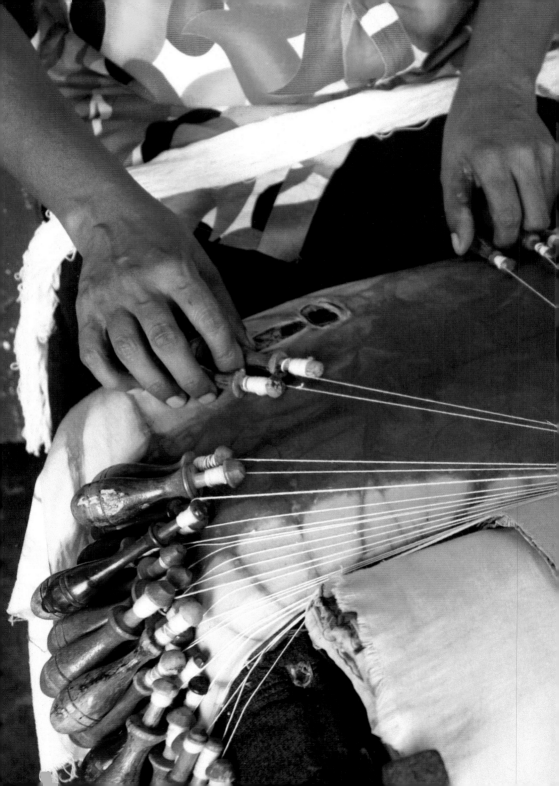

A One Woman Factory

Lace Maker
L.H. Shirani
Reanuka
Mansion House
23 Church Street
0773065339

Seated on a low chair by the entrance to the Mansion House on Church Street, Shirani Reanuka's fingers are working furiously, moving wooden bobbins of rich cream thread from side to side, creating the intricate patterns that she is so well known for. Colourful pins hold the design in place, the finished wonder not revealed until the last pin has been removed. Her colourful shirt stands out against the mahogany wooden wall of the shop that has pride of place at the end of Church Street, one of the busiest streets in Galle Fort, drawing many people wandering past into her lacy web, which she has spent 25 years perfecting.

Taught by her mother, Shirani designs everything herself, drawing it onto cardboard that she then marks with pinholes. The original patterns, often incorporating natural designs like the jasmine flower, are detailed and beautiful, resulting in the most gorgeous pieces of lace that people from miles around buy to adorn dresses and tablecloths with. She works all day, every day, often taking three days to finish one little piece of lace, longer if the many threads become tangled, as they often do! But, she says, she doesn't mind because she truly enjoys it, a passion that came through her blood. It was a skill that was always there; she never really had to learn it.

The finished design is not actually revealed until the last coloured pin is removed from the cushion.

Some post-colonial theorists have seen lace as a kind of Venus Flytrap minus the sexual connotations of course, in that it is meant to promote the ideals of home, nurture, care-giving and other such feminine traits highly valued by most who are mostly ignorant about the potential of the fairer and gentler sex. Yet, Shirani seems to have taken this most subtle and painstaking of arts and created a kind of empowerment using a sort of subversion that can only be felt when one comes into tangible contact with the fabric – its width, length and shape, the corrugations, the patterns – their beginnings, ends and merging of illusions until the epiphany of the mosaics and messages that are not generally immediately discernible.

As she was taught, now she teaches others, sharing her love of the art with youngsters who are just starting out. She tells me with a smile that lights up her entire face, "when others are happy, I am happy." Her dream is to have her own shop, a little haven of her creations. For now though she remains a one-woman factory, a designer, creator and exceptional talent.

"A legacy of the Portuguese, lace making was first practised by Dutch ladies during the Dutch colonial era and Sinhalese ladies learnt from them. Beeralu means bobbin, which is how it is made."

Mango Man

Mango & Spice
Seller
E.B. Munidasa
42 Hospital Street,
at the weekends

There is something very impressive about a man who pushes 1400 mangoes about 28 km every week. Mr. Munidasa loves his job and is immensely proud of his cart, which like his business has quite literally been built by hand, from scrap. As his cart trundles the streets of Galle he beams at everyone, a toothy smile, radiating with friendliness. You might see his cart abandoned in the middle of Law Court Square for ten minutes whilst he nips into one of the nearest kades for a cup of tea. The rest of the time you are likely to see him shuffling behind the powder blue cart he pushes. In his long sarong stained with fruit juice he is an easily recognised and deeply appreciated addition to the team of peddlers who roam the streets and squares of the Fort.

Mr. Munidasa sells slices of succulent mango or pineapple which he carves up before your eyes and in the centre of the cart sits a dark mound of tamarind nuts which coagulate, a cluster of dark brown beads with small tufts of rough hair sprouting along the seams of the shell. Mr. Munidasa says that he does particularly good trade on public holidays and religious holidays such as Poya days when he can sell almost all of his mangoes and goes home with a cart that is practically empty.

Even if you're not a fan of the fruit or the spice then you have to seek out this veteran of the streets just to examine his cart, which is his own creation and should be prized more highly than a vintage Rolls Royce for its sheer ingenuity. The wheels, which carry the cart, have been commandeered from an old bike and apparently perform a good six months in service before they require replacing. The whole contraption is a brilliant electric blue, which stands out even in the brightest sun, though the reason for this is not based on any eye-catching marketing ploy but rather because blue is Mr. Munidasa's favourite colour. All of the parts of this cart originated from the scraps of old fishing boats that line the small beach below the Fort walls. The tin roof that has been beaten into a basic apex

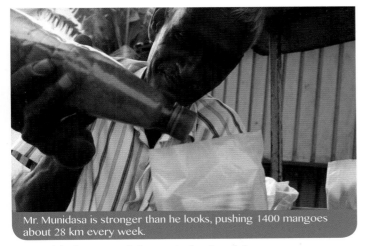

Mr. Munidasa is stronger than he looks, pushing 1400 mangoes about 28 km every week.

is roughly hewn and the main body of the cart seems a rather haphazard jigsaw of pieces of flotsam. But despite its seeming frailty, the cart can be seen traversing the streets from 8 in the morning until 5 at night; Mr. Munidasa proudly tells me that his trusty cart hasn't failed him yet.

Mr. Munidasa should also be sought for the simple pleasure of his company. He is a man who confesses to never being bored of his profession and who relishes the opportunities, which his trade gives him to converse with others. His father may have had the cart for a few years before him but it doesn't appear that his sons will take over from him. Indeed his children have taken to life with gusto choosing trades, which couldn't be more different from their father's. Can you really imagine that a civil servant in Colombo or one of the professional footballers in the team E.B Chianne (Mr. Munidasa says he taught this son all of his skills) can claim this extraordinary character as part of their lineage? As Mr. Munidasa pushes his cart into the radiant crimson gleam of the setting Sri Lankan sun through streets stained blood red with the embers of the day you wish with all of your heart that these same cobbles will bounce the wheels of his cart laden with its weekly load of 1400 mangoes for many years to come as he really is one of the great treasures of this ancient citadel.

"This cart also carries an old fizzy-drink bottle with a hole punctured in its lid through which the customer can sprinkle chilli, salt and pepper powder according to his taste. The contrast between the piquancy of the spice and rich soothing flavour of the mango is immensely cooling on a hot day."

Street Hawker

Lace & Wooden
Carving Seller
Krishantha
60 Pedlar Street
07707003466

As motorbikes dart around barking dogs, cars shoot past with their horns blaring and people stand in doorways watching the world go by, a smiling face and a bright green bag greets you on the corner where Church Street crosses Pedlar Street right in the centre of Galle Fort's busiest shopping area. Depending on the day or how he feels, Krishantha will either be showing you intricate lace dresses or elaborate wooden carvings: you just never know. He will charm and entertain you as you admire his wares, the shade providing a welcome respite from the ferocious heat of the Fort.

Krishantha chooses his selling spot carefully, not wanting to have to compete with anyone else but also finding somewhere that will bring most of the customers straight past him. He moves around a bit, always remaining inside the Fort and always at a junction, a crossroads where he can chat to every person who wanders past. He knows the maze of streets well having been born in the Fort. Now he lives outside the walls but says that there is nowhere else he would go as the Fort "is a nice place to live."

He remembers the Fort when it was quiet and peaceful, a far cry from the bustling citadel that it is today. He

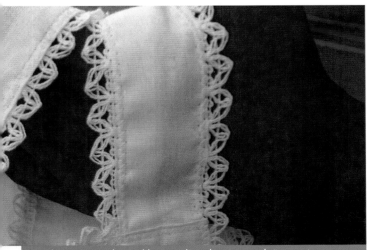

It takes an experienced lace maker about a week to create a metre of one-inch wide lace.

believes that the changes that have happened have been done so as to accomodate the many more tourists pouring through the archways that lead into the Fort. He tells me with a slight smile that of course this is good for business but it has definitely changed the atmosphere of the Fort.

Having been a street seller for the past twenty-five years, Krishantha has seen many families come and go and many homes transformed into shops. He enjoys the tourists who are a constant feature on every street as they are the customers who allow him to continue with what he loves to do. Such is the quality of what he is selling that many locals also buy from him, little lace baby clothes or a delicately carved elephant to adorn a mantelpiece.

He is the kind of man who you can just stop and chat to, even if lace isn't really your thing. Not a pushy character, Krishantha is happy to see everyone. So next time you're ambling down Pedlar Street, in need of a moment's rest, keep an eye out for the smiling seller tucked away in the shade as he will be here for many more years to come.

"Wood is a difficult material to work with as it has a high tendency to crack, to be damaged by insects or to suffer from changes in the atmosphere, which makes the pieces being sold even more special."

Galle Fort's Original Cave Man

Chaminda Kumara
aka Papa
Crêpe-ology

53 Leyn Baan
Street   0776422866

Dark, chocolate brown eyes greet me as Chaminda Kumara, locally known as 'Papa', sits down, his hands resting lightly on the table-top as he begins to tell me about his extraordinary childhood. His eyes glaze over at certain points and I know that in his mind, as he speaks, he can still picture his home and the life he used to lead. He is a member of an old Galle Fort family, one who has always lived, literally, inside its walls. For Papa's family were cave dwellers, living in the old Dutch gunpowder houses that are tucked away within the thick coral walls of the Fort.

Born in the hospital just outside the Fort walls, Papa's home was the caves on Triton Bastion, opposite what is now the Rampart Hotel, little pockets of history that have now been transformed into a row of souvenir shops. His family occupied one of the rooms in the cave whilst another lived next door. They had no electricity and one small lamp would provide them with the light they needed, both families helping one another to cook. Papa remembers his life there as one of great happiness and freedom, playing along the ramparts with his friends and his sister, fishing off the walls everyday, far away from the day-to-day petty troubles that most families face. It was a simple life but one which Papa clearly wishes had never come to an end. When I ask Papa if he misses his life in the caves, he replies, in less than a heartbeat, "of course."

His idyllic childhood came to an abrupt end about sixteen years ago when Papa was 15 years old. The government deemed the caves unsuitable for people to inhabit and moved all the families out. Much to Papa's mother's delight, every family was given a house but Papa says sadly, it was not the same. He always knew though that he would never leave the Fort completely. As he says, "my life's in the Fort." So although he now lives outside the walls that were once his home, he spends all day everyday within them, working, fishing

What was once Papa's cave dwelling is now a row of boutique shops that many wedding couples take their photos in front of.

and just enjoying his life. Having worked as a chef at the Serendipity Arts Café for two years, Papa is now the expert barman at Crêpe-ology, enjoying the tourists who come into the restaurant but always concerned that, in his opinion, they have the potential to damage the special nature of his Fort. He seems to be a modest man of many talents, shrugging off his cooking with a mere "I'm alright" when everyone tells me that he is one of the top chefs in the Fort.

He is still a fisherman at heart, and tries to go out everyday to catch octopuses and mullet for him and his friends. A truly selfless man, Papa does not sell his catch but prefers to throw big parties for all his friends so that they can share in his fortune. But for Papa, the Fort is his home: he cannot think of any reason why he would leave it. Papa feels that his life is richer thanks to his childhood in the caves, one without material possessions or desires, a time which he calls the "Fort's Golden Age." Papa is a Fort boy from an old Fort family and because of this, the magic of the Fort runs through his veins, a magic that you almost glimpse, shimmering in his eyes as he smiles broadly and heads out the door.

"Tunisian people still to this day build their homes like caves, to avoid the intense heat and strong desert winds. People who live in these structures, as Papa and his family did, are called 'troglodyte' people - in 2004 over 2,000 people lived like this."

The Lace Lady of the Walls

Lace Seller
Marliya Saliheen
73 Church Street
0775994616

With her plastic green bag laden with bright white pieces of finery and her shoulders wrapped in a midnight blue scarf, Mrs Marliya Saliheen sets out across the street from where she lives, climbing the small steps that will take her onto Galle Fort's historic coral walls. No longer running around the entire ramparts to sell her goods, Marliya tells me that she only walks between the 1938 British built lighthouse at the end of Hospital Street and the Rampart Hotel, seeking shade underneath the huge branches of the trees which form a place of sanctuary during the midday heat. She is a lace seller, a street peddler and an expert in the art of sales, sensing who may want to stop and have a chat and who is simply content with a smile.

Marliya has been selling lace inside the Fort for thirty-five years, starting up her job to support her family and her new-born son. Lace was the product of choice because of its popularity and quality within this area. The Portuguese initiated the art of lace making in the 16th century in southern Sri Lanka, a skill that continued throughout the Dutch rule. Local ladies learnt the art from their colonial counterparts and now today, the area that surrounds Galle Fort is renowned for its 'Beeralu Mostara' lace making. Six centuries ago when these ladies were busy perfecting their skills, members of royalty and the aristocracy donned lace clothing as a sign of their high status in society. Today much of the lace made throughout this region is used in television dramas that hark back to the days when lace was first introduced. It is also used frequently in Hollywood productions of the same nature for example in 'Elizabeth: The Golden Age' which sees Cate Blanchett sporting many a Sri Lankan lace-adorned corset and the amazing Queen's ruffled lace collar.

Marliya herself comes from a grand old family, three generations of whom grew up in 75 Church Street. It was a noisy and happy childhood as Marliya was the oldest of nine children. She moved with her youngest

It takes Marliya's nieces about a week to make one lace tablecloth.

brother 10 years ago to the house she currently resides in, Number 73 which belongs to her mother, given as a dowry gift on her wedding day. She says that this house "is like a train", long and thin and with life happening along its length. Pieces of her own needlework from when she was just fifteen years old hold pride of place on the mustard yellow wall, the first thing you see as you step over the threshold.

Nowadays though the lace pieces she sells are no longer sewn by her hand but by various nieces, one of whom makes the elaborate pillow lace and another who stitches the lace onto the fabric, creating beautiful nightdresses and tablecloths. It is an all female family affair, making the pieces that Marliya sells even more special. The Fort and its walls, she says, are her home, a peaceful place to live and work. She is starting to feel old, she tells me, no longer able to spend all day out on the ramparts. But she still loves what she does and, as I turn to go, she tells me affirmatively, "I will do this for as long as I can." And the youthful glint in her eyes makes it clear that she means it.

"If you go to Galle Fort's National Museum by the Amangalla Hotel on Church Street, you can see exhibits of an old handmade pillow and a sample of lace crochet work dating back to 1903."

Into The Deep

The Treasure
Hunter of Galle
Fort
Eranga Chamara
Hospital Street

Waves crash into waves, ocean into sea, reason into unreason, and the rational into the irrational and this is just part of the mystique of the deep blue sea that surrounds this ancient citadel. Various shoals of fish arrayed in magnificent disarray, swiftly brush past hunks of remaining reef coral, as life takes on the living. As ever the sea is testy, incorrigible, the final frontier of man, where you will find Eranga the fortune hunter of Galle Fort.

Man is not unwelcome but it is evident that he has no place here, unwanted in this world of endless blue. The wrecks of ships occupy the blips of torpor, menacing in their gargantuan rust, preening with unassuming treasures from a bygone colonial era, burping out the disturbed flurry of marine life. Treasure is now heritage, awaiting discovery, to be tethered to a bucket of rust, forever gleaming, glistening and gilded, forgiven for their obscurity but unforgiven for their loss, antiquarian in eminence and still black in a white market.

With a harpoon on his back this sinking, slinking plunderer marks time, searching for squid and cuttlefish. Dusk plays a game of solitaire and retracts its vice grip - darkness succumbs. The curled beings sleep in the warmth of relief. If ever you needed proof that man has evolved to suit his habitat then please look no further than Hospital Street's Eranga Chamara. He is the son of a fisherman and grandson of a man who used to make his living diving for shells, a product of a family attached to the sea. Seeing Eranga out fishing is like watching a golden eagle soar supreme in the starlit skies.

When he enters the shallows clad only in a pair of swimming trunks and fins, a piece of wire wrapped about his waist and a snorkel and mask covering his face he strikes that rather inelegant image of the ordinary man enjoying a spot of beach fishing. That is until he plunges into the water, harpoon clenched in one hand, cutting

Eranga's grandfather's house is a treasure trove in itself, reflective of a man who spends his life exploring the hidden and the ancient.

through the waves with a grace and speed that is beyond that of anyone you are likely to see in the Western world. Instead Eranga has an innate ability to find his way about clumps of coral with great ease. He is drawing not only on his skill as a swimmer but a fantastic memory of how the sea lies at different times of the day and how the rocks can accordingly be submerged at nine in the morning and jut proud out of the sea by six at night.

Fishing he tells me has also become more problematic since the tsunami that caused a seismic shock within the watery habitat of Galle, disrupting ingrained breeding patterns of many species. This is an issue, which Eranga is dealing with now, over ten years on. He believes that the new patterns of movement and breeding are becoming established showing how, like the Fort, the sea is also an ever changing environ.

You don't have to talk to Eranga for long to discover that this man is at one with the ocean that lives as the mistress of his heart, captivating his imagination and calling him to the water everyday. Eranga may leave the water without a scratch but by the time the coral had finished with me I looked like I'd been given a once over with a cheese grater, but its worth it to see the sea world first hand.

"During the season he also finds it better to fish at night by the light of a head torch which illuminates his dazed and sleeping adversaries before he spears them on a metal spike."

Life In A Cart

Vegetable Seller
Mr Priyantha
Can be found early
morning on the
backstreets of the
Fort

Mr Priyantha who offers the ultimate in convenience shopping, arrives with his mobile vegetable cart on Fort doorsteps at the same time every morning. There is no need to fill out order forms or even reach for a credit card; all the household matriarchs have to do is walk out onto their front porch having decided their curry menu for the day. Mr Priyantha begins his day in Galle, filling his sack-lined metal basket balanced on top of a three-wheeled wooden frame with produce from the original Dutch fruit and vegetable markets.

Everything finds a place in this travelling cart from twisted snake gourds, to leafy green plants used for medicinal purposes in cooking and sweet, yellowing papaya. Full of colourful produce, Mr Priyantha pushes the cart in through the tunneled entrance of the main Fort gate. Once inside the ancient fortress he works around in a clockwise motion making his way down every street. His rickety cart can be heard trundling along in the late morning heat as it is carefully steered around deep potholes. He cries out "elawalu, elawalu", ("vegetables, vegetables") rousing the wives and grandmothers from their household duties.

A veritable smorgasbord of raw freshness from the inlands of Galle.

He weighs shiny aubergine, potatoes, beans and carrots in the scales hanging from the roof of the cart and tosses them into waiting hands or plastic bags. He may also sell the odd lottery ticket dangling from the shady heights of his medieval travelling shop.

Mr Priyantha happily sells his wares to everyone, however, he is worried about his future as more supermarkets spring up and people indulge in this new Western phenomenon of bulk buying everything in one shop. This must not happen in the Fort, for the patterns elsewhere in the world show that it leads to bad health, laziness, loss of local and cultural culinary knowledge amongst the young generation, and eventually after a generation of extreme ill health there is a reversion back to small local businesses and fresh home delivered food. So rise up and support the local vendors and buy daily fresh vegetables like pumpkin, which is believed to clean the stomach and to be especially beneficial for smokers!

"Ever since their introduction to India in 1498, chillies have been included in many Ayurveda medicines, medicines that are still 'used' in the Fort"

Sweet Man of Galle Fort

W.J. Samankumara
Street corn Seller

The loud ringing of a golden bell is a warning sound that W.J. Samankumara with his steaming cobs of sweet corn is just around the corner with his travelling blue cart flashing piles of lush yellow corn, which is lit up at night with a parafin flame adding a golden glow to this carnival like character.

A large white bowl makes the steaming golden nuggets irresistible in this ingenious sea-blue contraption. Below the handles there is an opening, which reveals the cart's innards, where a small gas stove heats a water tank above it. There is a hole at the top of the tank through which steam pours up through small holes into the bowl. This has to be the ultimate travelling snack shop. A tupperware for the profits or old biscuit tin on some days, as well as an old ice cream carton containing some salt water sit on top of his moving stall.

Mr. Samankumara aka Mr Corn travels around the Fort every day from around 4pm, spending one day a week journeying to Monaratara, a hot, tropical area inland

The sweet corn man's lamp lights his way around the old city

from the Fort where farmers grow hundreds of acres of the wispy green crop. Getting them ready in the morning to sell is all part of his daily routine. He explains it is the perfect afternoon snack for the energy-zapped labourer, families walking along the ramparts or those returning home and hungry after a hard days work. It can either be eaten as it comes or dipped in the salt water for a different taste sensation. This smiley, good-natured vendor clenches his fist in a Popeye like gesture to highlight that the corn is healthy and good for building body strength.

He does not stick around for long and is always keen to keep moving on in search of more customers. He can often be seen passing out of the Fort after dark with an old flaming lamp lighting his way home, followed by fireflies and a few hungry travellers, which are always good for his last sales by the busy Galle bus stand.

"Grown by the Native American tribes and spread by European settlers in 1779 across the world, arriving in Sri Lanka via trade routes which bought many vegetables to the island."

Sri Lanka's Greatest Swinger

Flying
Carpet Hammocks
Captain Sunil
Serendipity Arts
Café
65 Leyn Baan Street
0777151570

Ten years ago it was said, "one day every garden will have one of Sunil's hammocks in it." Today this prophecy has pretty much come true. Over cinnamon spice tea he tells us the earliest hammocks were woven out of bark from the Hamack tree and when he started he only wanted to create muted colours that reflected his time working on a boat. It is this knowledge of ships and boats that makes him such a perfectionist at making the ropes hardy and strong enough to hang from anything. He calls his brand the flying carpet of Sri Lanka and unlike the flying carpets of India one swing and you do feel like you are flying through the air.

Sunil believes he got a second chance at life, one gifted to him after the awful events of the Boxing Day tsunami in 2004, when a quarter of a million people died across the Indian Ocean. Sunil was riding his bike along the coastal Sea road in his hometown of Galle when he was swept inland by a thirty foot wave, an experience that nearly killed him as he was dragged under the water with cars and debris coming at him from all directions. Surviving the disaster when 36,000 of his fellow islanders died changed his life completely. In Sunil's first life he was a bad boy sailor and for seventeen years he worked on various different yachts in and around the Galle area. But as he gazes into the distance, momentarily caught lost within memories of the high seas as a lover of women, you can tell that the tsunami changed his outlook forever on that fateful day. He is still a sailor and will always be a fisherman, aspects of his life that he will never lose. But his focus now is on his hammocks and on creating them in every colour under the sun.

The idea sprung from when Sunil saw a photo of a hammock in a magazine and simply thought, "I can do that, but better." And so he set out to prove his theory right. And prove it he most certainly has. With French reggae music playing in the background, Sunil and his ever-growing team make all the hammocks from his house in New Town Galle. As well as the three boys he has

Rasta man Sunil showing off a flaming orange hammock and the comforting contours of it which even the President has as a gift on the day he opened the Dutch Hospital complex 20th September 2014

employed to help make the hammocks, Sunil also hires a tailor and a carpenter to make sure that every aspect of the product is perfect. He loves making hammocks and it is where he's always wanted to be: "I'm happy."

Happiness is something that Sunil values above all else, not only his own but also that of others around him. In 2013, when Sunil decided to return to India to seek out his family there, his grandfather was originally from the neighbouring country, he ended up teaching ten people the skills and techniques needed to create hammocks to his own design, providing them with a livelihood they otherwise would not have had. Sunil doesn't make things because of money; that is something that "I don't want to touch. I just want to make." He has started branching out from hammocks though as he is a great believer in the future generations and is conscious about giving them a safe but incredible place to play. It was he who created the bright green rope bridge that you can see at the Thomas Gall International School in pride of place next to the cricket nets, happy children running up and down its length.

He jumps on his bike and says "for now I like being small, after all a hammock is to relax and have fun in."

"Hammocks grew in popularity in Central and Southern America because, by suspending their beds above the ground, inhabitants were better protected from disease transmission, insect stings or animal bites. Today you can swing into action at the Dutch Hospital Sri Lanka 'Hammock bar'."

A Miracle Home Brew

Ginger Tea Seller
M.R.M. Rizan
The streets of the
Fort
0717873750

M.R.M. Rizan is a mover and a shaker and his wife is a very good tea maker. During the time of the ancient Romans, a pound of ground ginger was so expensive that it was equivalent to a whole sheep! Mr Ginger Tea as he is fondly known rides around with a plastic bright blue crate and a hand painted wooden sign making this man and his bicycle stand out as he circumnavigates the Fort walls from 9am until 11 and then again from 3 until 6pm. Mr Rizan is Galle Fort's very own tea caddy service, and community news vendor.

Mr Ginger Tea has been coming in and out of the Fort for the last two years, making the scenic journey along the coastal road. Having been a builder of cement blocks for most of his life, he decided he needed a change, moving on to a job that allows him to wheel through life! He is a self-employed, self-made man who can go about his business whenever and wherever he chooses, stopping to chat to his friends seated in the Law Court Square or simply pulling his bike over to the side of the street and watching the world go by.

Mr Rizan may be the seller and the charmer but it is his wife who is the tea brewer. He tells me he sells two different varieties of tea, ginger and cardamom. His secret though is to mix the two together as the smell of the cardamom perfectly compliments the strong taste of the ginger. Ginger is what the modern day market would label as a 'super-food' but the people of the Fort and across Sri Lanka have been drinking the warming draft for hundreds of years as it stops fishermen from throwing up whilst braving the rough seas.

Mr Rizan tells me that he thinks ginger tea is best for fighting colds and sore throats but is also good for weight loss. It is proven to even help with the recovery from frostbite, as it improves your circulation getting the essential blood flow back to the injured limb. Cardamom too is an essential part of the Sri Lankan diet as it aids

Ginger tea man Rizan gingerly rides his old bike in the middle of the streets, a harbinger of health and comfort

"Legend has it that the first cup of tea was brewed in 2737 BC when dried leaves landed by accident in a cup of boiling water being served to the Chinese Emperor Shen Nung."

digestion and can help with any gastric problems that you may have. In reality, Mr Rizan is selling miraculous potions, liquid wellbeing served out of plastic white cups.

Mr Rizan's concoction is in high demand wherever he travels to. Though he used to station himself around the mosque and the ramparts that surround this fortress, he now travels through the streets, stopping to re-fuel thirsty builders refurbishing and restoring old buildings or tourists, fatigued after a day spent roaming through the streets. Mr Rizan says that the best part about his job is that he is free to move about as he pleases and, as he climbs back on his bike and heads off down Church Street, you can sense that this is a man who can never really be tied down, a man who will determine his own fate, wherever the wind may take him.

The Sultan's Snack Food

Patti & Samosa Seller
A.R.M Fais
The streets of the Fort

A.R.M Fais' rides around on the equivalent of the Rolls Royce of bikes, a timeless classic in its own right but one that in many Western countries would actually be worth a fortune. The bike that Mr Fais uses would have cost him about $30 maybe even less than that and yet the same bike, made by the famous English brand Pashley, would today cost you around $1,000, simply because they have now been labelled as 'vintage' rather than just old. Mr Fais' samosa-carrying carriage however is very much one of a kind. With a glass case strapped perilously on the back and a small silver umbrella hanging from the handlebars, Mr Fais has been journeying to Galle Fort on his thousand-dollar pushbike for the last seven years. He makes the journey around tea time to sell fresh samosas and patties, known as 'Short Eats,' to the hungry people after work within its walls, steaming parcels of deliciousness made with love in Thalapitiya, some two kilometres from the Fort.

Mr Fais used to work in a hotel as a waiter but is now a sort of deliveryman stroke salesman. He is not actually the chef however. The cooks are Mr Fais's friends from Thalapitiya who produce the food from their own kitchens using only the finest local ingredients, in time for Mr Fais to head to the Fort in the early evening, the back of his bike laden with delectable treats. Upon his return home, he distributes each persons' share of the day's profits before wearily heading home to his two daughters.

His bike has been ingeniously altered; the glass case that holds all the goodies does not have the slightest wobble as Mr Fais masterfully navigates around Galle Fort's narrow streets. The smell that wafts behind him is just too tempting not to try. When you stop to purchase a snack it is handed to you in a bag made from pieces of notepaper, recycled work from local houses and schools. Mr Fais tells me that despite all the many snack bars and cafes that have popped up all

The glass box with delectable crispy golden squares of savoury delight

"Samosas were introduced to South Asia during the Muslim Delhi Sultanate, which ran from the 13th to the 16th century, when cooks from the Middle East and Central Asia migrated to work in the kitchens of the Sultan and the nobility."

over the Fort, people still want to buy from him and he (nearly) always cycles home with an empty case.

Though Mr Fais has never lived in the Fort, he is very much a man who has been captured by its charm. He loves his job as he gets the opportunity to meet people as well as to explore the streets he now knows so well. It is a nice place to work and Mr Fais tells me strongly that he will keep on selling his scrumptious delights for many years to come. And with that he is off, no need to shout about his snacks, he simply lets the smell that tantalisingly follows him do all the talking.

The Octopus Catcher

A.S Mubarak
(Noor)
Flag Rock

A tall, thin man with a rod over his shoulder wades through the aquamarine waters in front of the ramparts. He moves so carefully, navigating over sun-warmed stones that barely a ripple appears on the water's surface. This is Noor, the octopus catcher.

He cycles up to the Flag Rock area of the ramparts sometimes twice in a morning, if the water has not been shallow enough on his first attempt. Second time lucky he glides up, puts away his bicycle and arrives, sharing a few words with his friends, the vendors, and excitedly raises himself up on tiptoes to inspect the water level. He does a few excitable jumps on the spot, suggesting an eagerness to be in the water. Noor has been fishing off the ramparts for thirty-nine years, and probably knows this subterranean underworld inside out, every nook and cranny among the rocks where his slippery, tentacled friends are hiding.

Whether wading or diving with a mask and snorkel, as soon as he sees his adversaries he taps them on the head with his rod to urge them out of their rocky hiding places and then holds out his arm, and they wrap their tentacles around it, as if to catch their predator. He then draws them up out of the water and either throws them in a bag if he has one with him, or slings them

Noor reveals that octopuses have three hearts

across his shoulder. It is a peculiar sight - a man with slippery black or white octopuses covering his body, gradually drying out in the sun. He is reminiscent of a character from a Greek myth, even his name, Noor, sounds Odyssian, other-worldly. There are two types of octopuses that he catches, one is black with yellow spots and the other is white with red spots.

After his morning session, he takes his catch of fish to the market in Galle, and sells the octopus to local restaurants outside the Fort or to private households. Sometimes he keeps one for himself and enjoys eating it in a light curry sauce. On average the octopus weighs about a kilo. However, the largest one he has caught was four and a half kilos and had a 3ft tentacle span.

A social, lively, saronged man on land, but a lone, solitary, statue-like figure who seems ancient, as old as the island itself when in water. Before there was any civilization on this rocky promontory, there were fishermen from coastal villages, who visited these waters everyday, wading in an environment of absolute calm and tranquility. Here Noor says you will always find harmony and real peace within yourself.

"After the tsunami it took a year for sea-life to return to normal, highlighting the extent of the disruption caused."

Flying Men

Fort Jumper
Chamara Sampath
Flag Rock

They start out like oversized spindly bats with splayed arms and fingers like hooking pegs for ends meant for latching on, bouncing their absorbed cosmic and soaked karmic energy sonar waves right off the face of the orange sun, fixed like dark matter for a fleeting moment lodged in the glistening york of the sun, only to then nosedive like a kamikaze bomber just been hit, before careening head-on towards a seductive pool of blue water surrounded by crashing white froth and dangerously jutting rock faces. Not quite possessed with the tragic ideals of Icarus, instead freestyle divers are blessed more with brazen braggadocio, full of a devil may care attitude, which allows them the confidence to pull off this death defying feat several times on a daily basis. To paraphrase the poetess Sylvia Plath, if dying is an art, then these daredevils play with it exceptionally well and what's more, these self-made entrepreneurs have made it a profession to aspire to, resulting in severe injuries for many foolhardy to attempt the stunt themselves.

Fort jumping started in 1993 and is the world's equivalent to the bungee jump only a lot more dangerous, because there is no elasticised rope to pull you back from the near death experience, or even a totally clear landing point! This hair-raising forty-five foot jump is based on the Fort ramparts at Flag Rock, between Point Utrecht Bastion and Triton Bastion. For those that like to dice with mortality and experience Fort life on the edge, nothing beats watching these five jumpers spring into action; Chamara, Lasantha, Chinthaka, Rawan, and Ranga.

It is amazing that even on a windy or stormy afternoon each diver always miraculously misses the deadly rocks below. A few visitors have tried and not surprisingly in most cases have ended up very badly hurt. This tragically includes a Japanese guy who broke both his legs and an Italian tourist who landed head first on the rocks smashing his face and arms to pieces. So Chamara and his friends would not reccomend that you, in a moment of bravado, attempt to try out 'The Jump'.

The jumpers see turtles swimming about, when they dive into the sea from Flag Rock.

Each lad has an amusing story to tell, however there is a deep sadness in their eyes as they recall the events of the tsunami in 2004. Chamara says "It was a busy morning on the ramparts, more than any other peak tourism season day as it was both a religious and public holiday." A local tourist group pulled up in a van and asked Chamara to jump and after negotiating a price he started to run as the water rose up to meet him at the top of the Fort wall. It was so high that even a small child could have done the jump that morning. It meant for the first time ever Chamara didn't need to climb back up the rock face, and within seconds of being back on his jumping spot he was even more alarmed to see the seawater recede. Chamara says, "It was just like the plug had been pulled out of the Indian Ocean. I could see everything on the seabed and was amazed that places like Elephant Rock had rocks underneath it in the form of legs and everywhere there were beautiful multi-coloured corals, fish gasping for breath and bodies. I knew then something was terribly wrong and ran as fast as I could straight home to check on my mum and sisters. Luckily they were okay, however it taught me one thing: to have an even greater respect for the sea."

"If I could have my life over again I would have only two wishes and that is to teach this [jumping] in every school around the country and lobby for this to be a national sport like cricket!"

An Instant Life Changer

Lottery Ticket
Seller
Dilip Nilantha
The streets of the
Fort
0722048906

Dilip Nilantha is a man who holds your fortune at his fingertips in the form of a simple set of numbers scribbled in biro on a notepad, a person who has the power to change your life in an instant. Mr Nilantha is one of the most valued people within Galle Fort because, as he cycles around each and every street that makes up this citadel, he carries with him the promise of change and good luck. He is of course one of the Fort's lottery ticket sellers, a beacon of hope, inspiring people to part with their hard earned cash simply to see if today may be their lucky day.

Mr Nilantha counts himself as a pretty lucky guy. It was in 2006 that he decided to leave his government job working for the Urban Council in Kurunegala, seizing an opportunity to change his life around. He, like so many of the street peddlers within the Fort recognised that there was money to be made and freedom to be had inside the fortress walls. And so, fixing a wooden board to the front of his trusty jet-black bike, he set out to the local lottery offices and the rest, as they say, was moneymaking history.

Mr Nilantha's job is however more important than most people wandering around the Fort realise as he carries peoples' destinies on a purple square notepad, its pages fluttering perilously in the wind as Mr Nilantha twists and

Sweep tickets, in reds and blues, promising a new tomorrow, forever within reach but ever elusive.

turns around each corner. He tells me that though his job is to sell the tickets, he is also the person who people have to come back to in order to check their numbers each day. This means that Mr Nilantha has seen a fair few winning tickets in his time and has been hugged and adored by each and every ecstatic winner.

When I inquire further about the winners of this fortuitous game, he tells me in a low whisper that though he cannot tell me who it was, someone who bought a ticket from him once won 20 lakhs (about 15,400 dollars) making them millionaires in an instant. Bear in mind that one ticket will only cost you 20 rupees (less than one dollar) and you realise why it is not surprising that Mr Nilantha is so popular within the Fort, both with tourists and locals alike.

He tells me that he works in a place that is full of his closest friends, completely free to ride around the five streets that he knows better than the back of his hand, a black cap pulled firmly down over his brow, the coloured tickets flapping in the wind, a lucky talisman to all.

"In 1567, Queen Elizabeth I established the first English lottery when she offered 400,000 tickets for sale. Prizes included china, tapestries and cash."

Menu a la Kade

Keerthi Kade
Mr and Mrs K. de
Silva
81 Lighthouse
Street

When I first walk past this kade I hardly notice it amongst the bustle of the town and the huge array of bright posters that drag your attention first this way and then that way in order to sell SIM phone cards or water bottles or yoghurt or electricity…

"Hello miss!"

Deep in the bowels of the kade on my right and seated in the murky darkness created by the posters and billboards that crowd the entrance is a wizened old man smartly dressed in a clean shirt and sharply pressed trousers at the side of a plastic table covered in a thin green sheet that billows in the slightest breeze. A kade (meaning tea shop and village grocers) is effectively what the old corner shops used to be in the UK and when I enter and sit down this man leaps to his feet in order to assist in any way he can. He explains that this is "madam's shop" and when I ask him a few questions about it he advises that I return later if I want to find out more.

It is clear from the first few exchanges about the shop that Mrs K. de Silva is incredibly proud of her establishment and she has cause to be so. Although she has not yet matched the record of her father who ran the shop for sixty years until he died at the age of 87 she has run the place for forty years and intends to do so until her son and then hopefully her granddaughters take over.

But alongside this sense of tiredness there is also one of resignation and acceptance that obviously runs in the family. She explains that her son works for a telecom company and doesn't really enjoy his job but like her has to continue working for his family and to survive. She is like most Sri Lankans in that she works for "small money" and life is often hard for those like her who "earn small". Her shop has a strong link to the outside town and many people who were born and raised in the Fort but have now moved outside, return to the shop out

Coils of golden rope for all purposes, a leftover from the now near defunct coir industry in the area.

of loyalty to buy their lunch and food. For many Sri Lankans without a family at home to prepare a lunch for them her shop is she explains a place at which they can find a good honestly priced meal and a place to talk. The community in this shop is fantastic and many people come to share their problems over a cup of tea and a bite to eat either to relieve a burden from their shoulders or else to seek advice.

"What we can do we did." murmurs Mrs K. de Silva when I mention the tsunami and the other customers agree and tell me in detail of how they took clothes and food to the hospital or else walked around the affected areas with blankets and bottles of water. The sense of togetherness in the face of adversity is palpable and is inspiring to witness. When I get up to leave I ask for a photo and Mrs K. de Silva blushes with pleasure. The other customers chuckle and begin to offer excuses as to why they cannot partake in the opportunity but when Mrs K. de Silva makes the matronly call to her husband to join her he looks as pleased as punch and pauses to tuck in his shirt and comb his hair in the glass front of the cabinet.

"Mrs de Silva's father ran the kade for sixty years, right up until his death aged 87. She has run it for forty years and intends to do so until the next generation is ready to follow in her footsteps."

Fishy Tales

Fish Crier
of
Galle Fort
Premasiri
'known as
Mr. Original'
The backstreets of
Galle Fort

"Malu, Malu, Fish, Fish" is Galle Fort's equivalent to the medieval dawn crier, as he wakes everyone up as he cycles by on his 1920s Singer bike, ready to sell you the dawn's catch of the day. Premasiri, the oldest fisherman in the Fort, is always fully geared up with portable weighing scales that hark back to the medieval period, blocks of ice to stop the fresh fish from going off in the tropical sun and a blood stained cleaver so big he could probably do you some serious damage if you don't buy his fish. After a good haggle over the price he will slice the fish up on an old wooden cutting board and will even de-bone it on special request, giving the left over tail or head to the incredibly spoilt Fort cats.

Listen early morning for his cry in tune with the sounds of a rusty bike pedal and bell. Despite being in his late sixties he will deliver directly to your guesthouse or villa. Premasiri like other fishermen, will happily take you out on a fishing boat for a small fee to experience night fishing under the stars or for a couple of hours in the day to go and see the pods of dolphins or whales, which pass by the Fort between December and April. If you would like to do this, go out of the Fort Old Gate and walk up along this pretty beachside stretch in front of the exterior rampart walls

As there is no supermarket in the Fort, fish is sold door to door

The best place to see the fishermen is right outside the Old Gate

where local fishermen barter over prawns, octopuses and exotic fish of all sizes and you can ask at one of the many stalls. You can buy anything there from giant lobster to crabs, and you can also try Ambul Thiyal, a pickle usually made from tuna.

The fishing industry is the oldest in Sri Lanka and the local stilt fisherman is so important to the island that he has become a national tourist icon, appearing on the cover of guidebooks and in all national airline promotions. As one tucks into fish with garlic sauce and spice, one has to marvel that a man balancing on a stick, which becomes a buffer against unpredictable seas, caught this at dawn. This is one of the reasons why this beautiful image of the stilt fisherman has been picked to be part of a giant mural centrepiece in the newly refurbished Maritime Museum.

Galle Fort is one of the few places in the world where you do not have to go to the supermarket as everything comes straight to your door, even sometimes old men with four-poster beds on their heads.

Go Nuts

Nut Seller
Mrs. Gunangani
Flag Rock

At Flag Rock the location of the original Dutch Fort Lighthouse you will definitely meet the lovely Mrs. Gunangani, who sells daily her delicious roasted and spicy snacks. She makes them out of rice flour or roasted lentils with spices and fresh curry leaves picked from her garden. She also sells freshly cooked nuts which are roasted in front of you on a wok with the local sand used to heat them up and then served piping hot out of little paper bags made out of homework sheets from her lovely daughter's old used school books.

Her tiny stall is decorated with a chain made out of dried chilies and limes hanging down from its roof to ward off evil spirits which adds to the charm of this blue cart that is one of the icons of food vending in the area. Some days she also serves chickpeas served out of recycled newspaper – a delicious and eco-friendly way to have a nutritious snack while sitting watching the boys jump off the old rampart walls or while trying to catch a view of the local turtles that nest and eat off the reef on a clear day.

The area around Mrs Gunangani's stall is alive with pop up vendors' carts, sometimes with as many as fifteen selling different goods at one time during the season. Goods include Mr Wimalarathna's mobile tuk-tuk

Lightly roasted crunchy peanuts full of nutrients and ideal as a tasty snack while biding time waiting for a bus or a girl.

selling wood-carved religious statues and popular ornaments such as secret boxes and elephants, which he has been doing for nearly thirty years. Before this he sold coral, but stopped when it became an illegal practice and is now famous around town for his mobile hand crafted blue tuk-tuk shop. Also Hussein, the mango seller can be seen slicing and dicing mangoes late afternoon with a knife, before plopping them into a bucket of water, rinsing them and then bagging them up for locals to enjoy on their evening sojourn.

The vending community also includes lace sellers, old coin-selling dudes with rusty boxes and others selling giant cotton tablecloths. Who knows what the traveller might discover at this makeshift ever changing market craft area, which is always full of surprises and stories of life in the old Fort. No one is more interesting on traditional trading life than Gunangani who is always full of fun and freshly roasted nuts that will give you plenty of energy to do the full one hour circuit walk of the old walls.

"The nuts for sale on the stall are roasted right in front of you in a large wok, using local sand to heat it up."

145

FORT
PROFESSIONALS

A Living Heritage

Tharanga Liyana
Arachchi
Galle Heritage
Foundation
212 1/1 Wakwella
Road
0777721547

Tharanga Liyana Arachchi, Project Planning Officer is deeply passionate about the Galle Fort and its surrounding area and his key concern is sustainable tourism as numbers grow, that means protection of the social educational values and without considering this you can't develop a deep level of heritage values. You must protect the environment or vanish under all the rubbish from the tourists and if Tharanga has one message it is, take your rubbish home with you! He also worries that everything is too focused on Galle Fort and yet there are so many amazing places of colonial interest in the surrounding area like Wakwella

Remnants of the colonialists were found entrenched and embedded within the very fabric of the architecture that is grand, magnificent and yet at the same time succumbs to the harsh weather of Galle Fort.

"The Heritage Foundation wishes the Galle Fort to be an architectural monument to history whilst being a testament to a living Fort unlike any other in Asia."

and by mapping and promoting these it will help those communities as well. Lots of valuable cultural areas like the Rumasalla Mountain will allow the spread of tourism across the Galle area.

Tharanga has worked with the Galle Heritage Foundation for nearly ten years, and has had the fascinating job of researching and restoring many of the original Fort historical buildings over the last decade and is also currently doing his PhD on

"It is absolutely imperative that we find the correct masons, carpenters and trained professionals for the restorative work."

Building Archaeology; colonial cultural landscape in the Galle area. Through careful work with master craftsmen, incredible finds have been made including from behind crumbling facades and badly built 1950s screened-up colonnades, which, when removed, have revealed magnificent Dutch and British merchant architecture.

Before working in Galle Fort for the Galle Heritage Foundation as Project Planning Officer, Tharanga did research and excavation work in the ancient cities of Polonnaruwa and Anuradhapura. In the process he found irrigation artifacts dating from the 2nd century AD. In 2002 he travelled around the country looking at original Portuguese and Dutch forts. At one stage, he reveals "There were 43 Portuguese forts in Sri Lanka and amazingly there was also a location at Elephant Pass."

Tharanga has, with the Galle Heritage Foundation, restored fifty-five historical Fort houses and helped with the opening of The Dutch Hospital, which was restored for the CHOGM Commonwealth Meeting of world leaders in 2013. To achieve the incredible level of restoration which he is renowned for, not only requires identifying the most important buildings but

In a testament to architectural restoration, local academics, local craftsmen and local labourers contributed to restoring Fazal's house.

"A lonely job that requires absolute knowledge and absolute patience to counter the number of hours that one spends second guessing what is best and what is historically accurate when deciding on restoring architectural gems."

also finding masons, carpenters, and painters with the right traditional expertise and then specially training them. The Galle Heritage Foundation only employs traditional craftsmen, who have a lot of experience passed down to them through family lines. But despite generations of knowledge, Tharanga explains, "the problem at first is that they do not know how to identify heritage or how to protect it and we have to teach them material identification and other specialist techniques." For example, "they might have a great skill for wood carving but until they understand the history, they can't identify from what period the original wooden features come from." The painters have to learn to use a special paint called Samara – mixed with lime – like the one used on the exterior walls of the Maritime Museum.

In May 2007, 24 Chando Street, a late 18th century Dutch house became the first of Galle Heritage's restoration projects. Tharanga explains: "the owner, Mrs. Daya Sudangama was the first applicant to apply, that's why the house was restored first. It was in a ruined condition. It had mixed Dutch and British features. The British changed the façade by putting

"Sri Lanka's first police station was established in 1848 in Galle Fort and this was due to the British being so debauched that one inspector was appointed and 19 PCs employed to control British drinking."

in small windows and using brick columns. But we took it back to its original Dutch state: a veranda with columns, large windows and doors and a central courtyard. When the Dutch first started building they used mostly timber as a building material but then converted to using lime columns. In contrast, the British used brick columns."

Another, perhaps more interesting, historical project is 56A Lighthouse Street, a building which dates from the beginning of the 18th century. In the British period it was used as a printing office and there were two presses in situ when the restoration work started. The company's name was Albion Press and it functioned from 1860 until the end of the century. Tharanga says, "In this building there were almost no changes from the Dutch period: it was almost totally unchanged from what it would have been like 300 years ago. A toilet was built in the façade in the

The 55 House Restoration Project changed Fazal's life completely.

20th century so we removed this, rebuilt the columns using coral and lime and converted the façade back to the original." This was a very expensive building to conserve: "25% was paid by Galle Heritage and the owners contributed the other 75%."

"As a monument" says Tharanga "I like the area from Star Bastion to Sun Bastion because it is a symbol of Southern Sri Lanka. The iconic clock tower is situated here and it offers scenic views over the old and new town and you can now see the prison with the models outside." Contrary to what most people think the Portuguese and Dutch worked closely with the local people, who were involved in building the rampart walls and original merchant houses. Tharanga explains, "The Dutch built the Fort not as a defense against local people, but to protect against foreign invasions by the French, Danish and the British."

"At 72 Leyn Baan Street – the local storyteller Fazal Jiffrey Badurdeen's house with the famous Dutch Café, Tharanga says: "When we destroyed the front façade of Fazal's home we found timber columns and doorframes inside the wall dating from the Dutch period."

153

The aim of building the Fort for the Portuguese and Dutch was to control Galle as a harbour city, whereas the British were more interested in using it for administration. With a smile he reveals, "The Portuguese's enemy were the Arabians, because of the competition for trade in gem stones, coffee and exotic spices." The harbour has a very long and fascinating history. It was originally called Gimheththe by the Sinhalese, which translates to 'bay of Galle.' Its history spans back 2,500 years. In the 11th century a monk called Chula Wansa wrote a document in Pali on palm leafs mentioning the harbour and although Galle Heritage will not be involved in its restoration they recognise that it is the key to the future of the Fort's success as a major tourism hot spot.

"In 74 Church Street, when Heritage demolished the front wall, they discovered an old British masonry brick wall and British-built arches. The original Dutch building would have had columns."

The job has many challenges from changing public opinion to educating people about the value of historical buildings. Tharanga says Galle Heritage's main aim is "to convert Galle Fort into a cultural tourism area, protect the authenticity of the buildings, protect the inhabitants and the heritage, to encourage the local people not to sell their properties by making them aware that they are part of the unique heritage, to take responsibility for protecting the living situation of Galle Fort, and to facilitate tourists and other institutes. Before starting conservation work, the most important thing is to protect the original families that have been living in the Fort for generations. This is a huge part of our aim. We give financial help so that people can have the chance to stay in their ancestral houses. The main asset the Fort has is its inhabitants. Without them we cannot protect the Fort."

Whatever the challenges, Tharanga believes passionately in his work: "I like the history of this Fort as a living monument. There are many fortresses in Sri Lanka, but most of them are not living. The only living monument is Galle Fort. Most of the inhabitants are now friends of mine. I feel strongly about protecting this heritage as it is the duty of our generation to conserve it for both the people who live here now and for future generations. Part of my job is managing film crews who are using the aesthetic values of Galle Fort Heritage and the people to be film extras allowing them new job opportunities and valuable income, who knows there maybe a future star

Number 94 was one of the houses involved in the project that has been restored to its former glory.

among them." It is important as tourism grows to identify the wider area of Galle Heritage sites and map them with a branding exercise to show the breadth of colonial involvement in the area and who knows we might be able to do canal trips by the Dutch built Railway station.

To find out more do go and visit the Galle Heritage Foundation tourist information office at Baladaksha Mawatha, Galle by the old gate. Here they will supply you with maps and the plans for the next ten years in which the community hopes through groups like Greener Galle to make the old citadel the world's first carbon neutral World Heritage Site. www.galleheritage.gov.lk

"One of the most important buildings, as stated by top architect Ashley de Vos, is 22 Hospital Street, because it is an archetypal Dutch building, built just after they arrived in 1640. Here inside, Dutch features remain untouched with large windows, timber floors, an open colonnaded courtyard and thick walls made from coral."

Saintly Treasurer

Lakshman Welikala
Treasurer
All Saints Anglican
Church
Church Street
0779959078

Generally when it comes to the duration of a sermon I believe that preachers should heed the advice of the Duke of Edinburgh and remember that "The mind cannot absorb that which the backside cannot endure". Here at the All Saints Anglican Church in Galle Fort however long sermons have proved to be a lifesaver—quite literally. On 26th December 2004 the travelling vicar who had been called to give the Sunday sermon spoke for far longer than any member of the congregation were really expecting or desiring him to do so. The sermon was so long that one or two of the older members of the Galle community fell asleep. Although they regretted it at the time, as a consequence of this long sermon the congregation were detained in the church, situated in the heart of the old city, whilst the tsunami hit the suburbs of the town in which most of them lived and would otherwise have been had the sermon ended earlier. The church

Despite weather-beaten white walls, the church observes piously - a solid, stoic stalwart of the Fort.

"Many of the congregation are converts from the multitude of other religions that reside within the Fort and its surrounding area, bringing a certain Sri Lankan openminded-ness to the church community."

therefore feels a debt of gratitude to the verbosity of the vicar that fateful December morning. They were also lucky to be inside the old walls as the water damage was limited and not one person died in the old citadel.

"It was an Act of God!" remarks Mr. Lakshman Welikala who is the treasurer of All Saints and like most of the congregation lives outside the Fort. This is a congregation who arrive for the Sunday service in the heart of the Fort by tuk-tuk, motorbike, car, bicycle and bus. The demographic of this extraordinary church's congregation has altered dramatically since the days when the Dutch Burgher families of the Fort thronged the pews and in recent years the influx of people to the church has comprised of Buddhist converts who are the product of the church's ongoing missionary work. This is an active church with a programme of action within the community, which lasts beyond the Sunday services. In addition to its Sunday school, the church has a youth fellowship of about twenty members and holds a Sunday lunch and breakfast at which the church's members can talk and build a solid community spirit, which can endure beyond the Dismissal.

All Saints' Church is keen to be more than a small urban parish in part due to its fantastic heritage and the magnificent building that it occupies. It is a building filled with soaring arches of dark wood and doughty pillars of granite, which support the graceful whitewashed walls with their intricate arches. Along the floor lies a close-knit pattern of Indian tiles upon which rests the Jewish-made pews of teak wood from Burma. It is perhaps the grandeur of the building and the richness of its heritage, which gives it such clout within the Anglican community of Sri Lanka.

"The service begins with a member of the congregation lashing the bell that was retrived from H.M.S Ocean Verity, a reminder of the Fort's maritime history."

The church is served, not by a vicar (although the congregation would like to have a vicar for their own purposes as a Parish), but by an Archdeacon who oversees the whole of the Southern province. In time the church envisages that the position of an Archdeacon will be too insignificant for the size of the Anglican community over which he will minister and therefore a Bishop will be enthroned in Galle with All Saints as his Cathedral. I ask whether as a part of this grand scheme the Anglican community of Galle would be prepared to accept a woman bishop and Mr. Welikala laughs.

"Perhaps one day, we are not set against such a notion," explains the broadminded treasurer "Though perhaps one day, as we move forward little by little here and at the moment we would prefer a man." The parish is not set in its theological ways but is progressive, which Mr. Welikala attributes to the fact that so many of the

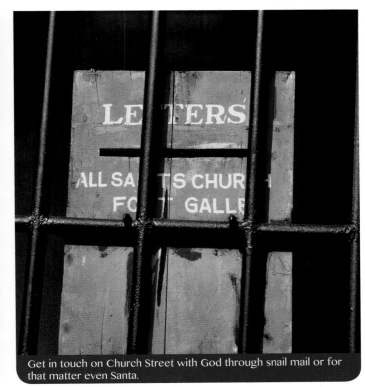

Get in touch on Church Street with God through snail mail or for that matter even Santa.

congregation are converts from other religions and therefore bring to this Anglican Church a certain Sri Lankan open-mindedness.

During the services the congregation usually removes their shoes as a traditional sign of respect in Sri Lanka. Also the servers carry large fans, traditionally used at pageants, up the aisle following the cross in order to respect this other cultural part of Sri Lanka's heritage. Mr. Welikala is a man who can speak as the voice of the congregation. He attended Sunday School in All Saints Galle during his father's tenure as the priest in the years 1949-64 and choirboy, server, warden and now finally treasurer are roles which he can put on his parochial C.V.

This is a church with vision and aspirations. For example they want to develop a larger choir to attract

"When asked if the Anglican community of Galle would be prepared to accept a woman bishop, Mr. Welikala laughs and says 'Perhaps one day!'"

"In the Portuguese era, the gallows stood where the altar now stands. As Mr. Welikala says 'we are remembering how Christ was executed on the spot where executions were conducted, so it seems quite fitting.'"

more people to services and they want a vicar who can speak English fluently to cater for the increasing number of foreigners who are attending the church. Perhaps their greatest goal at the moment is to raise the £15 million required to carry out repairs to this historic building. The sea breeze has taken its toll upon All Saints with severe damage caused to the roof and leaks now appearing in a number of places. The church is optimistic that they will raise the money but Mr. Welikala imagines that they will have to ask for help from richer parishes outside Sri Lanka in order to afford the restoration.

History lives within every facet of the building, which is suffused into any service that a visitor may attend. The service begins with a member of the congregation

The Anglican Church, a bird's eye view showing its central position on Church Street, identified by its very pink roof

"The Duke of Edinburgh once said 'The mind cannot absorb that which the backside cannot endure' but the lengthy sermon given on 26th December 2004 saved the lives of most of the congregation."

lashing the bell from H.M.S. Ocean Verity that hangs in one wing of the church, thus reminding one how this place, like the rest of Galle, finds much of its history in the sea. Perhaps the eeriest part of the heritage of the building is the archaeologically confirmed fact that in the Portuguese era the gallows stood where the altar now stands. When I ask Mr. Welikala whether this curio troubles him he smiles and says that if anything it seems apt.

"We are remembering how Christ was executed on the spot where executions were conducted—it seems fitting."

A Country To Be Valued

Supun Liyanage
Bank of Ceylon
2 Lighthouse Street
0912234219

The huge building that sits at the end of Lighthouse Street in Galle Fort is vast even by the Fort's standards. Step inside and you enter an immense central room, cool and official, lines of people clutching coloured papers snaking around the room. In a house that used to be home to the Dutch ambassador, women in patterned saris and men in yellow shirts sit behind low desks, solving the problems of those who seek their guidance, just as the Bank of Ceylon have been doing here for the last seventy-two years. One of the men working away diligently is Supun Liyanage, a serious, friendly young man who just so happens to know the valiant history of the bank as if he had lived through all seventy-two years of it himself.

The oldest bank in Sri Lanka, the British built the company in 1939, when Sri Lanka's economy was thriving and its export market, tea being the main success, was booming. They decided that they needed a way to accumulate this wealth through a recognised banking system that would be respected the world over. And so Bank of Ceylon was born seventy-five years ago. Its first and second branches were built in Colombo and Kandy respectively and, after consideration the third was built in Galle Fort. The reasoning behind this decision was that, in reality as Supun tells me, Galle has a far

longer history than Colombo as a commercial city as, in the 1940s, Galle was the second main port in Sri Lanka. For the British then, it was simply a practical decision.

The construction of such an important Art Deco building brought great excitement to the Fort, but it also provided them with a security they had not had before. There was no need to venture out. Now however, many of the government owned businesses have been relocated outside the Fort, seemingly to make it a more comfortable place for tourists. But Supun is firm in his belief that the "Bank of Ceylon will always be here."

The main bank itself sits on a roundabout at one of the entrances to the Fort, its bright canary yellow sign standing out against the stonework. It is the only Sri Lankan bank to have made it into the world's top one thousand banks, a feat that Supun is extremely proud of. It drew the rest of the world's attention to this small country's success. As the infamous "Gateway" to this magical land, so too does it sit at the gateway to the Fort, a guiding light in times of need and a reminder of the achievements of a country that seems to have forgotten how valuable it once was.

"The former home of the Dutch ambassador is now occupied by one of the world's top one thousand banks."

The Enlightened One

Venerable
Reverend Etmaloka
Panangala
Sri Sudharmalaya
Buddhist Temple
Rampart Street

When visiting Sri Lanka and other nations, where Buddhism is the major religion, there is a tendency to associate the faith with ancient rituals, unchanged over millennia and Buddhism's reliance upon simplicity and a basic, plain lifestyle, is sometimes entirely remote from our modern, busy and shallow world. With respect to these associations with Buddhism, I step barefoot into a room that is half-open to the elements, with a missing wall looking out onto a garden, and spy Reverend Panangala sitting in a low wicker chair, resplendent in his saffron robe and chatting in earnest on his mobile phone with today's newspaper folded across his lap and his reading glasses in his hand. When Reverend Etmaloka Panangala leaves to make us tea, Mr. Abeysinghe (who speaks in perfect polished English and acts throughout the interview as a translator), one of the educationalists and wardens for the temple, explains that this use of worldly goods is consistent with Buddhism.

"According to Lord Buddha all people are equal and therefore the Reverend is entitled to use things and act in a lifestyle that he thinks fit."

The room is open because this enables the monks to connect with the outside world and nature by sitting close to the plants whilst feeling the wind on their faces

The simplicity is even observed in the rather unassuming wall which is reflected in the stagnant water, reminding us like the mirror to look within ourselves.

"We suffer as much from happiness as we do from sadness."

and seeing the birds jump from branch to branch. This connection with nature is important, I am told, because Lord Buddha attainted enlightenment and wisdom under the Bo tree.

The Reverend soon returns with the tea and a plate of sweet jaggery, a particularly delicious sugary treat made from the natural sap of a tree, and whilst Mr. Abeysinghe and I drink from a cup and saucer he drinks from a bowl surrounded by Buddhist writings. The link to tradition is clear here and throughout our lively chat, as the Reverend explains through Mr. Abeysinghe why he became a monk, how he lives and why the temple fulfils its community role, it is clear that the following of precedents and scripture enables this community to function.

The temple was founded and built in 1886 using funds and land donated by F.A. Wickramasinga, a local village headman who earned his money by collecting taxes and working for the government. I was told that it is the Buddhist philosophy to earn mental improvement and wellbeing through good actions for the benefit of others rather than thinking of oneself and acting out of greed

"The stupa of the temple has Bo leaves carved into it and its shape is based on the Bo leaf standing upright. The idea being that pilgrims can also find enlightenment as they go clockwise around the temple."

and according to comfort. He says that tourists and newcomers come asking for advice and find comfort from the words and teachings of Buddhist scriptures that he and the other monks can provide. Mr. Abeysinghe says that the Buddhists were very grateful to the British for the protection that they offered to the temple and to the Buddhist religion in the Fort, saying that, following the end of colonial rule, many feared, in the strife that followed Independence (he cites the 1971 rebellion in which 30,000 died and the 1989 uprising in which 66,000 died), that the security of the colonial rule would be shattered. Although this seems confusing at first Mr. Abeysinghe says that the tumult of war and peace poses no greater challenge according to Buddhist philosophy for at all times Buddhism teaches us not to be proud of property or be filled with sorrow over its loss. "Reject all appreciation and then you can also turn away criticism!" extols Mr. Abeysinghe, "We suffer as much from happiness as we do from sadness for we fail to appreciate the happiness of mind rather than body."

This view seems rather harsh at first but when one considers the good work that the temple continued to do following the 2004 tsunami, by sheltering victims for over four months and continuing to provide food and clothing for a long time after that, it seems wrong to describe these people as uncaring. "All troubles are natural, whether war, tsunami, terrorism…" explains Mr. Abeysinghe.

At this point the drums and chants of the school children parading outside disrupt the quiet of our conversation, which causes the Reverend to laugh. The temple is embedded in the Fort both physically and mentally with at least 24,000 visitors a year and some three-quarters of Galle's population (mostly those living outside the Fort) following the teachings of Buddhism. The monks plan to renovate the temple, increasing the thickness of the walls and adding sound protection to enable the outside world to continue at its own pace without disturbing "natural serenity".

The intricate ornamentations and indentations on the face of the kotha - the highest part of the stupa or dagoba.

"The Bo tree is the first species of tree on the planet and secondly its religious importance came into its own after Lord Buddha found enlightenment sitting under one."

When I ask if such plans are underway I am told that at present they are stymied by a lack of funds. Instead the monks plan to build a public library within the grounds of the temple to enable people to rediscover philosophy and Buddhism. As I leave I am puzzled at why the Buddhist temple has flourished and not floundered as the Fort has increased the pace at which it lives and thrown itself into the world with a harder and faster sense of commercialism and materialistic wellbeing since the civil war ended in May 2009. Their immense flexibility and willingness to change that, which affects their material existence, ultimately stems from an unwavering commitment to keep their mental routine the same. This consistency of doctrine may explain why, despite the Fort's continuing and accelerating moves towards the modern world, their ancient religion remains a source of comfort and guidance to all that come to see them. In fact they are the key to the Fort upholding what is right for both the old city and the island.

Time Locked Trinkets

Hassen Ahmed
Dutch Wall Arcade
55 Rampart Street
0912227042

Time capsules in which time has come to a standstill is something Galle in the Southern province is famous for. Quirky antique shops with tokens, gifts, melodic troikas in lockets, key chains and watches, this dazzling array of treasures delves into the personal histories of men and women for centuries, of little known epochs in some cases, resonating love affairs and outlawed passions, testimonials to man's commitment to women, and vice versa, and their enduring seeds of emotions caught in vortexes of time, in locked trinkets we leave behind and that live on long after we are gone.

Wandering into the Dutch Wall Arcade is fascinating as it is a building that links right back to the Dutch period and is filled with local clay bricks that were made hundreds of years ago by the British mixed in with the old coral walls.

Along one entire wall there is an amazing shelf dedicated to our equine friends. On the top shelf there are heads of Jaffna horses of various sizes and descriptions all cropped at the neck in a way that gives the impression that you are standing beneath one of the hedges at Aintree. On the shelf below there are the horses in bronze, and cowering beneath them are wooden horses from Jaffna temples used in Dutch villas (as a result of Geoffrey Bawa

Jingly jangly oddities, still retaining some of their glimmer thanks to the clever.

setting a trend), rearing in anger with hooves poised in mid-air to pummel the floor as they fall back down to earth. Then there are china horses and porcelain models of carriages being pulled with their occupants shaded beneath parasols with their faces frozen for decades if not centuries beneath a cracked lacquer on which time has had its vengeance—and that's just the one on the wall.

Should you want yard-high 17th Century water filters from England then they're here in abundance and what about carriage and ship lamps for vessels that probably sank before your great-great-great-grandfather was born I hear?—well don't you worry they are on sale here too and old British safes that can double up as drinks cabinets as can now be seen in villas along the coastline. There are porcelain sets in the Chinese style with dainty blue patterns painted atop cups and saucers and teapots (with various chips and pieces having gone awry somehow over the years). If you need beetle trays then don't fret, (a beetle tray is a dish not unlike a foot-high bird-bath which is filled with tobacco and incense and cinnamon sticks and left in homes to enhance the scent) for here there are beetle trays that are made of wood, steel, bronze and brass turned green, blue, purple and black. I could go

"The dazzling array of treasures on display delves into the personal histories of men and women, of their enduring seeds of emotions caught in vortexes of time locked trinkets."

169

Imposing looking keyholes and door locks sit huddled, commiserating with each other now in their discarded old age, of intruders they kept at bay.

"The antiques trade is one which has a long past but has a very secure future within the Fort and Sri Lanka as a whole."

on endlessly in trying to name just a fraction of the goods that cram this weaving and wandering maze of the past. Here and there the corridors and pathways are blocked by objects and collections that are quite surreal like a three metre high glass cabinet filled with spoons and one enormous jar about four feet high and almost the same in depth, which even the most enthusiastic flower arrangers would struggle to do justice.

Dutch Wall Arcade Antiques flourishes in a trade that is rampant in Galle and one of its chief sales assistants says that with its long history and with the stamps of so many nations cluttering the pages of its past it is unsurprising that this is the case. It is due to the special appeal that Galle has developed by embedding itself in the past and its heritage that the antiques trade flourishes and therefore Mr. Ahmed cautions against any moves to modernise or alter the character of the place, after all old is gold. Galle has according to Mr. Ahmed established itself as the lead destination in Sri Lanka for antique dealers. Colombo is too busy as a place of trade and commerce to sit back and take at leisure the slow and gentle pace of dealing in this trade and anyway the draw that Galle has as a quiet retreat appeals to the elderly who in Mr. Ahmed's opinion are the main buyers. Although the majority of the sales go to locals the overseas market is also large although most tourists only buy smaller items like pieces of porcelain and fine crockery to take back home with them due to their luggage restrictions.

The challenge, however, of transporting the goods home is not insuperable and Mr. Ahmed tells of his proudest purchase in which he secured a shipment from a country, of a huge collection of items including amongst other things a large jar, two large tin horses and a printing press.

Many of the shop's workers have been here for decades and can talk (with a little coaxing) about their own preferences in antiques. Here Mr. Ahmed professes a love for Dutch and Chinese plates with their fine handiwork although he also fell in love with a Scottish whiskey glass that passed through the store many years ago. As for his favourite memory?—the time when a visiting Sri Lankan declared that he would buy a certain old armchair and promptly sat down upon its seat with a great firmness in his purpose. The result? The chair, which had only been jointed and not fastened with nails collapsed asunder and the customer was hurled spread-eagled onto his back to the amusement of all not least himself, who declared it must be a real antique to do this.

"Where else in the world can one city claim links to Portugal, Britain, Holland, the Middle and Far East, all along one street?"

It is a very worthwhile experience to plumb the depths of this treasure trove and to examine the sovereign beneath the sixpences and the tiara amongst the other trappings. Whether you buy yourself a bowler hat or Jaffna horse remember you are buying yourself a little bit of history and a memory of this time locked trinket. A word of caution though, don't spend too long or else like Narcissus beside his pool or the slaves aboard the Flying Dutchman it becomes impossible to escape without putting your credit card on life support!

The Queen of Banquets

Lucky Fort
Restaurant
7 Parawa Street
0912242922

During the month of January 2014, Lakmali had to temporarily close down her successful beauty salon. She'd spent 14 years ensuring her customers looked and felt beautiful on the outside, but now she's focusing on inner well-being. Business at her new restaurant has sky-rocketed; the result of her commitment to making sure customers have their stomachs satisfied.

But Lakmali certainly isn't complaining, and neither are the patrons that visit her new curry-house on the veranda of her husband's ancestral home at No. 7 Parawa Street. Lakmali's passion and creativity have combined to produce a flair for original tastes in the 10 curries she offers as a set on her menu. Her favourite dishes to cook are pineapple curry and aubergine curry, and her thoughtful attention to the tastes and preferences of foreign tourists has seen her swiftly develop the restaurant into Galle's no. 1. Sri Lankan curry destination.

Lakmali qualified with a diploma in beauty and bridal dressing, opened her salon 14 years ago. She is quietly confident, yet humble about her skills, whilst her daughter openly boasts about her mother's particular talent for singing and playing violin, amongst other artistic outlets. Lakmali is a savvy businesswoman, always anticipating

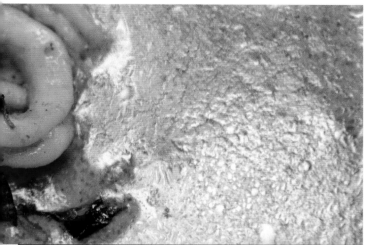

Lakmali's incredibly popular restaurant offers ten deliciously home cooked curries.

the next successful project. She recently started running cooking classes; her first sessions catered for a nicely egalitarian mix of 6 ladies and 5 men. What makes Lakmali so unique is her novel fusion of the traditional with the original. 'My curries, my style!' she explains, and 'my style' certainly seems to characterise her approach to business. However, she is adamant that she isn't the boss. The restaurant is family-run; her 18 year old daughter, Hansi, and her husband of 24 years, Ananda, have essential parts to play in the daily service and management.

The family's involvement also frees her up to dedicate some time to the salon, where she offers her speciality ayurvedic body massages and foot massages, amongst a wide range of beauty treatments. She has piles of photographs of the 35 beautiful local and foreign ladies that she has serviced on their wedding days, dressing them in traditional wedding outfits, styling their long tresses, and painstakingly applying their make-up. Moving from Unawatuna to the Fort when she married, settling into the 100 year-old Dutch-built house that her husband had inherited, she was immediately at home in Galle, comforted by the calm, communal vibe that was familiar to her from her childhood in a peaceful coastal village.

"Lakmali's quietly confident, leaving the boasting up to her daughter, who talks non-stop of her mother's talents which include both singing and playing the violin, amongst others."

Judgement Day

K.P.D. Gunaratna
Attorney at Law
Justice of Peace
Unofficial
Magistrate
President of the
Galle Bar
Association
18 Leyn Baan Street
0777596700

This year, K. P. D. Gunaratna, President of the Galle Bar Association, is resurrecting the annual Lawyers vs Doctors Galle cricket match, last held in 1986. Mr Gunaratna's desk proudly displays a photo of him walking out onto the Galle cricket field, opposite the bus stand, as one of the opening pair. Though he completed his runs without being caught out, it wasn't enough to secure a Lawyers' victory, and the Doctors won the match that year, which Mr Gunaratna attributes to the endemic liquor addiction amongst the lawyers, most of whom were already drunk before the match even began. Referencing the pre-game drinking, Mr Gunaratna says, decidedly 'I'll have to pay more attention to this matter – we have to win this year!'

Aside from presiding over the Bar Association, and writing letters to all the Doctors in town to invite them to the cricket match, Mr Gunaratna spends his time advocating on criminal matters in one of Galle's six courts, constituted by one High Court dealing with the most severe criminal cases, two magistrate courts dealing with minor criminal matters, and three district courts dealing with all non-criminal matters. The High Court is not equipped to handle the sheer number of criminal cases that come before it, so over 200 murder cases, for

The Law Court Square is where you get to brush past handcuffed convicts experiencing their final moments of freedom.

example, are filed away, still pending trial. But this is not for the lack of lawyers; there are over 227 attorneys in Galle, 140 of whom are women. 'Some days the whole Bar table is full of ladies' Mr Gunaratna says, of this impressive egalitarian parity, unique to this day even in western cultures.

Mr Gunaratna himself specialises in criminal law, which he studied whilst working full time for the Bank of Ceylon after leaving the Mahinda College in Galle. When he was just 15 years old his interest in the law was sparked after reading details of legal cases in the newspaper, and becoming curious as to the legal procedures that led to the results of the court cases. He started to hang around the courts at the top of Leyn Baan Street in Galle Fort, sometimes sneaking into the High Court to hear the judgements passed on murder cases. 'The idea to study law was already inside myself without my knowledge' he says, continuing 'I thought that I could use words as power in society, instead of physical strength'.

After studying law in Colombo, he returned to Galle, his hometown, in 1986, and he has been practicing in Galle Fort for 28 years. In that time, there have been many

"Before 1974, members of the legal profession were known as Advocates and Proctors. After January 1974 when a new law came into being, fusing the two, the result was that all the members were now known as Attorneys-at-law."

controversial murder cases, though he suspects that the Galle area is marginally safer than Colombo. In one recent case, a husband and wife were both stabbed to death by an angry mob comprised of their neighbours, who had been lying in wait for them to return from their tea estate. The husband had been buying up all the neighbours' land by threatening them with his gun, so the mob took it upon themselves to take revenge when they knew he would be travelling without any weapon to defend himself.

In one of the most famous and horrific cases to ever come before Galle's High Court, a local beauty queen, Premawathi Manamery, was targeted by two army officers, after she got involved in the political riots with the JVP movement in 1971 in Kataragama, a holy town inland east of Galle. The officers arrested her, and then, in a series of barbaric acts of brutality, forced her to strip naked and then paraded her in the streets in front of crowds of army officers and locals, before shooting her, dragging her on the ground, still alive, to her final resting place, where they shot her again, before burying her. The officers were themselves arrested and came before Galle High Court, because the case was deemed too serious to appear in the local court in the Hambantota area.

The officers were charged with murder and received a sentence of the death penalty. The recently inaugurated President at the time, J.R. Jayawardana, against the wishes of the people, extended to the officers a Presidential pardon so that they may serve time in prison rather than face execution. One of the murderers died of natural causes in prison, but the other served his sentence and was released in 1989. He returned to his village in the Matara area, where there was still ongoing political violence. Just three days after his release, he was murdered in his home by JVP activists, taking justice into their own hands. The local population had never accepted the Presidential pardon, and so, to them, by killing him they had served only the death sentence he had been due.

"The Sri Lanka Law College was established in 1874 to provide a formal education for those wanting to be lawyers in Ceylon. It is the only gateway to the legal profession in Sri Lanka and it is a partner university with the University of Wales in the United Kingdom."

A moment to catch up on small-town gossip as female lawyers decked in white saris have a moment's respite from the hustle and bustle of legal affairs.

"The last time the Doctors challenged the Lawyers to a cricket match, the Lawyers lost, badly. Mr. Gunaratna says that they are now ready for a re-match."

Since everyone agreed justice had prevailed, there were no suspects in his murder case, as no one would turn in the JVP activists.

Back in 2014, in his office at 18 Leyn Baan Street, Galle Fort, Mr Gunaratna still uses old-fashioned typewriters, in perfect working condition. They are more reliable, he explains, than modern computers, since typewriters can still be used when electricity cuts out in one of the many Fort power cuts. The image of attorneys, clients and secretaries huddled in his small office, talking and typing up criminal matters by candlelight, is quite an amazing thought, and probably not too far from reality in this old Fort, where anything and everything happens, and where you can be sure the lawyers will know about it.

Fires of the Imagination

Millennium Gems
Mahesh
Liyanaarachchige
70A Church Street
0914381621

The spinning wood sends up small sparks as a dark curly haired man focuses intently on the detailed work in front of him, oblivious to the hustle and bustle of Church Street shoppers. One would think he was an alchemist making fire, not drilling holes into priceless pieces of jewellery, made using only the finest Sri Lankan gems. The spinning contraption that he is drilling with is as simple as tools get, made from a few bits of wood and scraps of cloth. It is this emphasis placed on the logic in the practicality of daily science, where one has to make do with whatever is at hand and therefore has to rely on sheer determination to conjure up magic from what would hinder most that is priceless. Everything in the Fort is recycled, right down to the cuttlefish bones found on the seashore that Mahesh uses as moulds for casting the jewellery.

Upon walking into his charming shop and workshop you can see why he sticks to the island's original ancient techniques. Glittering leopards, little silver tortoises and gem-studded elephants are just a couple of his creative designs, proudly displayed in glass

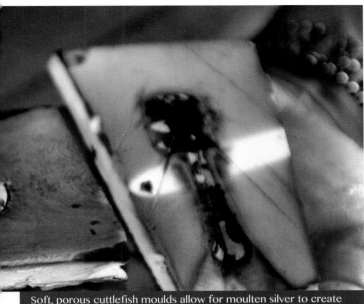
Soft, porous cuttlefish moulds allow for moulten silver to create alchemy.

"It is only when I hold a gem in my hand that I can decide what to make it into."

cases, which reflect Galle Fort's proximity to the Yala National Park and its rich wildlife. And if you buy from Mahesh, you know you are getting something completely original as his family have been in the business for generations. Not a man for pouring over latest catalogues or fashion magazines, Mahesh simply says that it is only when he holds the gem in his hand that he will decide what to make with it. A strong believer in the power that gems possess to heal, Mahesh speaks intently of the life giving properties of gems. They are potent not only in the value that money gives them, as Mahesh tells me, the king sapphire, one of the rarest and most valuable gems in the island, sells out the minute he gets one. He believes that each gemstone has its own ability to heal.

He is not only a jeweller but also a magician who created the first silver 'tortion' ring, an incredible piece of jewellery that involves balancing a gem between two pieces of metal. Having seen how other jewellers in Europe, mainly Germany, used tension

"Jewellery came with the colonial invaders and before that gems were used for their healing powers and even today Shamans use them."

to create beautiful gold and white gold jewellery, he decided that he wanted to find a way to be able to do it in silver. The problem was that silver was far too soft to be able to hold a gem in place. And so he devised a way to strengthen the metal, enabling him to create exclusive silver tension jewellery, the likes of which are not seen anywhere else in the world. Mahesh is careful to explain to every customer who wanders into Millennium Jewellers, especially those from out of Sri Lanka, exactly how every piece is made. But when I ask what his strengthening method is, he simply chuckles and says that it's his little secret!

Growing up in a village like Tangalle, meaning 'gold rock', he spent his life surrounded by the 'tap tap' noise of the finest jewellers in action, creating filigree

Blowing fire in his cramped room, the magician weaves money spinners.

"Mahesh's philosophy for living is entirely focused around Galle Fort: 'The best thing for life is choosing the right place to live.'"

jewellery the likes of which are no longer seen. It was a difficult and time consuming business, one that required great skill and patience. It didn't take him long to decide to follow in the family footsteps. The problem is that time is very much money in this industry, as Mahesh points out, so many people cannot spend as long as they used to for perfecting their skills. The gem trade itself isn't dying out, not in the slightest, but the skills that were once so prided, are starting to. Luckily for this little town, many of its finest artisans like Mahesh are still continuing the ancient traditions, which you can view when you go to his shop.

Little Hearts, Big Dreams

Mrs. Sadiqa Haneef Little Hearts Nursery
40 Middle Street
0914380380

With over 30 children under 5 running around and making as much noise as a herd of elephants, it wouldn't be surprising if the lady in charge of this rabble had a slight headache. But Mrs. Sadiqa Haneef, the Directress of Little Hearts Nursery school on Middle Street is as calm as can be. She loves her job, she tells me, as children simply "do what their imagination tells them." There is never a dull moment at Little Hearts and Sadiqa doesn't want it any other way.

She started the nursery in 1996, just after finishing her A Levels. While most of her contemporaries were lazing around, trying to decide what to do with their lives, Sadiqa was busy achieving her dreams. A Galle Fort girl she believes that it is an incredibly special place for a child to be able to grow up in. She has seen a change since the end of the war in the characters of the children who pass through her door. Where they once used to be very quiet and withdrawn, doing everything they could to not be seen, now they are "more active, happier and expressive," and extremely intelligent. They have embraced the freedom that was not available to their predecessors.

Young hearts and minds, in that carefree age that we all sometimes yearn for.

Sadiqa is "very proud" of every single person who has come through her nursery. The first pupils she had are now about to finish their A Levels and Sadiqa beams as she tells me that many are going on to study medicine. One of the younger old boys has just taken the Grade 5 scholarship and besides being enrolled to Mahinda College, he has come first in a number of his exams, proving that Little Hearts may only be little in its name but not in its achievements. It is the power of the word of mouth that keeps her admissions book overflowing with names. Amzar one of the characters of the school and the Fort being from a family that goes back nine generations says "I learn new things everyday and love making Mr Men out of sindus, old cds or creating a fluffy rabbit picture with cotton wool, which I play with on the Fort walls after school."

Little Hearts, thanks to Sadiqa and her team of incredible teachers, is making a big name for itself.

"Sri Lanka's literacy rate is 92%, the highest in South Asia and only 1% less than South Africa."

Stony Enticer

Ameen Hussain
Laksana
(Jewellery shop
since 1980)
30 Hospital Street
0777900170
+94 – 91- 4381800

Laksana's glittering gems and shimmering stones catch your eyes as you walk along Hospital Street and inside this uber cool showroom shop you will meet Ameen, a swashbuckling Galle Fort debonair gem designer and jeweller. A Galle Fort merchant who has a secret passion for painting exotic flowers in his office that can be found above his shop, gifted to him 35 years ago by his father who called it Laksana, which he believes derives its meaning from the Sri Lankan word beautiful. The shop is in a word fabulous.

Weirdly Ameen at school selected dancing over art, which he deeply regrets as drawing is his passion today. "After school I started to paint fishermen but only with the hat to symbolise the icon of the area." "I feel strongly as a Muslim that I must stick within the religious criteria of not showing the human form." Ameen is clearly deeply religious sticking to the fast throughout Ramadan, not eating or drinking from dawn until dusk. "I refuse to sell anything that would bring me into conflict with the Koran. As a devout Muslim I can do concentric designs and unlike other Fort shops I don't sell elephants, crosses or any religious designs, animals

Ameen's secret hobby is flowers painted in dreamlike, vivid Technicolor on canvas.

in any form as I believe one should stick to the rules of one's religion and respect others."

"Some of my earliest pieces I created are now in the Historic Mansion on Leyn Baan Street, a popular local museum from the 1980s. One piece on display is a stunning pair of ruby cabochon earrings with a simple links design." Looking around his main boutique gem shop on Hospital Street he explains that "One of my top sellers and early designs I made is with a Smarty's effect with all different coloured stones looking just like the sweets dropping from the elegant link chains in the choker, which allows you to wear any colour of outfit." The piece uses seven kinds of semiprecious stones. On average Ameen creates 10 to 15 new pieces every week and his best sellers have sold several hundred necklaces in specific designs such as in the three different lengths of 60 inches, 40 inches and 20 inches pieces, known as the Gia necklace.

Asking for his secret tips and inspirations for his designer collection pieces and hoping to glean some real insider

"Loved by women and feared by men, Ameen is one of Galle Fort's most popular gem designers."

185

Ameen showing off his latest ring designs.

"Some clients ask for rose quartz as they believe it has some sort of cooling system but I don't think jewellery heals. I think it makes someone feel great as it shows off a person's natural beauty."

knowledge I ask him where he gets his ideas from. Ameen says unlike lots of jewellers "I never read magazines or look at TV, I just have a special sofa where I draw at home in Akuressa Road." Clearly with the Midas touch, as several people are shopping while we interview him, I learn that colour and fashion do matter, but Ameen defines it and does not follow others' trends.

As Sri Lanka has an ancient history of shamans using stones for their healing powers before jewellery arrived with colonisation I ask if clients look for stones that will protect them or absorb serious illnesses. He admits, "Some clients ask for rose quartz and they believe it has some cooling system, but I don't think jewellery heals but only makes someone feel great as it shows off a person's natural beauty." Agate stone is good for drawing diseases out of the body and there is a lot of talk about this among crystal healers. Ameen does not believe stones would kill like the one in Harry Potter's cursed ring.

The makers of his pieces are based in modern Galle and the eight to nine mastercraftsmen use each of his drawings and gems, carefully bagged up from his blue box hidden in his showroom where like a painter he mixes gems in both size and colour. Ameen surrounded by his sketches says, "I am always drawing and now my ten year old son is sketching and my daughter did this floral design and they are both different from my design ideas," which he was surprised and yet deeply proud about.

Prices of gems always go up by 150 per cent every two years and so way better than leaving cash in the bank.

Sadly since the war "Synthetic sapphires have been sold in Pedlar Street and with fake certificates so people have to be very careful and selective in what they buy as return business is key." Ameen has so much repeat business even though he does not go for exhibitions or fashion events to promote his work. "I prefer direct long term clients."

"I have had many interesting clients often the most casually dressed are the biggest spenders."

Semiprecious stones may be more fashionable as you can buy bigger for less. Yet it is the royal blue sapphires that continue to drive women crazy as Kate Middleton (and before her Princess Diana) keeps them very much on centre-stage of the world fashion pages. With more than 50 types of gems to pick from, thousands of unique designs and King Sapphires locked away in Ameen's bank size safe, it is not surprising that people have flocked to the island where Sinbad the Sailor rightly noted that the rivers run with gems.

"Ameen would argue that 'women can do without food but never without something pretty and sparkly."

The Museum of Maritime Archaeology

Queen's Street

Visitors to Galle Fort may well have found themselves intrigued by a rather conspicuous Dutch building, stretched out along the Fort's boundary on Queen's Street, curiously displaying a sign for the Museum of Maritime Archaeology. Fortunately, if the meaning of 'Maritime Archaeology' eludes bewildered tourists, it won't be for long, since the very first gallery of the museum, which opened in 2010, explains exactly that.

Maritime Archaeology is the investigation of human activity in relation to the sea, and as a historic international trading port, Galle has much to offer of interest in this respect. The building itself was built in 1672 as a warehouse store for spice and other items due to be exported by the Dutch East India Company, and remains the longest building in South Asia, colossal with 6ft-thick walls. It now houses an exhibition of artifacts salvaged from sunken shipwrecks around the Galle harbour, accompanied by fascinating educational displays and model reconstructions to guide your dive into Galle's rich maritime history. The museum project began in 1993, when an archaeological team from Britain, Australia, Sri Lanka and UNESCO excavated the giant 'Avondster'

An impressive vista and a perfectly horizontal grid with the red tiled roof balancing the saffron coloured walls.

trading ship, which sank in 1659 after running into rocks in the Galle harbour. The storey-high original anchor stands pride-of-place in the basement gallery of the museum, beside models of what the ship would have looked like in its heyday. This basement contained 'Avondster' artifacts long before the museum opened, and tragically, but also somewhat ironically, many recovered items were swept back out to sea in the tsunami.

The collection of artifacts has since developed and, perhaps strategically, is now exhibited upstairs in three large galleries. In the first gallery, in addition to the general introduction to Maritime Archaeology, there is the life-like reconstruction of an ancient Holocene coastline settlement and a soil profile of land in Kinnole showing ancient fish fossils along with the incredible image of the ancient 'Map of the World' painted on the ceiling of the Kottimbulvala Temple near Balangoda. Many nuggets of information about ancient societies and their relation to the seas and the worlds beyond, can be inferred from the astonishing details of the map, presenting you with the perfect opportunity to try your hand at maritime archaeology yourself.

"The museum project began in 1993 when an archaeological team from Britain, Australia, Sri Lanka and UNESCO excavated the giant 'Avondster' trading ship which sank in Galle harbour."

සමුද්‍ර පුරාවිද්‍යා
கடல்சார் தொல்பொ
MARITIME ARCH

මධ්‍යම සංස්කෘතික අරමුදල සංස්ක
மத்திய கலாசார நிதியம் கலாச
CENTRAL CULTURAL FUND   Minis

"This gallery is a testament to the importance of maritime archaeology for its efforts to track the changes and influences on coastline civilisation."

In the second gallery you can find examples of artifacts excavated from Indian, German, Dutch, Chinese and Persian shipwrecks. The oldest artefact is an over 2,000 years old stone stool, engraved with Brahmin letters, whilst the most popular attraction is a towering stone slab recovered from a 14th century Chinese ship, inscribed with writing in Persian, Tamil and Chinese characters.

The third gallery completes your personal tour into maritime archaeology by exposing, through models, artifacts and displays, how maritime culture in the area has been influenced and severely changed by the deep history of colonial invasions. A Hindu Vishnu statue and a large Buddhist meditation stone, represent and inform how the local religions arrived, by ship, from Sri Lanka's neighbouring kingdoms in India, whilst displays of the now-traditional southern industry of lace-making exposes that this trade originated with the Dutch colonisers. A model of a well-groomed 19th century Sri Lankan couple, wearing familiar European style clothing is a reminder that the local dress was completely overturned; in the traditional society, both men and women would only have worn clothing on the lower halves of the body. Even the

This may be the museum, but the floor of the Indian Ocean houses several skeletons in its closet, damned from human sight.

traditional Sinhala painting displayed on the wall is the product of colonial influences, no longer reflecting the original style of painting. This last gallery is a testament to the importance of maritime archaeology for its efforts to track the changes and influences on coastline civilisation. The project and the museum credits many supporters and founders, most notably, the famed-science fiction writer, Sir Arthur C. Clarke, though it is unclear from the display whether this support was in the form of financial encouragement, or whether the writer himself actually actively partook in the early excavations of shipwrecks in the Galle harbour.

Tourists can book themselves on to a guided scuba dive to an archaeological excavation site on the coral reef around Galle, to explore shipwrecks. This exciting new initiative, along with the basement demonstration laboratory where visitors can see first-hand how the shipwrecked relics are put back together and preserved, provides a holistic experiential insight into maritime archaeology, in line with a new concept for the modern museum.

"The oldest artifact in the museum is an over 2,000 years old stone tool, engraved with Brahmin letters."

The National Museum

Manjula
Karunathilaka
Officer in Charge
Church Street

Manjula Karunathilaka's very first job was as the Officer-in-Charge of the Galle National Museum which serves all of the Southern Province curating the nation's treasures.

The Galle National Museum since 1986 is housed in a listed Dutch building and is an 'archaeological monument'. Originally used as a military weapons storehouse, it was built in 1686.

There are three galleries exhibiting displays of colonial antiques, relics specific to Galle history and industry, and items relating to Chinese-Sri Lankan relations, which date back to 1405. In the first gallery there is a scale model of the Fort today. Manjula points out the 'Black Fort' or the 'Zwart Bastion', built by the Portuguese in 1505, the Old Gate built by the Dutch in 1646, and the New Gate built by the British. Galle Fort stands on 96 acres of land, surrounded by a 3km long wall, 50-80 feet high.

There are displays of turtle shell objects, ranging from jewellery boxes to a luxury fan, and also how some of these items were made, using the heavy metal press, which would shape items between a wooden mould. There is

Ordered within the white columns is the chaotic world of thoughts and ideas contained in the prisons of antiquarian physical realities.

"The National Museum building was built in 1686 and originally used as a military weapons storehouse."

also an antique ebony box, and a tiny antique Senakkale table from which people used to eat. The gallery also contains items of 'pillow' lacework utilizing the Beeralu lace technique, unique to Galle. A stone inscription states, 'The first stone of this bridge was laid by The Honourable Fredric North, Governor of Ceylon. 28 June 1802.'

In the second gallery you can view an antique Dutch Almirah wardrobe, still in perfect condition, of the kind only ever made in Galle, from teak, jack wood and with ebony detailing. Then there are the cake moulds, used by the Dutch. The third gallery room is decked out in an orientalist style, dominated by a life size model of Chinese merchants, standing by their ship, and a gleaming gold cast of the head of Fa Xian, a Buddhist monk who travelled Asia, between the years 337 – 422 AD. There is a stone slab originating from the old Chinese court in Galle Fort, inscribed in 1409 with writing in Persian, Tamil and Chinese. The Chinese coins all have holes through their middle so that they could be worn on a string, which was typical of Cantonese merchants.

A Kingdom of Spirits

M.G. Wolter
Security Guard
Lloyd's House/
Clan House
27 Church Street
0775768037

A bright blue gate protects the entrance to this hidden historic crumbling building on Church Street, behind a gate that is manned by the finest moustache in Galle Fort. A huge landed property that in 1863 was worth only thirty five thousand rupees, but today is priceless in its value. It is where M.G. Wolter, security guard and owner of the said finest facial hair, spends his days, whiling away the hours, observing life on the most exciting street in Galle Fort. An old chalk shipping board and an ornate sign seem to be the only reminders of the shipping company that used to operate out of this building. But step inside, through the sapphire gateway and you are transported back to a different era.

Windowpanes are missing from almost every frame and plants grow in abundance making it feel like the ancient ruins of Angkor Wat as trees grow through structures, roots winding in all directions. Old red and white signs for a staff canteen and a buttoning room hark back to the businesses that were once run from here, old scraps of cloth betraying the secrets of a once flourishing garment factory era. Huge Italian Palladio-like columns frame the square courtyard, holding up a wooden veranda that would have run around the entirety of the second floor. Across the courtyard, a tiny passageway takes you back to

Clan House marks the inception of blue-chip corporates with new fangled names and giant killer multi-nationals eventually vying for space in an open market economy.

an entirely different part of the property where the wildlife have taken charge and the stairs are cracked.

You can almost picture the Dutch Commander in the seventeenth century striding through what was once magnificent courtyards barking orders at his staff and tripping over children who play hide and seek throughout this colossal house. The ghostly pattering of small feet fades away, replaced by the hustle and bustle of a shipping company in full sail. It was, at the time, known as Clark Spence, a headquarters that would eventually become the foundation of what is today Aitken Spence PLC. The company made use of the tallest tower in Galle Fort to monitor their ships' progress into the harbour and to also keep an eye on what the neighbours were up to. As the ethereal businessmen turn into seamstresses, the building becomes a garment factory where old machines whirr away, creating the fashions of yesteryear. He sees the Fort as a place where he has come to seek "silence and rest," an escape from the noisiness of reality.

"Aitken Spence was one of the first companies to 'go green'. Journals of internal memos dating back to the early 1900s show that the company was advising employees to use the back of old envelopes for internal notes. Galle Fort property has gone so green, it has gone native!"

195

The Member's Club

Mr. Abeywickrama
Galle Fort Library
14 Church Street

Like a summer outhouse found in an Edwardian garden and the interior rooms which feel like that of an Oxbridge library, the chief librarian Mr. S Abeywickrama proudly sits.

The library celebrated its 175th anniversary back in 2007 and was originally built as a reading club for the officers of the Ceylon Rifles Regiment until the Governor of Sri Lanka disbanded the regiment in 1879 over fears (prompted in part by the Indian Mutiny of 1876) that this regiment of Muslim/Malay fighters could one day rebel. Illustrious members include Dr Anthoniaz (who was the Galle Fort Mayor in whose honour the clock tower was built), Wijaynanda Dahanayake (who was the longest serving MP for Galle and also served as its Mayor), and literary giants like Nora Roberts, author of "GALLE As Quiet As Asleep" (Colombo, 1993). At present the President is the Minister of Agriculture and the Vice-President is a senior lawyer within Galle.

Every month membership depends on whether in the Library Committee's estimation you are a person

The Galle Library standing tall and proud like a pre-Socratic philosopher

"The Galle library at 14 Church Street has 115 members, all of whom live in or around the Fort."

with sufficient interest and knowledge of education and literature. As if to emphasize the traditional "Gentleman's Club" feel, the membership is voted for using white and black balls. Here this extraordinary gentleman answers some of my absurd questions. "I don't read novels. I don't really have a taste for them. I don't have any idea what they are all worth, it doesn't interest me."

As "the hub of all cultural and research activities", it's literature is primarily academic although I notice that some recent titles have been allowed to enter the collection like "Eat, Pray, Love" and "One Day". His favourite book is "Historical Relations of Ceylon" by Robert Knox. The oldest book is the 1803 "An Account of the Island of Ceylon" by Robert Percival. It may be quirky, elitist and a slight anachronism but if such things are to condemn an institution to the pages of history then the world will become a much smaller place rather too quickly. I honestly mean this, I'm not just trying to butter up the committee before my membership application is up for consideration.

Behind The Veil

Ifriya Anwar
Fort Banker
87 Leyn Baan
Street

Surely there can be few settings to rival this: a soaring nineteenth century British colonial lighthouse painted white but with specks of pink coming through the flaking paint framed with palm trees laden with coconuts against the stunning backdrop of the shimmering Indian Ocean all set beneath a brilliant aquamarine sky and Fort beach. Across from this view sits the Lighthouse Inn and waving from the balcony out of which creepers tumble studded with hues of crimson and magenta is Mrs. Anwar. Entering the foyer of the hotel I see that the bright floral trend continues with plants bursting with colour everywhere one looks creating a jungle feel and definitely pointing to a woman's touch and care. Mrs. Anwar is proud of her plants and tells me that she waters them regularly and carefully to keep them in such a healthy state despite the often sweltering heat.

She walks through the door in a bright blue outfit with tiny mirrors across the chest, which wink in the sunlight and together the colour and these plentiful bright eyes remind one of the tail of a peacock, Sri Lanka's national bird. As she enters, Mrs. Anwar casts a scarf over her head for she is a Muslim lady and she

Celebrating an annual alms giving, on this day all the hardworking women gather to Mrs. Anwar's house, the strength of their inner convictions etched into the very fabric of their energetic presences

explains that this tradition of covering one's head in the presence of other people is one that she strictly observes. Mrs. Anwar's religion is very important to her and she views the five prayer times a day as a compulsory minimum and she explains that she attends the local ladies mosque rather than the grand central mosque around the corner. Mrs. Anwar also has prayers in her house every Sunday evening, a tradition which has been observed since the time of her mother's mother over one hundred years ago. She also believes in being generous to others and has an almsgiving to the whole community every year in order to demonstrate kindness to the community.

Last year's almsgiving was particularly special as it celebrated the centenary of prayers in her house. Her family is an old family and stretches so far back that she cannot tell you when they first arrived although she adds with a shrug that her eighty-six year old mother who lives upstairs may be able to give some assistance.

"Ifriya Anwar's husband is a banker full of interesting historical facts like the fact that in 1655, during the Dutch period, copper coins bearing the monogram 'VOC GALLE' were minted for the first time in the citadel."

199

Mrs. Anwar deep in thought in front of the 1782 Dutch Magazine, an ammunition storage space, where the colonial rulers kept cannon balls and later gunpowder to protect the fort from possible invasion.

"Mrs Anwar's husband is a banker. In 1939 when the Bank of Ceylon opened its branch in the Fort, only a few people would have had accounts. Others would have kept their money locked in 'almirahs' (bedroom cupboards) or hidden under matresses at home."

Despite her observance of tradition and her strong faith it is obvious that Mrs. Anwar is a thoroughly modern and educated woman. She proudly tells of how she studied Advanced Levels in Colombo in order to become an accountant and is insistent that both her children be educated with both her son and daughter also studying Advanced Levels. Mrs. Anwar gave up her job as an accountant and opened the hotel almost ten years ago when she had to stay at home to raise her children and although she tells me that she enjoyed her time as an accountant she says she wouldn't return to it, as raising a family is more important.

She thoroughly enjoys the sociable nature of her work and meeting and getting to know all of her guests. She says 90% of her guests are normal, decent people and it is only a tiny fraction who are as she puts it "odd" (she also remarks that a large number of these "odd" customers are old). Her warm and sociable nature manifests itself to even the most casual observer as she engages in long conversations with all those who call past the door.

"Everyone knows everyone!" she declares when I remark on this and she cites this unity as one of the

Fort's greatest assets. She dismisses the idea that there could be any tension or differences between the different communities and insists that in the time that she has lived here the Fort has not become more dangerous or unpleasant. Even tourism has not greatly changed the nature of the Fort and Mrs. Anwar's only criticism of tourism is that it does not provide a steady income but comes in fits and starts according to the season. Her businesslike nature comes to the fore now as when I suggest that she would prefer a less busy season at certain times of the year when Galle is crammed with tourists she shakes her head firmly and says that she likes a good income. Mrs. Anwar shrugs and says she is incapable of predicting the future and what it will bring although she hopes that in the aftermath of the war and the coming of peace, tourism will flourish and continue to provide her with prosperity.

Mrs. Anwar does not have any illusions about what makes the world move around and says that although it is sad when old families move out of the Fort to sell their homes at a good price such change cannot be stopped and shouldn't be; however she hopes to remain in Galle. She loves the view of the sea and the sunset over the waves with the beach barely a thirty seconds walk from her front door.

As a member of one of the Fort's families she is happy with new families coming from abroad with their different cultures. She ponders for a moment and thinks hard as she has done to all of the questions she has been asked before asserting that Galle thrives upon the unity of its people and therefore upon decency and understanding, so long as newcomers come armed with such openness she has no qualms about their arrival.

"Mrs Anwar's husband works for Bank of Ceylon and interestingly one chamber of the warehouse that is now the Maritime Museum was used for storing money and precious metals called 'geld winkel.'"

The Light of the Fort

U.D. Harischandra (Principal Lighthouse Keeper) M. Sembakutti (Assistant Keeper) K.P. Boudhi (Junior Lighthouse Keeper) Hospital Street

The lighthouse in Galle may just be the Fort's biggest let down, though I don't mean this literally (although at twenty eight metres in height it would probably win hands down). Rather I mean that despite conjuring images of a seaman huddled beside a beacon that glares out to sea with a single solitary eye as he sees out into the night in solitary but glorious isolation lest his manpower be required to rekindle the light within this guardian of seafarers, the existence of those who man this lighthouse is rather more mundane. When I ask for the boon of a trip up to the top of the lighthouse for instance I am told that they don't actually travel up there save in emergencies when they are required to switch a bulb and in the meantime turn on the emergency generators—it all seems a far cry from the lighthouses of the 18th century. Indeed it's rather like being told that the Ferrari in the front drive has had its engine replaced by a hamster in a wheel.

There are aspects of the original lighthouse-keeper's life that linger on though. For one thing the keepers work in shifts that last from four in the afternoon until eight in the morning when for two of them the shift ends; the final man waits until he is relieved by the next watch at four. These hours may be long but the keepers do not say that they are troubled by this in the slightest as not only do they get every other day off due to the working patterns between the two shifts at the Galle Fort Lighthouse but they also appreciate that when judged against lighthouses in which they have formerly worked the workload is relatively light. The junior and assistant keeper explain to me that when they used to work out on the lighthouses at Great and Little Bassis (islands off the south east coast of Sri Lanka) it was expected that they live on their own in the lighthouse for one and a half months at a time. When I remark on what a lonely experience this must be the keepers shrug and Mr. Sembakutti confesses to enjoying the intimacy between the three keepers out in the middle of the sea.

The lighthouse built by the British in 1938 is still fully operational.

The trio do agree that the Galle Fort Lighthouse with its white stone and pink facade is far more sociable than the lighthouses at Great and Little Bassis although this does have the added disadvantage in that the tuk-tuks, ice-cream sellers and all the other multifarious contributors to the eternal racket that is Galle can ensure a good night of unbroken sleep is not so easy to come by. The other advantage of living out at sea?— "No mosquitos!" grumbles Mr. Boudhi and the other keepers raise their eyebrows in an expression of mutual dislike for their winged nocturnal friends. The switch from Great Bassis was caused by nature's destructive force when during the tsunami the lighthouse's facilities were wrecked by the power of the waves and it was decided that it would be better to replace the arrangement of live-in lighthouse-keepers with a solar system. On that fateful Boxing Day Mr Sembakutti recalls waves that were twenty five feet above sea level moving past in two bursts of four and feeling intimidated by the sheer power that the water seemed to carry. These men telephoned to Colombo (the radios weren't working) and then waited for four days in

"To climb to the top of this lighthouse you have to get permission from the Harbour Master because allowing people to photograph the Naval Base is considered a security risk."

205

"The 1938 lighthouse replaced the Dutch one and is on Hospital Street, which often confuses people who walk up and down Lighthouse Street expecting to find it on Flag Rock."

isolation until an army helicopter came to the rescue—there is no risk of such an isolation happening in their current station which they all admit is a relief.

At sunset the great eye is switched on to beam its protective gaze across the desolate ocean waves until that other, greater, natural eye returns at dawn. The lighthouse is also the base for the radio operator who keeps watch over the harbour on a twenty four hour basis and for the radar beacon that also keeps a constant signal (of G for Galle) transmitting over the waves.

These responsibilities are separate however from those of the three men who take turns to keep it going whilst the others watch for the moment when the light fails and they are required to resort to the emergency generators. The room in which the keepers live is situated in the small and unattractive little yellow blob that lurks in the shadow of its greater and more glamorous neighbour, and contains three iron bedsteads crammed together with little bedding and only a thin pane of glass keeping out the noise of the street. Even if the glass were to offer greater protection the heat is such that the keepers normally leave the windows open at night—"Therefore there are many mosquito bites!"

One can only imagine Alfred Hitchcock and Sigmund Freud at the top of the tower having a picnic over vertigo.

"The lighthouse is still fully operational and it gets switched on just after sunset."

remarks one of the keepers. Below in the small room in which the keepers live for most of the day there are few homely items to distract from the loneliness of a night on one's own including a few faded Sri Lankan and Buddhist flags that lurk behind the door and a small stuffed animal that hangs in an alcove wearing a pair of dark glasses like some ancient and rather ineffective guardian. The ceiling also bears the weight of a plastic carrier bag that seems a focal feature as it is suspended above the centre of the room. The reason for this bag? "Dinner packs!"—if it weren't bad enough being left on your own for all that time, the lighthouse keepers also eat meals that are created by adding hot water which is hardly an enticing culinary delight. What then drives these men to seek out a job such as this that is in so many ways detached from the comforts of a normal life?

"I love the sea." confesses one of the keepers "and at night as I look across the bay I remember just how beautiful it is all over again." That is of course until a mosquito decides to remind him that he's on dear old land.

The Shutter's Close

Puiyahtua Pezesa
Photographer
Studio Up
67A Lighthouse
Street
0718271333

Mr. Pezesa confesses that he lives in a business that is declining and well past its heyday. Sitting and talking to him is an experience in which human mortality plays the part of the elephant in the room and it is like talking to a Dodo who sees a sailor approaching with a large knife and licking lips or else musing to a dinosaur about that funny looking shooting star that appears to be headed towards us. His office occupies a small corner in the front of a large house and hemmed in by piles of papers and a stuttering fan (it too is apparently tired of its occupation), it is clear that I am entering into a business whose days are numbered. As if to emphasize the point I can see no cameras in the office save for a small old-fashioned film that sits discarded and unloved beneath a stack of cardboard files, crushed in a world in which it no longer fits.

Ten to twenty years ago was according to Mr. Pezesa the time to be a professional photographer and he looks back with relish upon those days in which his business flourished. Part of Mr. Pezesa's trouble may be his limited scope and market; he only does photography for weddings and has no wish to expand. Instead Mr. Pezesa sees his problems lying in the chronic decline of his industry (he references the decline of large Sri Lankan photography firms and also large American businesses like Kodak), accelerated by globalization and digital photography which

The Galle Fort is one of the most photographed sites.

has made photography no longer the hobby and pursuit of the talented elite but rather the sport of the masses in which artists like he cannot hope to compete.

Like his father who worked as a civil servant (and thus the family moved to Lighthouse Street, Galle in 1978 due to a government posting) and took up photography as a well-paid hobby Mr. Pezesa is clear that his love for cameras and their produce will stay with him forever. Converting his home into a guesthouse with twelve bedrooms he is confident that he will succeed in hospitality because of the size of his house.

When asked if there is any particular wedding that stands out to him he shrugs and explains that after a while there is little difference between this union of lovers and another.

The sights which form the best backdrop to his photographs are the Amangalla Hotel and the clock tower as the architecture here and the natural surroundings (the large and verdant trees with their branches descending from on high in a myriad of severed cat's cradles and the turquoise ocean respectively) really attract couples on their wedding day.

"Photography means writing in light and the best time to shoot this historic citadel is late afternoon when the sun turns to gold."

209

Galle Fort's Entrepreneur

Ziham Hussain
Jack-of-all-trades
Olanda Antiques
30 Leyn Baan
Street
0912234398

"God didn't give horns to the horse!"
This traditional Sinhalese saying was quoted to me when I suggested to Ziham Hussain that he was an incredibly skilled and successful man to be managing a chain of luxury rental villas, a school directorship, an antiques and reproduction shop, a boutique and his own building project simultaneously, to say nothing of looking after a set of ponies and twenty-odd goats. Oh, and then there is the added factor that he is a single father of two children. Ziham runs the Olanda Empire (Olanda Villas, Olanda Antiques, Olanda Boutique), which takes its name from the Sinhalese name for Dutch. I'm told that the moral of the equine saying is that we are each able to do a set number of different tasks according to our own abilities. It's a good saying but it still doesn't detract from the fact that Ziham is capable of managing a huge number of different projects always with a smile on his face.

In each villa built by him there is a tastefully created pool with natural stone steps and a view of the sea, like the one at Olanda Beach, which is simply breath-taking. At one villa you can see the Unawatuna Bay with its glorious postcard setting of the Indian Ocean, the sun and the

The mystery of the four happy grimaces-the perfect visual expression of the Sri Lankan 'joke is on you' humour.

"Ziham's horses roam the old rampart walls just as his goats run wild at his workshop."

sand. These villas are part of the business empire that Ziham has taken on from his father old Mr. Hussain who, like his son manages to set an example of not only how a dozen different things can be looked after by one person at once, but also how each and every project can be made into a thriving success story. Mr. Hussain took over a hardware and building empire and now sits in semi-retirement as a quirky collector of antiques having handed over his hardware firm, building company, property and land to the next generation. The older Mr. Hussain is a living legend of Galle Fort and for years carried the title of "Officer in Charge of Rich Foreigners". This stemmed from Mr. Hussain's ingenuity in being the first man to introduce foreigners to the Fort in 1974 for the purpose of tourism. He explains how in 1965 he began to rent out the house bought by his father Mr. Rahim in 1926 (his father ran a fleet of lorries as part of a hardware business) to the managing director of the Ceylon Tobacco Company. Through running this property Mr. Hussain eventually got in touch with the managing director of another firm called W.D. Wills, a Mr. Lukar for whom he was asked

The skeletons may be in the closet but the boats that are in the way form the perfect tanning bed-anyone?

"Not all his antiques are for sale such as the Hindu Kovil cart and brass racing chariot at the entrance and just inside Olanda Antiques on Leyn Baan Street."

to find a house near Unawatuna (which he duly did). Shortly afterwards two foreigners staying as guests at the Unawatuna villa (by the names of Charles Hulse and Gordon Merrick, the first serious foreigners to buy in the Fort) asked Mr. Hussain to purchase a property for them in the Fort and so he obliged, helping them purchase a house on Rampart Street for the paltry sum of four and a half thousand lakhs (around $4,000US).

From these humble beginnings Mr. Hussain was to gain the reputation of the Fort's "Mr Fix-It" soon able to boast of rubbing shoulders with film stars like Knut Husebo and architects such as Geoffrey and Bevis Bawa. Ziham vividly remembers how on his visits to the family home Mr. Bawa at seven and a half feet was far too tall to enter through the front door without stooping!

But once Bawa, the island's most famous architect, had entered the house he was in for a real treat. In the family bungalow that centres around a small pond in the courtyard there is a collection of valuables and antiquities that would make Aladdin's Cave seem like a cheap bring and buy stall. We sit in dark art deco chairs which arch back to form curves and semicircles, instantly reminding one of the roaring twenties whilst hanging from the ceiling is a metre long glass lamp with an ornate moulded base which can be lowered by a simple weight mechanism in order to be lit. In the outside shed there is an ancient buggy cart of the sort which old Mr. Hussain can remember riding to school in. To accompany this fantastic vehicle with its leather seats and brass fittings there is a collection of old lamps of every shape and description. Apparently Mr. Hussain used to treat local people to rides and used the cart quite frequently despite the fact that the family have had a car since 1951 when they purchased a brand new Austin A40 shipped from England, which features in all of the family photographs.

Despite being fond of antiques due to their beauty and the way in which they depict the skill of a craftsman, Ziham confesses that it is not possible for him to keep all the pieces that he admires. He has an enormous warehouse on Leyn Baan Street filled with curios, as does his father, and he does his best to fit out all of his properties with antiques, such as doors saved from the demolished wreckage of homes. In Olanda Antiques he attempts to pass on and preserve those pieces, which he finds and admires; in both his opinion and his father's the art of antiques is about conserving the treasures of the past for future generations to enjoy - it is Ziham's aspiration to open a museum one day.

Ziham is the epitome of the new and powerful economy of Sri Lanka freeing itself from the troubles of the past to flourish anew, but always remembering that it is important to be part of a community in all senses of the word. If each businessman who is part of this economic boom shares the strong moral code of this man and his passionate belief in a personal duty to do well at everything that he attempts then this nation battered by three decades of civil war has good cause to be optimistic. This horse isn't being put out to grass for a long time to come as he certainly more than takes the bull by the horns.

"Top cricketers have stayed at his villas, because they include professional snooker tables and homely luxury settings like the epic bathtub at Olanda Beach, which is big enough for a couple."

THE ARMY WIFE
Mrs. SOLDIER.

You know
Who you are
You're a wife.
A mother, a lover
A maid, a cook.
And a dish, clothes and f.
Washer.

You're a packer, a chauffeur
And a diplomat.
Today you're often a member
Of Sri Lanka's Work force
Well above all.
You're an individual
You're the power behind
Your man in GREEN

Join the Army & See The World

Army Camp
Rampart Street

Finding the army camp in Galle Fort is easy as it has a 'no smoking' sign in what looks like a rural idyll and underneath in big red letters 'DANGER' as there is still live ammunition kept in case the need to defend the Fort ever presents itself. Opposite sits the army camp in the highest point of the Fort. As I walk across the walls to the main gates I have to say I had never considered entering the Sri Lankan army until I was asked if I had come for an interview, which, following a lot of confusion in which the guard at the post thought I was asking to sign up, I was finally granted a chance to sit and talk to a camp commander.

Like most of the high ranking soldiers in the Sri Lankan armed forces this officer is a very intelligent man and has an academic record to prove it (in this particular instance he had studied in the UK and gained an M.A. from a Welsh University) and he is proud to say he has now been in the Sri Lankan army for 15 years. According to the army officers based in Galle Fort the camp is very unique as it has a close bond both historically and socially to the Fort and its people. It occupies a windswept spot overlooking the Buddhist Temple from behind soaring

At attention and at ease, greens melt into subdued yellow-just another day in the life of war heroes-get the drill.

iron gates, which was once the magistrate's home. Although there are training operations at the camp its main purpose over the past 50-60 years is to protect this unique citadel's cultural heritage and also help in the restoration of it when required.

The army have dealt with every type of risk, not just artificial threats, such as the thirty-year civil war, but equally serious, the natural disaster of the tsunami in 2004. The people of the Fort have recognised the work of the army in the community and learnt to trust the men in dark olive green with their eclectic display of brass, buttons and peacock badges, as people who are working with them as friends rather than dominating them as oppressors. During the tsunami it was particularly encouraging for the soldiers to find that civilians were actively assisting them in their humanitarian work, which often involved taking great risks to save lives from the wall of water that smashed modern Galle to pieces. During the aftermath of the tsunami the extreme bravery of many of the soldiers in the camp was recognised by the President, who has decorated

"The highest military decoration that can be given in Sri Lanka is the 'Parama Weera Vibhushanaya', the equivalent of the British Victoria Cross. Only established in 1981, it has been awarded 29 times."

some of the troops for their outstanding courage. The army recognises that today most of their work is essentially civilian oriented such as building schools, hospitals and restoring other public buildings for important events such as the Commonwealth meeting, but still feels that the Fort needs the army to be there with their guns and drill routines to remind people they mean business.

"This is a Fort, it has to have an army otherwise what is a Fort for?!" exclaims the officer, "We have our guns because they are part of our essential equipment, we wouldn't be soldiers if we didn't have them." The officer views the arrival of more tourists as an opportunity to show a different view and hopefully tell the world of the peace and security that now exists within Sri Lanka, dispelling the rumours abroad that the nation teeters from one crisis to the next in a state of military rule, which for anyone whose been here is clearly untrue. I discover that the Sri Lankan army came to this idyllic spot in 1959. Formerly the main house, which is now the officer's mess, was a high court judge's residence.

"The Dutch built a defensive wall around Galle Fort with four defensive towers: Triton Bastion, Neptune Bastion, Clippenberg Bastion and Aeolus Bastion. They were designed to provide long-range protection against attacking ships."

The officer explains that it is normal in Sri Lankan army camps for the staff to keep a few animals as pets. There are painted Francis Bacon and Shakespeare quotes on some of the buildings, 'Infantry is the nerve of the army' (Bacon) and 'Cowards die many times before their deaths; the valiant never taste of death but once' (Shakespeare), which are supposed to provide inspiration to the soldiers. On opposite walls pieces have been written about the role of the army soldier and his dutiful wife. The Army Wife poem is particularly helpful in knowing one's place and goes as follows:
You know
Who you are
You're a wife
A mother, a lover,
A maid, a cook
And a dish, clothes and floor washer

The solitary penance of the lone gunner-the icon of the Sri Lankan Army.

You're a packer, a chauffeur
And a diplomat
Today you're often a member
Of Sri Lanka's workforce
Well above all
You're an individual
You're the power behind
Your man in Green.

"The Aeolus Bastion is still used by the Sri Lankan Army as a look out today-it is above one of the old ammunition stores that still holds live ammunition!"

With a parting cup of tea I learn that part of the army's philosophy is not to be overbearing, and in this officer's opinion this is partly due to the Buddhist teachings which are ingrained in Sri Lankan society, advocating peace over conflict and welcoming respect over hostility. It is part of their job to make people feel safe although the army recognises that using guns and force to change attitudes cannot achieve this. As I leave the gates of the Fort (thankfully without any conscription papers) I reflect that this is a good moral to have and an amazing job in peace times as it allows you to see Sri Lanka's most wild and remote places.

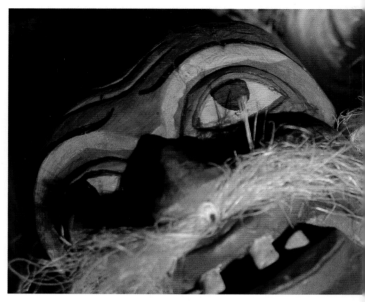

All The Colours of the World

Janaka de Silva
Sithuvili
56 Leyn Baan
Street

Dutch Hospital,
Hospital Street
0777914277

Janaka De Silva's artwork, whether created with a porcupine quill or brushes made out of cats' hair, embodies a painting tradition rich in heritage and culture. If the art gallery shop where he hangs his work conjures up the image of a wise old sage or mad monk with a weather-beaten creased face, straggling white beard and shrinking hairline, struggling to mix the paint on a palette, then nothing will prepare one for the gangly young man with a bandana lassoed on his scalp like a turban, decked in faded jeans and bush shirt working out the variety of wood on an old Dutch chest or discarded door panel or fashioning out his own paintbrush from a quill or stick. Always inventive and looking for new ways to appreciate the master artists, his work harks back to the era of the great Kings and the Dambulla cave painters.

From winning awards to having his own art shop at the Dutch Hospital complex in Galle Fort on Hospital Street, Janaka's merging of the ancient with unusual canvases like curio boxes and wooden blocks have left an indelible impression in the South and also on fellow art aficionados like the Barefoot Gallery who have

The existential panic of the Danse Macabre, where the devils and demons dance to drive off evil spirits from those possessed

"Janaka produced the paintings for Prince Charles' Commonwealth visit, including his spectacular image of the Tree of Life."

commissioned his work and are regular bulk buyers of his vivacious stylings. At the more exclusive end of things he is becoming well known for beating temple gold into paintings for boutique hotel shops and re-creating Jaffna horses for the front verandas of stylish fashionista Southern villa owners.

Always looking back and yet moving forward with different items to paint on from door stops looking like colonial characters to Dutch chests with the tree of life on, challenging us all to think about where it all went so wrong in the 21st Century. His main studio shop on Leyn Baan Street is always a hub for creative types, fellow artists and artisans as he also sells masks for the devil in you and puppets for those who always fancied creating their own Punch and Judy show, Sri Lankan style. During the day you will find the master craftsman carving and one can even book a two-day course to create one's very own mask through Janaka direct or through trekurious.com. Day one is learning how to carve and day two is learning how to paint them with natural forest dyes.

"Janaka has built his own house in Ambalangoda and uses his Dutch chests to store his cooking pots in."

Artist Janaka de Silva has been working for over ten years in this field and has been described as a Sri Lankan artistic version of Modigliani. Wander through Janaka's current art collection and it shows he has moved away from the brightly coloured traditional Ambalangoda medicine masks, to using them as a canvas to paint historic temple themes and framing them in some cases like artworks or in complete contrast turning them into ordinary household items like plates or candlestick holders. Janaka has also created a freestanding mask that can be put on

Note the expressions of alarm in the carved heads of the fish, the cow and the lion, fashioned out of wood and given various sheens

"Janaka launched his official website in the presence of the President of Sri Lanka, Mahinda Rajapaksa at the Dutch Hospital in the Galle Fort opening ceremony."

shelves or act as a centrepiece for a room. Each piece he guarantees will last a lifetime as he uses natural herbal paint taken from the wood of the trees in the surrounding Sinharaja Rain Forest. It is fascinating watching him mix the grated pieces of bark with clay and vinegar to make a range of earthy warm colours, which are reminiscent of the works done by 5th century artists at the Sigiriya rock fortress in the Cultural Triangle.

FORT NEWCOMERS

STICK
NO
BILLS

Walled In

Juliet Coombe
and her sons,
Samad and Amzar
Careem
Sri Serendipity
Publishing House
42 Hospital Street
0776838659

A car, careens around a snaky Fort street to come to an abrupt, screeching halt and clad in a colourful sari wrap, a woman in black high heels, whilst carrying giant hand painted picture frames in both her hands, juggles two adorable little urchin-boys. Once inside the Serendipity Arts Cafe and Gallery, she attempts to tone down her manic energy for an instant, as her boys ask for ice cream and she hangs one of her photographs in a curated exhibition, which forms a unique celebration of life in the Fort. The same woman can be seen at the Lighthouse flirting with the sun at dawn, coaxing it for that exact shaft of light falling on and illuminating a railing depicting a war, turning the final photograph into a blazing sonnet to history. Towards dusk on the ramparts, her form contorts as she lies on her back, getting the right amount of exposure, twisting the aperture, framed sometimes with a film of negligee, to accommodate the acrobatics of those crazy men flying off Flag Rock and ultimately capture a moment of time as an incendiary work of art. It should also be mentioned that these feats were managed while carrying two demanding human monkeys literally clambering on her back and she claims, with the biggest smile, are her reason for living life in the Fort full throttle.

Juliet Coombe with her arty framed photographs of the Fort.

Unpredictable, brilliant and just a little out of control, author and photographer Juliet has made a home for herself and her boys inside this magnificent Fort and has lived within its walls ever since she first stepped foot in the country over ten years ago. As an international journalist, Juliet has travelled the world and experienced things only others can dream of but, "Despite travelling to 143 different countries around the world, no other place has persistently seduced me more!" It was, she says, "the kindness of the people, the incredible diversity in wildlife and stunning places to see and things to do" that made her stay.

Since then, Sri Lanka and the Fort in particular, have incredibly changed around Juliet as the years have passed. The country itself may have transformed quite considerably, experiencing the devastating effects of the 2004 Boxing Day tsunami, the end of the civil war, and the rise of a world-class cricket team. But she believes that the most significant changes have occurred within the walls of the ancient citadel: "The Fort has gone from a sleepy impossible to get to village with goats and cows meandering on the walls, to a much sought after historic

"In the 10 years that Juliet has lived in Sri Lanka, she has written 11 books."

227

Amzar Careem is the cheeky youngest son of Juliet Coombe, the author of Around The Galle Fort In 80 Lives.

As part of my marriage ceremony I was given gold, not as a dowry but as an insurance policy to look after the children if anything ever happened. Hence the phrase are you worth your weight in gold?

citadel that is having the most incredible commercial renaissance, putting it firmly back on the international travellers' list of places one must go to." There may still be a few goats hanging around but for the most part, the Fort is now full of those wanting to explore and learn about the incredible history of this place. And Juliet is right there to help them do that.

When she first started her publishing business, many people questioned her decision to run it from a seemingly sleepy town on the South Coast of a country that was, at the time, in the midst of a bloody war, that had divided a country for thirty brutal years. For her though, it made complete sense: "I realized how rich Sri Lankan literature was and just how many important academic papers would vanish because of the war. I also recognized that publishing was very limited compared to India with its huge publishing houses. Out of a love of books I carried on despite all the challenges and the simple reality that there is no big money in writing, but I was enriched, in so many more important ways, through what I learnt about the island, the team I work with and the daily feedback I get back from readers who range from 8 to 80 and simply love the depth and breadth of the Sri Serendipity Publishing House publications that range from racy to deeply intellectual."

She may have found her place now but life in Sri Lanka has not always been easy for Juliet and her sons as she still has to battle for her right to citizenship and fight to earn the respect of her contemporaries within the country. Her business, she feels, can never be secure or guaranteed a future until she is assured that she can remain in the country indefinitely as a citizen rather than simply a visitor. She tells me that "In many ways the last decade has been terribly sad losing my father his Honour Judge Coombe, my husband to insobriety and the underworld, receiving death threats, having a baby cut out of my stomach, and losing one of my best friends in a freak accident but simultaneously amazing, having given birth to two very special healthy little boys, who are deeply proud to come from the Fort's amazing merchant history. But I don't quit even when everything seems impossible as I realize the importance of documenting this extremely important living city and one of the reasons I continue to run Sri Serendipity Publishing House against all odds and equally importantly, I can see how the books have changed people's lives across all backgrounds in incredibly powerful and useful ways. Despite everything I am very honoured to live here as I have met, alongside the worst scum of the earth, some of the most brilliant people in the world and what I have learnt through them has been both priceless and humbling. I just pray the younger generation turn against drugs that could precipitate the country's latest and most serious war, and instead embrace the reasons their Kings were once revered throughout the world."

Along with these experiences, Juliet's diverse and multicultural life has only served to enrich the young lives of her two sons. The eldest son Samad frequently acts as a translator, being able to speak a multitude of languages for someone so small, including English, Sinhala, Tamil,

"I never imagined that I'd have to kill a cock on the day I moved into my house, kill a cow on the birth of my son and set fire to the house to get rid of evil spirits."

Arabic and a smattering of French. It is Samad whose name means global warrior, who is going to change the world, as his name has already decreed. "I want to be the president and have a helicopter to take me around the country, so I can help the people in the most remote areas," he once said.

He notices realities about his country that normal seven year olds would not usually appreciate as he tells me so wisely, "I feel sad as people talk badly on all sides and I want to change this because it is ignorance that causes this and then makes people fight for no reason, because of lack of respect and the simplest thing of all, learning to speak each other's language."

Amzar, very different to his brother and the baby of the family, is able to turn his movie star smile on and off depending on whether it might secure him an ice cream at his favourite spot, Dairy King, or maybe even secure him Mr. Dairy King's little princess of a daughter! Amzar is a comic genius in his own right, who has already starred in several movies and has big plans to continue along this line as he tells me, "I want to make people laugh and love working on films like Bombay Velvet as I got to be dirty and get paid for it!"

Juliet sees her two sons as a bridge in what is becoming a global world. They are a powerful double act whose bond is palpable as they put their heads together and plan their next adventure. Their hybrid identities will only serve to help them in the future as Asia booms and begins to catch up and potentially even overtake Western counterparts. Samad and Amzar are constantly reminded of their heritage, both English and Sri Lankan, a birthright that they understand and respect. They are constantly learning, whether it be from the samosa seller, the Imam at the Meeran Mosque or from one of the many international interns who frequent the spare room at 42 Hospital Street. For Juliet, however, the most important lesson that her

> Amzar her youngest son had a serious vehicle accident just after learning to walk and Juliet was overwhelmed by the help and support she received from people from all walks of life to save his life, and it demonstrated to her just how brilliant Sri Lankan doctors are, as today hardly anyone notices the terrible scars the accident caused.

The boy wonder playing jungle boy or like Newton waiting for the apple to fall in the Law Court Square

boys should learn is to always act with integrity and "To see things from all sides, to have the courage to stand up for what is right, to know their cultures, both Sri Lankan and British, inside out so they can argue knowledgably, be kind, environmentally considerate and have empathy for others and be grateful for being born into such a special historic place at such a historic time. Most of all to laugh, live life to the fullest and be part of the changes that need to take place if we are to move the world into a better place."

Juliet set up Sri Serendipity because she noticed that there was a perfect gap for it but she runs her business for the benefit of the Fort, every penny going back into the Fort's steadily thriving economy. "I never cease to be in awe of this complex historic spot that just got forgotten over time after the British moved the main port to Colombo around 1870. I love sitting on my roof looking out at the ever-changing light on the working lighthouse built by the British in 1938 and watching the fishing boats coming into harbour. Swinging in my hammock listening to the clattering of Singer bikes below, street peddlers hawking their wares mixed in with the call to prayer just after sunset. Spending over a decade in such a place is an honour, as it is so old and full of so many fascinating characters. It is like one never-ending story."

Samad loves catching crabs and can be found at Lighthouse Beach in the Fort most days with his brother Amzar riding the waves on their boogie boards, or going in search of one of the turtles that frequent these ancient waters.

The Poster Mavericks of Galle Fort

Stick No Bills
No 35 Church
Street, Opposite
the Galle Fort
Hotel
0912242504

They are everywhere. Peeling off weather-beaten, coral plastered walls and billboards grazing the sky before becoming life-nourishing fodder for the local goats at the end of a movie run. Each masterpiece promising magnificent, life affirming escapes to the La Dolce Vita or, for the younger mind, sci-fi utopias brimming with superheroes. Yet they are increasingly given the red-carpet treatment in the high-end art auction houses of the West, where the rich and famous clamor to acquire the Mona Lisa equivalents among the world's finite supply of original releases of King Kong, beating his chest as he flies through the air (1933), square-jawed Flash Gordon saving the universe (1980) or a bikini-clad Raquel Welch being pursued by some nasty looking dinosaurs in One Million Years BC (1968).

We are talking about posters, not just vintage and instant classics but specifically the spectacular kind, boasting epic vistas and apocalyptic scenes populated by smoking hot chicks, gun-toting, machete-wielding villains and heroes with ripped chests fulfilling their Herculean quests against a gaudy backdrop that exudes exotic glamour.

Outrageous posters, weather-beaten surfboards and Aviators, putting a new hip in the anatomy of cool

This is all true to the dynamic You-Only-Live-Once style of the Stick No Bills' husband and wife leadership team. The diamond from their engagement ring was not, for instance, forever. Instead they sold it to buy the posters you now see adorning the walls of their gallery in Galle Fort amongst which Diamonds Are Forever, ironically, takes pride of place.

The art of the movie poster – big, brave and beautiful. So leftfield yet so universal is this burgeoning art form in its appeal that one doesn't have to be a fine art historian to appreciate the visual content. Even pretty boy Leonardo DiCaprio is trading these rarities when he is not out there trying to save the environment. And it is off to the races with Christie's and Sotheby's leading the way, prompting investment to boom in this Alternative Investment Market (AIM) 'star performer'.

But the stakes are high in what must be one of the most unregulated marketplaces of all, wherein fraudsters selling fakes too often undermine the efforts of bona

"Posters were only ever made to be temporary ads for films. Most enjoyed just a two or three week display life at the cinema before they were torn down and replaced with the next advance promo. Some Sinhalese and Tamil poster artists even hand-painted their replicas onto large walls whilst being suspended from coconut wood scaffoldings in order to reach all four corners. Unused posters sent to cinemas were supposed to be sent back to the production company who would then normally burn them to save space."

233

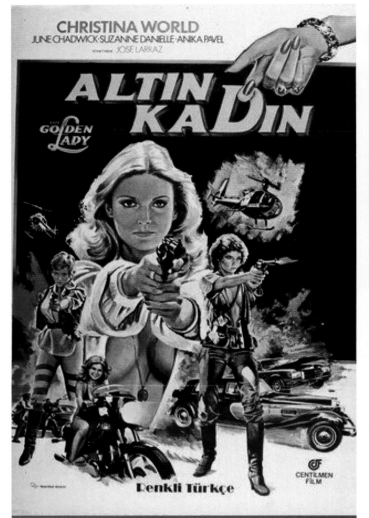

CHRISTINA WORLD
JUNE CHADWICK · SUZANNE DANIELLE · ANIKA PAVEL
JOSÉ LARRAZ

ALTIN KADIN

GOLDEN LADY

Denkli Türkçe

CENTILMEN FILM

Sultry bombshells taking on all comers in a big budget action extravaganza, portraying the eternal thrill of escapism and fantasy

"Posters have been used for many different reasons, the most powerful of which are often for propaganda or political purposes. America alone during WWI produced about 2,500 poster designs and approximately 20 million posters - one for every four citizens - in 2 years."

fide curators and collectors. All taken in the stride of this go-getter British couple who bring Philip's obsession with authentication and Meg's expertise as a risk analyst to bear on every bid they make.

Talking to the Stick No Bills co-founders I discover that if you were smart enough to buy an original, mint or even just very good condition, 1964 release James Bond Goldfinger card stock poster ten years ago for $500, it would now be worth about $5,000. An original 1933 released three-sheet poster advertising the first King Kong movie starring Fay Wray was sold at an auction in Dallas, Texas for a mighty $388,375 in November 2012.

Phil the owner of the gallery explains "In the mid 20th century nobody had any idea that they were often either ripping up or incinerating precious historical artifacts, the value of which would soar in due course. I've even been told that the majority of the island's entire archive of movie posters was lost forever in one fire. If this is really true then that is a tragedy, a tragedy that makes the Ceylon collections we exhibit all the more important. We found some of our most historically valuable pieces quite literally peeling off the walls of Sri Lanka's most forgotten cinemas".

From its inception Stick No Bills specialized in vintage Ceylon and Indian travel and movie posters. This was largely by virtue of the gallery's location on Sri Lanka's southern coast. It was only a matter of time however before the founders' passion for classic movie posters from Europe and America had to be unleashed.

The sale of the diamond from their engagement ring funded an investment odyssey that saw the couple source new posters and lobby cards from over twenty cities spread over five continents.

So, step inside a shop that celebrates sex, violence, thrills and heartbreaks. Here intellect collides in an unparalleled visual bombast, an extravagant panoramic feast for the senses capable of inducing ecstasy in the already initiated, shock and wonder among novices, diffidence among the unappreciative and finally appeasing hunger temporarily among the posters' greatest fans – the Galle Fort goats. Investing in vintage poster art is the zeitgeist. Get on it!

"The modern poster as we know it dates back to 1870 when the printing industry perfected colour lithography and made mass production possible. Textual posters have a much longer history having been used to advertise Shakespeare plays as well as upcoming jousts."

That Magical, Mechanical Whirr

Shanthi
Wickramsingha
74A Pedlar Street
091 4900262

As you meander down Pedlar Street, one of Galle Fort's main streets, you can hear the faint mechanical hum of a permanently whirring sewing machine. In a spot that perfectly catches the daylight, a small white Singer sewing machine takes pride of place as a raven-haired, bespectacled lady sits, huddled intently over the work in front of her. Shanthi Wickramsingha didn't grow up in the Fort but she has managed to find her calling in it.

Twenty-three years ago, Shanthi moved to the house at 74A Pedlar Street. Tucked away next to one of the many kade shops within the Fort, Shanthi decided to pursue her dream, which was to learn how to sew to spin the white web of her dreams. So eight years ago, she started going to private sewing classes, perfecting her skill and learning how to produce clothes that were of a high enough standard to sell. Shanthi's ambition was unstoppable, her passion for her craft driving her on to keep learning bigger and better things. And now, people are in her house every day, with different designs and patterns, asking her to make them custom clothing.

Shanthi takes her time with each customer, carefully taking their measurements and finding the perfect shade of duck egg blue to match the floral fabric that she has chosen.

The perfectly ordinary looking sewing machine, scissor and cloth ultimately conjuring a perfectly extraordinary sense of fashion

The piece currently being created by Shanthi's magical fingers is a small nightdress, just a pile of cuttings for now but slowly and perfectly, the design is taking shape. A messy mosaic of colours and textures to be chipped away at like a sculpture to meld and solder together with the fabrics using the eye of the imagination and the plentiful inspirations that flit past the stage of memories drowned in a whirlpool of calm and bliss that awaits one at the end of creation. She is truly a delight to watch. Currently a one-woman show, she says that she can handle the demands of the customers because "sewing is my passion." She can't think of anything she would rather do or any place she would rather live.

The Fort for her is a fantastic place, nowadays anyway, to run a business. She tells me that it used to be a dirty, unclean place to be, the roads not a joy to walk down as they are today. But now it is "beautiful and clean," a place where everyone can run a business and earn their living. As we leave, I turn back to see Shanthi, head down, completely focused on the work in front of her. It is this dedication and love for the craft that results in some of the most beautiful, bespoke creations that the Fort has to offer.

"Take any design you like and any fabric and Shanthi will create tailored clothes that are completely unique."

Everyone's Mama

Mama's
Malanee Perera
67 Small Cross St
0777510485

The thing about Galle Fort, as Mama's daughter Dinesha tells me, is that everyone has time for everyone else. You get a very homey feeling as you walk into Mama's restaurant, cooking school and guesthouse on Small Cross Street. Mama or Malanee as she's named, has only been on this Street for about a year, having been on Leyn Baan Street when she first started and within a decade became a legend in the area for her rice and curry. The move was hard at first and yet now everyone knows where she is and they flock to try her wonderful food and cooking school.

The daily classes find Mama taking centre stage moving about with vigour, her passion like a whirling dervish creating a literal tornado and then setting in motion a series of well executed cooking activities, as spits, sizzles and crackles of local spices punctuate the hot air. It is simply magic watching her slice and dice food, adding the most fragrant and daintiest of sauces and gravies, and there is always the sounds of dishes clanking and clinking when being plated up.
Clay pots take pride of place as Malanee demonstrates how you use the island's spices. Having earned her place in the illustrious Lonely Planet guide, Malanee no longer needs to worry about customers, even during

Fresh vegetables and matured condiments along with the loving touch to coax magic out of the produce, the wonderfully wacky world of cooking

"Tourists flock to be taught the secret cooking tips and reasons for using the island's spices."

the off season. When I ask Dinesha, if she intends to follow in her mother's footsteps she replies of course, "I might even do better!"

This is in essence a pivotal Sri Lankan family dynamic in action where the incorrigibly brilliant mother is seen spurring the burning ambition of her offspring through a fierce mix of pride in heritage and tradition combined with a unique understanding of how important it is to adapt to what is hip, giving a new meaning to the war between the generations, the old ably guiding the young. Having made a video of the classes, which visitors can now purchase to impress their friends back home, Malanee is putting Sri Lankan cooking on the map, making it accessible to everyone.

And the mystery ingredient? Unroasted curry powder added to each and every dish. For such a small country, Sri Lanka really does have everything but it is cooking which, Dinesha tells me is special here. And in the end you simply can't beat Mama's cooking!

Waxed & Wicked

The Chandler of
Galle Fort
Ahmed Mokhtar
60 Leyn
Baan Street
0770771871

You could be forgiven for confusing Ahmed with one
of the many Arabic traders who wander the streets of
Galle Fort. Slicked back silver grey hair and piercing
blue eyes betray a mysterious side to this international
photographer and now infamous spice candle maker.
Working from the garden of his cottage, Ahmed
creates exotic wonders using the Eastern spices that
are considered good for the mind and body. For a man
who was once at the top of the advertising photography
world, it is no surprise that his choice of destination
was met with exclamations from his friends such as
but it "only has 5 streets!" But, he keenly tells me that
there is a peace about this enchanted Fort that he was

" Creativity, artisan skills, fragrances, innovation and patience are the essentials of today's Luxury Candlemaking... With a hint of Daring !

Slick and meaning business, this candle-maker is a consummate professional from the get go, something very evident from his workshop and attire

so looking for, a certain magic embedded deep in the historic coral walls that bewitches every person who enters through the old gate.

The peace of the Fort of course didn't counter the reality of the millions of mosquitos that also inhabit the walls. A hatred of citronella found Ahmed looking for a mosquito repellent that wasn't so unappealing to the nose. It is surprising to note that even one of the most deadly and irritating flies from the tropics can serve as an inspiration for a show stopping scent and a perfect backdrop for those shadowy windy nights spent in a star caressed Fort. He experimented with several dozens of essential oils and after much trial and error landed on the perfect anti-mosquito candle, one hundred percent efficient with absolutely no citronella. He just made one but soon friends were asking where they could get the fabulous candles from and as he says with a nonchalant shrug, it just flowed from there. He unintentionally tapped into a niche in the market, working with five star and boutique hotels, tailoring his scented candles to their brands. Having left his heart in Paris, it was only natural that Ahmed would go straight to the heart of the perfume business, to Grasse in France, to create his uniquely gorgeous range of scented candles.

"Ahmed Mokhtar's philosophy: Simplicity is the ultimate Luxury."

Ahmed cites himself as an artisan, his candles an artistic enterprise as much as a practical one. Creativity is what he does best, a statement clearly displayed by his twenty-five extraordinarily successful years as a black and white photographer. Travelling all over the world for his craft, Ahmed found his calling somewhere between Paris, "his base, his core" and Cairo, his hometown. After growing coffee for six years in Costa Rica, two years alone with his camera in the desert in Egypt and witnessing a revolution in Cairo, Ahmed can't be blamed for wanting to find a bit of peace and quiet. But as he says, photography is not something that you can just pick up and drop: "Photography is in my soul, my blood, my genes."

His photography reveals a wonderfully multicultural life rich in layers, that have left him with several diplomas and speaking five different languages, facts that have only served to benefit him in Galle Fort, he says. In such a small place, Ahmed feels completely at ease with foreigners and locals alike who quickly accepted him by absorbing him into the community. He works just like the rest of the inhabitants of the

Candles that terrorize drones of mosquitos by assaulting their olfactory senses.

"With the invention of the light bulb in the 20th Century candles became more decorative and Ahmed has made them both beautiful and useful whether it's warding off mosquitos or creating uplifting smells."

Fort, living the same life as every other local, using the same resources and constantly finding people with whom he can exchange and relate his philosophy and rich views on life.

A descendent of royalty, his father having married a princess, there is a certain grace about Ahmed as he strolls around the Fort, exchanging greetings with everyone. His candle business is only going from strength to strength, unsurprising really from a man who, everywhere he goes, manages to end up at the top of his game. The stories he has told me leave me in amazed silence but as I thank him for sharing such a fascinating life with me, he simply smiles and with a little shake of his head says, "It's not amazing. It's life."

Tintin Returns

Krishantha's Elita Restaurant
75, Hospital Street
Galle Fort
0772423442

In Sinhalese there is a saying that a leopard never changes its spots, despite changing the forest. Be that as it may one obvious question that can be asked in the case of Krishantha - the owner of Elita Restaurant on Hospital Street overlooking the historic walls is why on earth after 18 years in Europe has he returned to set up the most successful fish restaurant in the Galle Fort.

This may be the latest novelty addition to the ever bursting at the seams Galle Fort restaurants – and yet its one I feel will last as Krishantha is an outstanding Sri Lankan chef and combines incredible cooking with a unique historic view of the port, gun bastions with charming art and day beds in the warehouse attic roof top, from which you can watch the ships come into the harbour or simply fall asleep in. Perhaps the reason is that if one's youthful wanderjahren takes you to that land near Luxembourg – Belgium in his case at the tender age of 20 – the land of Tintin, Van Dyck and Brueghel smothered among mountains and mountains of praline, icing dusted waffles, mussels and beer, incidentally also practicing that habit much lampooned and the sole cause of much agreement in Tarantino's Pulp Fiction - the habit of dousing and lashing French fries in a sea of mayonnaise something

STAURANT

The unpredictable Tintin staring out of a paradise of his own making, delectable wonders constantly being cooked in the kitchen behind him reflecting his years of being a chef in Europe.

English tuition classes used to be taught from this house

he does to accompany incredible fish dishes - a land which is primarily a melding of the hedonistic decadence associated with the Flemish hailing from the Netherlands or Holland and the refined excellence in culture and cuisine that signifies the aristocratic France, bolstered finally through the gradual creeping in of the more fiery and earthen German elements.

So why on earth would you leave Europe, the land of opportunity, big money and high flying lifestyle to come back to Sri Lanka and what could possibly prompt such an uprooting after nearly two decades of being a much sought after chef? After all isn't it every Sri Lankan man's dream to marry a pretty Western girl and get a passport out of here. However in the end the nature of self-imposed exile and travel is also characterized by an often intense melancholy, yearning and longing for one's roots – a return from seeing the vastness and impenetrability of one's external world characterized by various experiences to coming back full circle to weigh anchor and moor in the shores of one's internal existence, plunging into the depths of one's inner life, the very origin of one's being, nature

245

A whole butter fish surrounded by a smattering of colours, this is food fit for a king

Sangakkara the famous cricketer is his next-door neighbour and during the restoration of his house popped over for a quick shower.

and character. And hey, cliché or not this is literally one land that is simply like no other and as such it has that seductive enigmatic quality that pulls one into it repeatedly, hook, line and sinker. Also, the heritage and cultural practices of the Dutch Burghers, the second colonizer, remains now very much soaked into the fabric of the people, encompassing everything from delicious fish with wasabi sauce to chicken lamprais a gift from the Dutch invaders, mesmerizing lace work, love cake and the pithy humour found in novelist Carl Muller's observations of the jam fruit tree and the yakada (iron) yaka (devil).

As one sits in the earthy warehouse terracotta tiles amongst the wooden carvings of ebony elephants and life size turtles which perch about the restaurant hidden atop a twisting staircase one feels like one has entered a lost world, a secret room, a haven from the heat where you can watch the boats at night coming into the harbour and by day travellers exploring the old historic walls with the magnificent 1938 lighthouse beaming out like an icon from the British colonial period. Here in the Elita Restaurant Krishantha wants his guests to unwind and indulge in a Sri Lankan feast with a Western twist. Perhaps of greatest interest will be the tiny oil lamps, which are redolent of an age in which the Galle harbour as one of the beating pulses of trade in the Indian Ocean bore witness to ships held together by hemp and smelling of tar and canvas.

The restaurant Elita is much more than just a family business (it is named after Krishantha's daughter and whilst he cooks his sister waits on the tables); it is the culmination of Krishantha's lifelong ambition to open a restaurant in Sri Lanka. The influence of Krishantha's travels can be seen in his food which he describes as Sri Lankan "mixed up". There is all the flavour, the spices and the vivid, extravagant colours of the cuisine that one expects from this island's rich culinary tradition but Krishantha is proud of the Western twist in his food.

Krishantha enjoys the blend of cultures and history in the Fort and remarks on how fortunate Galle is with its heritage and its colonial style. He says "When you walk through the second gate into the square with the old banyan trees and the court buildings you can only say wow! It tells such a story of life through the centuries....". So do come and discover the latest addition to Galle Fort culinary experiences, Elita with its new world chef and old world ideals you won't be disappointed. His restaurant is a foodie haven and in a word pure magic!

Krishantha sells various traditional masks from his restaurant and they all have different meanings: cobra is for prosperity, peacock is for good luck and parrot is to guard against the evil eye.

Shahzad Malik

The Fort Printers
39 Pedlar St, Galle
Fort
Phone: 0912247977
Fax: 0912247976
theprinters@sltnet.lk

When asked about his statement about the Fort Printers in the last 'Around The Fort', he responds with his usual wit and charm "It's a bloody mistake come good." Shahzad Malik, is a man of questionable heritage, but unquestionable taste. He is a true citizen of the world, spending his post insurance banker days popping between Singapore, Galle Fort and Thalpe, and surely a slew of other covert destinations, armed with an investment mind and his keen eye for a good deal. In 1999 he spotted a rough cut gem in the form of the old printing workshop on Pedlar Street, and built it up from a derelict building containing ghostly shadows of its past life, like a large vault from its days of being the Bank of Ceylon, and mechanical monster printing presses. Now, you can't help but be charmed by the rounded deco corner façade of the Fort Printers, the colonial shutters, the archways and the twins out front; two black Morris Minors. Shahzad has seen the Fort grow in stature "In my time here, it has changed tremendously, there are villas everywhere now, designer shops and finally a great range of places to eat out." Whether marks of improvement in their restoration or sacrilegious in approach, Shahzad remains only slightly diplomatic: "They've ruined that historic home." Who they are, will remain locked in the vault.

Shahzad feels the Fort needs a more nocturnal energy; he's rustling the intelligencia out of their homes with exciting nightlife attractions from exhibition openings of Vintage

From James Bond's action packed doomsday scenarios to the exploits in space of Flash Gordon and the private hell of war and what it does to a man's soul in the star-studded Vietnam war epic, Apocalypse Now, in movie posters life's illusions and delusions unfold deliriously. The exhibition is just one of the many yearly exhibitions at The Fort Printers.

After being a college, the building was the home of a traditional printing company; the original press stands outside the main door

Posters to Russian contemporary art, groovy Austin Powers book launches like Drawn To Galle Fort and large private dinners backed by leading banks, enticing the Colombo crowd down the one hour expressway as an alternative to the equally long transit through traffic from one side of Colombo to the other.

Two more villas have been added to the Fort Printers, where you can stay across the road, like a canal in Venice and swan over for dinner in the evenings under grand and contemporary art pieces adorning the huge white walls and arches. If the beach beckons, turn off your phone and escape from it all at Frangipani in Thalpe, where Shahzad stays with his children if they're in town, a place of seclusion with all the trappings, offering an endless summer with the family. Although this is Shahzad's choice, he still has a love of the Fort, the magical sound of the call to prayer and a soft spot for the functioning lighthouse passing its gentle light over the Fort buildings, churches and streets. This view can be seen from the Headmaster's room in the Fort Printers. He is famous for saying in the civil war years that getting involved in Sri Lanka was a big mistake, but now repents, smiling, "it's been a mistake, rectified."

Mr TEA

Orchid House
A.G.M. Yameen
Hussain
28A Hospi-
tal Street
0915453344

A tea tasting experience? Within Galle Fort? An idea that seems to be a no-brainer in a country renowned for its tea, but one that no one really seems to have latched onto inside the Galle Fort. Until now that is, as Yameen Hussain, owner of the Orchid House shop on Hospital Street, is so excited to tell me. His third store in the Dutch Hospital boasts of a tea tasting area that comprises of at least sixty different varieties of tea. Yameen believes that it is essential that people don't buy the wrong flavour of tea because "If people take the wrong tea, they will never drink Sri Lankan tea again!"

Orchid House was officially opened after Yameen decided to return from London on Christmas Day in 2008, after just three days of preparation, stocking only a few boxes of tea, a case of jewellery and one rack of clothing. Yameen tells me that around 96% of all the stock in the shop is made in Sri Lanka by small scale businesses. The only thing that isn't is the tea, which he explains, is because "it has to be perfect."

Yameen's shop is also known for his exotic collection of spices that are pre-packaged and prepared so that anyone can take a little bit of Sri Lanka home with them, carefully sealed inside airtight bags. The spices he tells me are

Orchid House is the best place to buy spices in the Fort and one of three shops created by Yameen Hussain

handmade by a husband and wife team in their kitchen in Thalpitiya. With the spices he is a perfectionist, selling only the freshest ones he can get.

He is inventive with his designs always looking for ways to expand and change a product to suit the latest international fashions. His most recent idea was leather and jute bags that have two different sections: one that is lined with a waterproof fabric and one with cotton, allowing for the bag to be used at the beach as well as every day, as both are useful and uber cool.

He is worried now though that the Fort is turning into a commercial city, one that may never again regain the atmosphere that people were so proud of in the past. He is incredibly proud of the Fort's UNESCO heritage and is desperate that others realise that it is an honour that must be respected. No gaudy signs litter the road in front of the shop, as Yameen does not want to, or need to, shout about it. Those who know of Orchid House will always keep coming back and for all you first timers out there, you'll love what you discover at 28A Hospital Street.

Vanilla is actually a plant that derives from the orchid family, primarily from the Mexican species, flat-leaved vanilla

The Island Tests You

Mango House
Sophie and Hugh
3 Leyn Baan Cross
Street, Galle Fort
Call 0912 247 212

The name is business, strictly business, and you certainly better mean it even with a winning combination of colonial stylish rooms with delightful Italian verandahs and an Aladdin's cave of colours and silks that make it the most charming spot in the old town.

So armed with the experiences of previous people who have made the island their home, Sophie and Hugh decided to give Galle Fort a go, realising that after years in the Middle East this was a perfect half way point. Talking to them as they open their stunning place it may seem a little unoriginal for the managers of a hotel to refer to it as their baby but at Mango House they have more cause than most to refer to it so; not only was this project one into which Hugh and Sophie have fused their shared ideas and creativity but it also took nine months (rather than the anticipated three) to grow.

As we sit on a terrace beneath this beautifully converted Dutch cinnamon warehouse it is clear that Hugh and Sophie are fanatical about ensuring that this hotel lives up to their dream home away from home. The attention to detail is beyond meticulous and no fragment of this ancient building or the objects that furnish it are beyond significance. Long elegant saris hang from the tall exposed beams of the original Dutch roof but the building doesn't have the cramped and dark feeling of some of the older houses, instead it has a liberating fresh and open feel. This may be down to the skylights which let the sun flood into

Mango House is named after the luscious fruit, embodying the heady vitality of the tropics

It is as far away as one can imagine from mass-produced corporate hotels or the run-of-the-mill guesthouses churning out so many guests a night.

the large open foyer or it may be because the furniture is alive with bold purple colour from the pieces of Sinhalese art and to a bright lime green wardrobe filled with all the practical essentials that travellers need like sun cream and mosquito repellent. It's these little details that mark Sophie and Hugh out as travellers of real experience and they confess that part of the reason that they have decided to "put down roots in bricks and mortar" here in Galle is because they feel the Fort can act as a home to those who are used to the open road. It's clear that the couple have realised that a life spent living out of a suitcase with barely a few nights here and a few nights there (Hugh is a writer with some experience in culture and art) is not one that can continue indefinitely. Now in their thirties they wanted to find their own plot in which to settle and live thus starting an adventure tied to a single location rather than spread across a world, and so they turned to Sri Lanka.

"It's something about the mix of cultures here," explains Sophie. "It makes Sri Lanka the ideal home for the traveller and Galle Fort has always been an international crossroads." The pair go on to describe how they feel the whole nation resonates with the history of movement from its past as an island of commerce where the exotic east collided with the power and might of the West to create a melting-pot of people. And why Galle?

253

There are only seven rooms here but each has been individually furnished with a different set of art on each wall, a separate design of door handles on each wardrobe, bright linings on the insides of antique reproduction cupboards and a completely different tile each time that you put your foot down. The tiles, I am told, came from an original producer of natural clay tiles in the centre of the Sri Lankan jungle and Hugh can point to the unique imprints of paws and claws of numerous unknown and unnamed beasts who left their mark before the tiles were sent to be fired in a wooden kiln. The hotel is a bright star on the backstreets of Galle, the silence only broken by the call to prayer, a place to rest for those who are always on the move and a place for those constantly in transition to settle.

"Hugh is also in a rock band and so thrives on challenges. His next one being a father!"

For Hugh and Sophie the highs of taking on a business that was entirely new to them have definitely cast away the initial difficulties of the project. They had never run a hotel before coming to Mango House and even with all the advice of predecessors initially found real difficulties in tackling a mound of bureaucracy over planning permission, building control and legalistic red tape—as if to confound such difficulties Hugh was struck down by Dengue fever at the same period.

"We felt the island was testing us!" laughs Sophie, "But we hope that we're through the worst now."

This low point has obviously been banished from their minds and it is clear that they revel in their new profession. They describe the surreal moment when the first guests walked up the path through the secluded garden and instantly fell in love with the unique and intimate character of the experience at this close-knit hotel. Here guests can live as they want to by taking meals on their own balconies which overlook the unique Sri Lankan rooftops of dense and disorderly clay tiles, coloured with age, through groves of palm trees which add that exotic holiday sensation to every view.

Hugh and Sophie have clearly unleashed the full spirit of this ancient building by harnessing the colonial splendour and

The owners at the official opening ceremony of the hotel

"We were looking for somewhere to settle but we kept on being drawn back to the Fort, it was something about the feel here that so many different cultures can get along in peace and unity rather than causing divisions. It was something about the history, the village community, both good and bad, and the sense that it was a place where travellers could stop and feel at home." Perhaps this is what is so special about Mango House.

sheer size of this enormous building with its soaring rooftop a dazzling distance above those historic beams crisscrossing the foyer far below but retained a sense of togetherness and cosy-comfort which is truly modern and fresh. For those visitors who wait with bated breath to sample the fruits of the mango trees that give the hotel its name and soar through the quiet and peaceful splendour of the garden, wrapped and cosseted in fairy lights, a disappointment lies in store.

"Yes, we have to buy in the mangoes," laments Hugh with a rueful smile, "the purple faced monkey always has a tendency to get to our fruit first!" If this is the only monkey business they have to face in the exciting months ahead they consider themselves lucky as the latest people to join Galle Fort's excitingly diverse community.

A Risk Worth Taking

LankaRealEstate.
com
Ivan Robinson,
Director
1 Magistrates
Square
0777235775

"Even though Sri Lanka is a country with a lot of risk, people want to take the risk." So is Ivan Robinson's proclamation for the future real estate of the dynamic country that is Sri Lanka, an area he has specialised in for many years. He is the Director of LankaRealEstate. com, a business he set up in 2002 with his friend Giles Scott after spending many years visiting the country on holiday. He used to run it from a small office in Colombo and from his home. But he decided he needed a place where the public were free to wander in and out, browsing his incredible selection of properties like kids in a sweet shop.

The business grew faster than he had allowed for and so three years ago he bought Number 1 Magistrates Court, which became the company's new home. Ivan deals with properties mainly in and around the Fort, although he tells me he doesn't sell as much in the Fort anymore as most of it has already been sold! He both rents and sells villas, catering to any customer's needs, whatever country they come from. He believes that it is a key part of his job, as a foreigner in Sri Lanka to explain to the many hoards of excitable prospective buyers, just how different the country is, both in its history and its culture. He wants to make

Buy a house and a painting at the fabulous Saskia Fernando Gallery

sure that people don't buy ignorantly, keeping both the buyers and the locals happy.

Ivan feels that Sri Lanka is very much a country of ups and downs: you'll fall in love with it if you manage to accept the good with the bad, much as you would with a potential spouse. He absolutely loves running a business here and tells me, "the challenge is amazing!" He especially loves working from the Fort as he feels that the Law Court Square is the heart of the citadel, drawing people and business in from all over the country and not just the surrounding area. The country is constantly moving and growing and Ivan says, the "development in the country is amazing" for example in 1996 a house in the Fort would cost you $30,000 and today the same house would go for about $1 million or more in the case of the Galle Fort Hotel.

The Fort, he feels is becoming more commercial every year but Ivan is not one to dwell on the negative aspect of this advancement: "Nobody likes change but it isn't fair to stop people progressing."

Galle Fort Hotel as a house was sold during the war for $500,000 and resold 7 years later, after re-branding as a hotel, for $7 million

A Spicy Sorcerer

Spoon's
Shamil Roshan
Careem aka 'Babi'
100
Pedlar Street,
Galle Fort
0779383340

The bright ruby red sign beckons you inside, catching your eye with its larger than life spoon as you meander down Pedlar Street. Shamil Roshan Careem, known to his friends and family as Babi, is working away in the adjoining kitchen, pans sizzling and pots bubbling away. He serves one of the best rice and curry in Galle Fort, a fact that is verified when you speak to anyone who lives in the area. Spoon's was formerly called the Serendipity Arts Café, but it is now hot on Serendipity's heels, giving it a run for its money. Babi has been in this business for a while, however he doesn't try to sugar-coat his profession when he says that "it's not easy running a highly successful restaurant, it's tough."

Shamil "absolutely loved" growing up in the Fort but when he was given the chance to travel, he seized the opportunity with both hands. His good fortune came in the form of a well-known Sri Lankan TV chef domiciled in Australia, Peter Kuruvita, who in 2010, was visiting the country and decided that he needed an assistant to make a TV cooking series My Sri Lanka. So Babi went off to the meeting, apprehensive but also excited. They got on immediately, says Babi, as Peter was an exceptionally "friendly and generous man." After that they set off on a six-month tour of the country to make the most successful cooking series ever on the island. His eyes widen as he tells me "Now

On a rustic stove, a local delicacy of prawns in creamy sauce, simmering and thickening over heat

I have seen the whole island and tried every type of food!" His favourite place he went to? "Nuwara Eliya because the weather is good and so are the people!" But he is honest when he says that, whilst he was experiencing the most amazing things, "when I was with Peter, I missed this place a lot."

Most of the friends he grew up with in the Fort are still all here, getting together at Babi's for New Year's Eve parties and sitting on the ramparts watching cricket, only 20/20 games though as "I hate test cricket! It takes far too long!" Babi is a man with big dreams and an even bigger future ahead of him, a person who just maybe the one the thick coral walls of the Fort will not be able to contain and confine. The selection on the menu at Spoon's is adventurous to say the least, yet there is something for everyone. The rice and curry is a must try but more unusual would be the lush pumpkin soup. For now though, Babi is just content with living in the present, not worrying about what may or may not happen in the future. As he leans back in his chair and gives me a cheeky smile, it is clear that he is very much Peter Kuruvita's protégé in action. So get used to that bright red sign at the end of Pedlar Street because it, and its illustrious owner, aren't going anywhere soon.

The longest test cricket match ever played was between England and South Africa in 1939. It went on for 9 days, drawing to a close because of rain and because the English had to catch their boat home: they only needed 42 more runs for victory. Despite it being a 'timeless' test, a draw was the agreed result.

Galle Fort's Van Gogh

Dr. Janaka Ruben
17 Pedlar Street
0773058485

As two little girls play with a camera, passing it back and forth, twisting, bending and jumping to get the perfect shot, their proud father looks on delightedly. There is no doubt too that the photos taken will be works of art in themselves as creativity runs through these girls' veins. And when your father is Dr. Janaka Ruben, artist, musician, awe-inspiring photographer and respected doctor, you have a pretty impressive role model to learn from.

Dr. Janaka has an attitude that many, in the commercialised modern world, would cast aside as it is his feeling that "knowledge is worth more than money." Regardless of what life throws at you, if you are rich in your mind then you can do whatever you want to do. He did not become a doctor in the first place for money and his decision to give up surgery and become a lecturer at the Karapitiya medical faculty was not motivated by material gain either. Having done surgery for more than twelve years, Dr. Janaka decided he wanted to further his education and it seemed only right that, having studied as a boy at St. Aloysius College in Galle, he remain in the Fort's surrounding area. He tells me that his dream is simply to become an effective teacher and researcher, paving the way for the future generations to be able to develop and deepen their understanding of the world, allowing them to make their own decisions.

The lighthouse hoists the sun, spreading its singing rays one final time, before the world ends by Dr. Janaka Ruben

Dr. Janaka is now embarking on his next mission, a PhD, in which he has decided to explore the psychological effects of chronic diseases and the importance of the protocols that enable the treatment of such diseases. It is a mammoth task but one which Dr. Janaka plans to devote his full attention to. He says that the benefit of no longer practising surgery is that he now has the time to dedicate to his research so that, eventually, people across Sri Lanka will be able to reap the benefits of his paper.

You would think that a man undertaking such a task would not have time for anything else. But Dr. Janaka is a man who excels at many things, not just saving lives, as if that wasn't enough. He has an aptitude for playing every single one of the fifty musical instruments he keeps in his house and a Van Gogh like eye for artistic detail. He believes that art is an essential part of every child's development so that is why he stands back and allows his two daughters to scamper up and down the perilous, stone staircase, his precious camera swinging precariously from around their necks. His is a rare outlook, however, in a country that still places a huge emphasis on traditionally 'good' and well respected professions like the law and medicine. But Dr. Janaka feels that attitudes within Sri Lanka are slowly changing and he hopes that, whatever his

"Photography is an industry that is only booming but with new technology allowing anyone to be able to take an impressive shot, it is still artists like Dr. Janaka Ruben who stand out from the crowd."

Galle Fort in daytime, a nightmarish time lapse, an endless ghost town emptied of life, taken by Dr. Janaka. To get this spectacular panoramic shot Dr. Janaka had to climb to the top of the 1938 British built lighthouse

"To get this spectacular panoramic shot Dr Janaka had to climb to the top of the 1938 British built lighthouse in the early morning"

daughters decide to do, they will merely be happy in their professions.

Having grown up in the Fort in his parent's house on bustling Pedlar's Street, Dr. Janaka's heart has been well and truly stolen by this ancient citadel, the soft lighting and dreamlike aura making for the perfect artist's home. For now, Dr. Janaka still offers his friends his professional wisdom but it is his PhD and lecturing job that are the focal point of his life, though as he tells me with a slight grimace, "you spend half your life building your house!" yet another task that Dr. Janaka is currently undertaking.

It is easy to see why Dr. Janaka has always indulged in his passion for photography, even whilst the chaos of normal family life and a medical job goes on in the foreground. His photos are spectacular and his shots of the Fort at sunset perfectly capture the magic of the historic coral walls and carefully restored buildings. Some of Dr. Janaka's work is exhibited on the walls of the central coral courtyard of the Historical Mansions. In reality, he tells me, he would like to explore classical painting further but he says, "I do photography because I don't have time to paint!" First and foremost, in his heart, he will always be a doctor but if the photos shown grab your interest you will be able to treat yourself to a little slice of Fort magic in the form of Dr. Janaka's book of photography.

"Photography literally means writing with light and many people think Dr. Janaka's photographs are more like paintings as they so beautifully capture the moment like the sun setting on the top of the Fort lighthouse built in 1938. Some of Dr. Janaka's work is exhibited on the walls of the central coral courtyard of the Historical Mansions."

A Witch Doctor's Legacy

Venod
Weerasingha
35 Lighthouse
Street 0775622299

In a house that is still today known as the Veda Gedara it is no wonder that a certain magic still moves through the air. The word veda comes from the traditional practice of Ayurveda medicine that Venod's grandfather, as he tells me, was one of the Fort's masters at. Small green-lidded bottles and white pots full of mysterious, remedies are lined up in an old glass cabinet just inside the door, a reminder of the illnesses and diseases that, over the last forty years, were cured in the front room of this old house.

The house has various features from both the Dutch and British periods, the high ceilings and square archways lending to the building a light, open and airy feeling. Venod is the third generation to have lived in the house, as it was his grandparents who first bought it. Venod grew up in the house until he was twelve years old but had to move out of the ancient citadel when his father's business required him to. Venod remembers his younger childhood with great fondness, able to run around the corner to his friend's house whenever he felt like it to scamper along the ramparts, terrorising the inhabitants of the citadel. He tells me now, however, that he is delighted that he is now back

Part medicine man cum shaman, part alchemist, what becomes of these men and the wealth of indigenous knowledge in the stampede of 'development'

living in the old house though the sentiment is tinged with sadness as his grandmother, the sole occupant of the house for many years, passed away in 2013.

Venod is part of a generation who are leaving the Fort to find professional jobs elsewhere, unable to find something to satisfy themselves within it. There is a feeling amongst this generation, some of whom are currently, like Venod, awaiting exam results and going through university, that the Fort cannot offer them the opportunities that can stretch them nor provide them with livelihoods that will enable them to live a life that their education has so prepared them for.

This is a sad reality but it is simply one that is a product of a changing world. Venod is adamant however, that, regardless of whether or not he decides to work outside the Fort, it will always be his home. He echoes many of his Fort contemporaries' own sentiments when he declares that he will always come back, wherever his life may lead him.

"Venod's generation are one who, though they may go elsewhere to seek professional employment, will always remain loyal to the ancient citadel."

The Carpenter Family

'71 Pedlar Street also doubles as a beautiful B & B to make a booking Tel:0779619822 or email Eve Turner on evet1102@ gmail. com or Tel: 0776960238'

"I bought this house really to stop Ninni running off with the sexy Italian tennis coach!" says Tom chuckling slightly as he looks over at his wife who simply raises her eyes to the heavens and says "fact number one, I've never even played tennis!" The good humour and love surrounding this family are what has made them into one of the most appreciated and respected foreign families in the Fort, as they are some of the few who are still here ten years on from when they first bought the property at 71 Pedlar Street.

December 2004 changed their entire family's life for, when the tsunami struck the island, the Carpenters were all on Christmas holiday in the south. In the aftermath of the event Tom and Ninni's children Erik and Laura and Erik's wife Simone were so deeply affected by what had happened that they stayed on, helping to run Project Galle from the house from January of 2005. As Ninni says "all my four grandchildren are now here because my children were here during the tsunami and it had a deep effect on them all. They became attached to the people and this house became a base for all of them at different stages."

Vivid colours set ablaze the obvious joie de vivre experienced by artist Kristian Carpenter

Tom remembers the moment that they made the decision to buy their house and the undercurrent of risk involved in the purchase: "Buying here was a leap into the darkness and in the immediate aftermath of the tsunami one wondered how would Sri Lanka rebuild itself and could it rebuild better with new ideas. That was always the big question."

The person they are most proud of is Azeez of Pedlar's Inn fame who, they say, when they first arrived merely had two tables outside his bedroom and "he didn't even do eggs for breakfast! The only food he served was toasties which he learnt from working at Project Galle!" Over the years he developed his house into the wonder that is Pedlar's Inn Café and from the profits of that, he then set up an ice cream shop and a successful hostel. The Carpenters have watched him evolve dramatically turning into the shrewd but kind businessman that he is today. As Ninni says "everything he touches turns to gold!"

They say that when they bought the house they were at a period when they had the energy to restore it and turn it into the family home. But now as they get older, Ninni

" Ninni and Tom explain that the attraction of the Fort "was the large number of different nationalities all with the same spirit, and so many different religions and denominations, and the reality that they all co-exist harmoniously."

Pop art, here depicted through a futuristic flower-child, full of the exuberance of youth

"Ninni says one of her favourite places to go in the Fort is The Rampart Hotel because 'it is one of the few places that is still exactly the same and, because we are so close to it, it feels like our own dining room!"

says the heat does get to them and the new pavements laid down to make the Fort's streets more appealing to tourists may look good but they have turned the Fort into an oven. They do stress that, though "Change is all for the good, I loved it when we bought the house with goats eating the rubbish and cows meandering through the main street."

The house itself has also changed in its uses over the years as now it has become the base for Ninni and Tom's five children and four grandchildren which they say, out of everything is the "biggest change that has happened." Ninni says "all my family are here so in reality it wouldn't make sense to sell up and leave." Sri Lanka has captivated every single one of their growing brood with several of them running extremely successful businesses in and around the Galle area, including their son Kristian who, with his partner Eve are permanent residents of 71 Pedlar Street running it as a B/B.

Kristian is a trained artist, having studied fine art at both Chelsea and Brighton and his latest works hang on the walls of the house, funky pop art inspired images that capture his family in a fun and quirky way. Ninni says that he is only getting better and better and now, with his studio above the Stick No Bills poster shop on Church Street, he has the time and freedom to keep developing his artistic talent. Ninni believes that Sri Lanka has only been beneficial to Kristian and his work because "there is a lightness to his work that he has done here that he didn't have at home." Home for the Carpenters is an isolated farm in Wales, a place not known for its colour and vibrancy, two features that would be the first words to spring to mind as you admire Kristian's work. The dream for Ninni would be for him to do enough work to host an exhibition in the house, making it into a creative hub for people to come and visit as she does feel the Fort lacks in many stimulating cultural activities like live music and art shows.

Kristian has made this place his home but Tom and Ninni are unsure as to whether they could ever live here permanently: "sometimes it can feel a little claustrophobic." The only thing both of them hope is that it doesn't become a tourist jumble site, overrun with cheap rubbish: "It has become more like Saint Michel since the war ended with a lot of tat, portable goods and things that have nothing to do with the craftsmanship of Galle Fort. It detracts from the heritage."

As the conversation draws to a close, Tom is reflective as he says that the Fort is "a model of a unified world" a place that, should they ever choose to leave, will remain with them forever.

"Jewellery is a divisive subject in the Carpenter household but Tom says 'Ninni's very good now as she doesn't have to start her day with a visit to Laksana!'"

Stephen LaBrooy

Dutch Burgher
In the Dutch Fort
of Galle,
1, Middle Street

"I remember coming here to the Galle Fort quite often as a small boy from Colombo and my father would always stop the car before the main entrance and say "Stephen, this was built by our Dutch ancestors," and for me at that age it was like entering hallowed ground. I remember the Fort being very impressive and exciting and the N.O.H (New Oriental Hotel) - the grandest of buildings; I am going back 60 years now, when it was in its heyday and everyone who was anyone went there. I remember thinking as a child just how beautiful it was. I was in complete awe of the Fort playing war games on the ramparts, imagining myself to be a VOC soldier protecting the Fort from the wicked British by attacking their ships with imaginary Dutch cannons. In my childish version of history, the Dutch hung onto Sri Lanka!"

Although the ramparts of Stephen's childhood are the same, much of the Fort has greatly changed; for example, he remembers the wooden floors, the original veranda tiles and its massive doors as the only things left of the NOH since it became the Amangalla. He rues the loss of the ambiance of the NOH with its decaying colonial elegance and feels that the hotel restoration

A quiet dining room somberly awaits the cacophony of life

in its common areas could have been done more sympathetically in keeping with its heritage.

Stephen LaBrooy's mixed heritage makes him both part coloniser and part colonised. He is on the one hand a proud Dutch Burgher whose ancestors came here nearly 300 years ago and stayed on after the British took control of the Island; on the other he is a fiercely proud Sri Lankan with a passionate love for his country. Several years ago he decided to "go back to his roots" – metaphorically - and make his home in the Galle Fort. In 2006 he bought a plot of land in Middle Street and two years later was finally given permission to build a colonial-Dutch style house overlooking the Dutch Reformed Church opposite his beloved N.O.H, which still brings a sparkle to his piercing blue eyes. The house took him 4 ½ years to build and on its completion in December 2012 he finally realised his dream of living in the Fort.

Educated in England during its iconoclastic heyday of the 1960s, a time of rock and roll, a time of new and fresh ideas, a time when youth was celebrated, he

"Stephen has spent more time away from the island working as an International Commodity Trader in London, Colombo, Singapore, back to London and finally in Hong Kong. He quit the trading business in 1996."

explains that it was exciting times. "Every icon was being smashed in England, every norm and every "sacred cow" was being thrown out or dismantled. Youth was, if you like, the 'centre of the universe', the music industry particularly was re-born and even today it is still my generation's music like the Rolling Stones, the Eagles and Led Zeppelin which is still being avidly listened to by generations who were a long way off being born at the time it was created." Nevertheless, during his education he came back home at least once a year and continued to do so throughout his career until he decided to return home for good.

"Stephen returned home to live permanently in 2002, owing to a deep love and passion for the island and its people."

Stephen loves the heritage aspect of the Galle Fort; initially he looked for an old Dutch House to restore and then realised he would have to spend a lot of money on quite basic stuff – getting rid of wood worm, dry rot and rotten roof timbers - before he could do any renovation. "Also, I realised, looking at many of the houses up for sale that there was an endemic damp problem in the walls owing to the hygroscopic nature of the materials used such as shells and coral at the time of their construction. I thought to myself, wouldn't it be nice to have a house exactly the way you want it without any of the inherent drawbacks. I saw this site – at the time it had an un-prepossessing jewellery shop cum workshop built in 1989, but it had a great location right next to the Amangalla and behind the Dutch Church. The rules for the heritage site in the Fort were that you are allowed to demolish a building deemed to be not of historical interest provided that you replace it with something that is in keeping with the architecture of the Fort, so I asked renowned architect and this country's "guru" of colonial architecture, Ashley de Vos to come up with a concept drawing (and subsequent detailed drawings) which he did. It was approved."

"Tropical Amsterdam" as it has been called, is not strictly speaking a correct view of the Dutch in Sri

The columns balance out the horizontal play of doors and windows, of hellos and goodbyes

" The house on Middle Street is a masterpiece of craftsmanship in its own right, one can feel the historic roots in the marvelous timber furnishings, and giant bolts with perfect Dutch replica lamps."

Lanka. It was not Holland, the country, that came here but the Dutch East India Company (VereenigdeOost-IndischeCompagnie), a public company that operated under the Royal Charter. Holland being a very small country, the V.O.C employed people from all over Europe (Dutch, Belgians, Luxembourgers, French, Germans, Austrians, Poles, Swiss, Scandinavians, English - and some with Iberian names too). Most of the VOC personnel in Sri Lanka were in fact not of Dutch ethnicity but their common denominator was that they were Protestant and (probably) anti Catholic! LaBrooy himself admits that his immediate ancestry was a mix of French Huguenots-kicked out of France in the 1680s-on his father's side and on his mother's paternal side from Germany-Koch being the family name. Both of his grandmothers' families, however were Dutch – Wambeek and Kriekenbeek who came here in the 1690's.

No house with history is complete without a sturdy bookcase and enough books to impress its vision of an ideal world upon those fortunate to enter it

"I decided to photograph an original Dutch chandelier and took it to a wonderful metal craftsman in Bentota who made copies in brass, extrapolating the dimensions of every part from the photographs."

"Contrary to what a lot of people say, the VOC was invited here by treaty in 1637 by the then King of Kandy to get rid of the Portuguese; the VOC's interest here was to take control of the spice trade, which at one time was as valuable as gold. It was a trade route that had been under the control of Moors first and then with the Portuguese for over a hundred years, and finally under the Dutch for more than 150 years." As a successful trader himself, Stephen points out that the Dutch East India Company, formed in 1602 is arguably still the world's most successful company, having paid out an 18 per cent dividend to its shareholders for nearly 200 years! The causes of its final demise in 1796 lay in internal corruption, the rise of the British

East India Company and the Napoleonic wars. When Holland was overrun by Napoleon's troops the Dutch gave Ceylon to the British for "safe-keeping" on the understanding it would be returned, but realising its strategic importance, the British kept it for 152 years.

For LaBrooy, however his dream retirement home in Galle Fort is not all he imagined it would be. "Living in the Galle Fort is far from my idealized memories of a sleepy town, as today it faces noisy traffic congestion from the school runs and tourist buses making it very difficult to get around at certain times of the day. Quiet enjoyment of the ramparts can only be done in the early mornings as in the evenings they are so crowded with people. Sadly for me, I still constantly have to prove that I am Sri Lankan even when I speak reasonably good Sinhala. For six months after I bought the property, the land registry had not registered it to me, because they thought I was a foreigner! I suppose I shouldn't blame them as there are so few Burghers around nowadays that anyone with pale skin is deemed to be foreign but I have to say it saddens me as I never consider myself anything other than Sri Lankan." Stephen is not frightened however to take these issues head on. After three hours of cogent argument in Sinhala at the land registry, he walked out with the registration certificate in hand having had many abject apologies from the relevant staff therein for their mistake!

The year 1956 proved to be a cataclysmic year not only for LaBrooy's family and the Burgher community but for the whole country. It was the year of the Sinhala Only Bill, which changed the administrative system overnight and would eventually ban the English medium of education in schools. As a result, a great many of the Burghers emigrated, mainly to Australia. "They were not economic migrants" he insists. "Believe me they loved this country so much. I even think

"All the long door latches are copied from originals. I had a master craftsman make special hinges for the doors and very faithfully copied all the Dutch style fastenings and finishes."

" I wanted to get as much detail as possible to be as authentic as those of the master craftsmen our ancestors would have employed."

they would even have put up with all the draconian socialistic nonsense of the 1970-77 period – had they only been allowed to educate their children in English - given also, the fact that, it is our community's mother tongue - a not unreasonable stance!"

If not for that legislation he believes that about 80 percent of his community would still be here. It is unlikely the Burghers will ever return as their children have grown up in Australia, and after 30 years your life is in another country. Quite apart from that there is the pragmatic aspect. We are a country of several disparate ethnic groups. We could and should have followed India who knew that they had to keep English as the unifying language making them one of the world's superpowers today."

Enjoy the detached calm and recharge your batteries as you indulge in an afternoon siesta in this beautifully designed house

"Sadly, the Sinhala Only Bill and its abolition of the English stream of education was the death-knell for the Burgher community. Those that migrated to Australia in such vast numbers are now Australian or if not them, their children certainly are; those that stayed have largely been assimilated into the majority community. Though official statistics number 39,000 Burghers, that figure largely consists of Sinhalese people with Burgher names. After several generations of marrying into another community, you take on the identity of that community. For example Sinhala becomes your mother tongue; you speak only Sinhala at home, listen to Sinhala music, and watch Sinhala films on TV. I myself have met young people with Burgher names who are absolutely Sinhalese in every other respect. A truer estimate of the number of Burghers left in this country would be around 15,000."

His mother understood the intellectual and cultural wealth of this country and when her husband insisted that they move to Australia in 1956, Stephen recalls. "My father went on ahead and had been there a few months when my mother decided she would visit to see what it was like. She only took 6 weeks to decide that Australia was not for her (and therefore not for me!). She thought Australia at that time to be quite shallow in culture and very un-genteel – and in stark contrast to her way of life and the circles in which she moved in back home. We came back after 6 weeks there and in the end I was schooled in England. A few years after I returned the country had turned to a very doctrinaire Eastern-European form of socialism. I decided to go back to London in 1971. In those days you had to get an exit visa to leave the country which involved a Tax Clearance certificate from the Inland Revenue Department, and a certificate from the Department of Exchange Control affirming that they had allowed you foreign exchange for your travel. I remember a few harrowing meetings with the Exchange Control people during the first of which they even refused me permission to pay for my ticket! Eventually it came, I still had a British passport; sold my car, sewed the proceeds - £80 - into the waistband of my trousers and left.

> Also, as a long time convert to Buddhism myself, I deplore the politicisation of Buddhism in our country.

Stephen sitting looking out over his colonnaded garden understands the complexity of the country and its turbulent history "I have always loved Sri Lanka not just the countryside, but also the history and the people most of all. I have always felt that this is my country (even though most Sri Lankans look at me as though I don't come from here). Apart from all of that I came back for the incredible food. 'Sinhala Kaama' is my favourite food in the world. Every country in the world has its pluses and minuses - Sri Lanka is not without its frustrations: rampant indiscipline being the main one. Also, as a long time convert to Buddhism myself, I deplore the politicisation of Buddhism in our country. On the other hand however, the unsolicited kindness one experiences so often here is so rarely found in other parts of the world. It really does get to you-like the Galle Fort and its historic ramparts layered in rich history. Sri Lanka is my home and a very special one at that."

Stephen goes onto say "I have to say that I am not sure as a new arrival to the Galle Fort community, how long I will stay. For the most part it is not stimulating, and also very cliquey. I would love to be part of the entity that looks after the Fort and its interests. I do have a passion for old buildings, artefacts and antiquities and in the case of the Galle Fort that is not just the product of an academic interest but a highly personal one." He explains that there was once a Burgher tennis club in the Fort

A realm of comfort resting in the lap of old world luxury and the sound of feet and shoes, echoing their odd music, disturbing the dense silence

When Holland was overrun by Napoleon's troops the Dutch gave Ceylon to the British for "safe-keeping" on the understanding it would be returned, but realising its strategic importance, the British kept it for 152 years.

indicating a large number of Burghers who lived here until the 1960s, and now there are none - bar himself.

As an all-encompassing footnote it can be said that to tackle racism and reverse-racism, essential cogwheels in a colonial and post-colonial context, requires guts and intellect fed by real Dutch courage to survive. Stephen LaBrooy is just such a man and one can only hope that as the only Burgher in the Fort he will stay and keep the Burgher history a living one.

Shoba Life To Hands

Women's
Cooperative
Society

67A, Pedlar Street,
Galle Fort
Tel: 091 2224351

Shoba celebrates locally handmade crafts and is famous for its intricate lace work demonstrated at the shop daily during the season on the second floor. Shoba "Life to Hands" developed from a gallery into a Women's Cooperative after the 2004 tsunami and it concentrates on empowering of women in the Galle area, teaching them new skills and trades.

One aim is to support disadvantaged children and Shoba provides artisan and craft training and materials to create bags, tops, jewellery, lace and textile group workshops. These efforts result in a shop full of traditional and modern designs. Chamanthi runs the project and says, "Our main target is for the women to make a livelihood." All these groups are developed in the local area and many women have progressed to running their own small businesses. Funding is supplied by the Trans-rural Trust that approves microfinance and interest free loans. Their sister-group, the Himalaya Natural Fibre Foundation in Nepal, supplies the fabric used in Chamanthi's design of a cushion cover she is making on the old Singer sewing machine in-store. "I am mixing three different livelihoods into this one piece; lace, nettle and

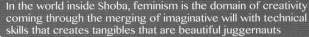
In the world inside Shoba, feminism is the domain of creativity coming through the merging of imaginative will with technical skills that creates tangibles that are beautiful juggernauts

needlework." The shop is a beautiful little alcove with lace makers click-clacking upstairs giving the place both mood and context.

'Beauty that is created by love, peace and happiness' – this is what Shoba means and under this motto the Women's Cooperative Society helps women because "everybody should have a chance in this world." Charity projects are often run with a bitter taste of pity but as you enter the Shoba shop on Pedlar Street, displaying and selling handmade items by underprivileged women from the Southern province in Sri Lanka, the positive and happy atmosphere of the society's president will fill the room with hope and laughter. Chamanthi is a powerful woman who says what she thinks. She is proud of this shop and says that the idea is not to just be a gallery but a living space of great artisanal work. "It is a gallery of hope and the future dreams of unemployed Sri Lankan women. You can purchase manufactured household items, linen, bags, clothes, greeting cards and lace products for a good price and a good deed – allowing many of them to build sustainable businesses".

"I know how tired and fed up people are when they constantly hear about poverty and unemployment in Sri Lanka", says Chamanthi. "But we want to show the other – the positive – side of the coin when social projects carry fruits and show why women in Sri Lanka are so amazingly creative!"

The Traders Truest Treasure

Collectibles
Mohamed Hassen
53/1 New Lane 1
0773946500

On the 18th January 1946, Mohamed Fahmy Hassen was born in a bunker in modern Galle, where his family had taken refuge from the World War II military presence inside the Fort. He's a gemmologist by profession, and his dedication to self-realisation propelled him from Sri Lanka to Hong Kong, to Nigeria, to London and back again to the Island of Jewels. After almost 50 years earning and learning all he could in London, he has finally returned to Galle Fort to spend his 'retirement' collecting and selling coins, stamps and gems, from his shop at 53/1 New Lane 1.

He knows the secret to success: always act according to the situation. This philosophy grounds his motivation to frequently move onto new projects and places, abandoning situations that haven't proved fruitful. His flexible attitude and skills have seen him working for Gala Bingo online, W H Smith, the U.K.'s top stationary store, and the software companies he set up 10 years ago in Colombo with his son. This charismatic entrepreneur was the fourth generation

The intricate and ornate rhythms of feminine grace and charm woven with silk thread as seen in this gorgeous sari

"To prevent smuggling, the Dutch East India company ordered special coins with the VOC monogram printed on them. Only these pieces were valid in Indonesia."

to be brought up at 68 Leyn Baan Street, and spent much of his childhood competing in local sports and running around the ramparts.

'Everywhere I go, everyone knows me here' he says with the biggest smile 'I was the best goalkeeper in the Fort!' He may be settled, but his thirst for new experiences and opportunities is insatiable, and a conversation with him is a whirlwind including historical anecdotes, tours of his coin collection, and nostalgic reflections. Against a backdrop of 'old-world charm' in the Fort, he stands out as a modern man who used to visit 5 car boot sales every Sunday in London but now buys and sells coins and stamps on Ebay, an unusual occupation in a Fort where they still make police reports on Remington typewriters and Trip Advisor is seen as a weird Western thing in which people can no longer tell people directly when they have a problem.

The collector, as he is fondly known on 'rope' street, is a bit of a gem when it comes to old coins and chest-loads of junk-turned-treasure due to the passage of time. He mostly sells old copper Dutch VOC coins as souvenirs, though they have almost no value as collector's items, and all but the tiny 'Half Druit' were never actually used in Galle. The only coins he keeps for himself are the mint editions, like the British coin issued in 2004, currently valued at £700, which he keeps in a safe in Colombo, and the 1856 and 1859 limited edition gold $10 American coins he will give to his children.

'Anything you can think of – I've got it!' he exclaims, referencing the secret collection he keeps locked up in a secure suitcase inside a treasure chest next to his bed. 'I don't collect properties anymore' he explains 'it's such a headache – I have to spend so much money cleaning up after the monkeys' and of course the bills today are no fun, not to mention the court cases if you forget to pay one. Whether it's to see his treasure chest, swap a coin or learn what is really important about life, meeting the Galle Fort

> "The art of accumulating knick-knacks brings to mind the famous explorers of the Dark Continent and the pyramids and tombs, where these eminences on many an occasion confused treasures with curses and curses with marvels."

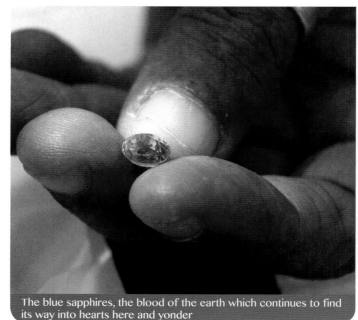

The blue sapphires, the blood of the earth which continues to find its way into hearts here and yonder

The beaming innocence of a girl passing by the gleefully painted wall of Collectibles

"The desire to possess these oddities is truly a case of curiosity killed the cat but as the cat has nine lives the finder keeper too finds himself undergoing a process of transformation, rejuvenation if you wish at the sight of and the primal experience of coming into contact with these tiny dreams created by the equally possessed mad geniuses found resting in many unassuming pockets around the world."

collector is worth all the chests of treasure that can be found in the shipwrecks that surround this exciting sea port Fort. A man who has returned to his hometown after making it big, because he realises the greatest value lies in the place of his birth.

The Best of Both Worlds

Fortaleza
No. 9, Church
Cross Street, Galle
Fort 0912233415
reservations@fortaleza.lk

Liam Hill's family history is intriguing and yet it is clear from the outset that the past has no hold over this man; he is his own person forged by his own life experiences and clearly reliant upon nobody, well except the lovely Natalie Rogers, his right and left hand woman.

The son of a Sri Lankan model born into an aristocratic Kandyan lineage who admits that his early days in Sri Lanka were filled with staff, servants and a fleet of cars. But then the very fact that a stunningly beautiful Sri Lankan daughter of a traditional line would marry a British photographer albeit a model one is in itself very out of the ordinary even in London's swinging 60s. Liam dismisses any notion that his background is worthy of great note saying that his mother was thoroughly Westernized by the age of fifteen when she went to school in England and that it was a natural consequence of their shared profession that his parents would have met, but living between two worlds did not give them a model marriage, even with two bouncy adorable and now very successful sons. A chasm that existed between his mother's family and his own was largely insuperable due to the different attitudes with which they had been imbued. It was however always his intention to join his mother in Sri Lanka (unpretentious and unafraid of work she had returned home to the

A warehouse turned into suites, with a leggie blonde buried in a book facing the window overlooking life size replicas of dinosaurs down below

country of her birth after her divorce and founded a guesthouse in Kandy) but confesses that his plans to operate a business in Sri Lanka were accelerated by his mother's death.

"This came up!" he explains calmly and gestures at the stunning background of a 17th Century Portuguese spice warehouse now converted into one of the finest and most popular restaurants in the Fort. They have opened another eatery and an amazing Galle Fort SPA at 63 Pedlar Street on the second floor. Liam accepts that part of the reason that he has enjoyed success is Galle's existence as a "funny" place with a market of tourists ranging from rich expats to impecunious backpackers and a growing line of domestic tourists particularly coming from Colombo's elite jet set. Liam sees the Fort as someplace that has flourished because over time different groups have taken over the Fort, established a presence and then dominated the life of the Fort before eventually being replaced by another crowd. Of course like all great characters his secret to success is the woman behind him Natalie Rogers who is both the brains and the reason the place is so beautifully run.

"This elegant colonial building, once a spice warehouse, was built around 1600 in the heart of Galle Fort by a Dutch merchant. More recently it has been converted into a boutique hotel with rooms and a superb outdoor restaurant."

The Galle Fort Hotel

The lair of the
Comte de Mauny
Galle Fort Hotel
28 Church Street
091 2232870
091 2245780

The Legendary Galle Fort Hotel is an award winning UNESCO restoration that is renowned for the Comte De Mauny apartment overlooking the spectacular Palladio central colonnaded courtyard and pool. The Comte was a rogue who was famous for his exploits in the 1920s, and was infamous for being 'faux noble', and yet a 1920s architectural genius and bon viveur.

The Comte De Mauny (1866-1941), was it seems a lover of all things grand and exotic and nothing is grander than the Grand apartment at the Galle Fort Hotel on Church Street, where nightly fine dining allows one to enjoy his roguish architecture. A dashing man in his fifties, who escaped to Ceylon after his English wife found him in bed with his valet. Few foreigners transplanted by fate to Sri Lanka's shores during the past century have managed to surround themselves with such mystique as the Frenchman and naturalized Briton who made Galle his home and lavish playground in the 1920s and 30s. Those Sri Lankans and visitors who have come to know

The Galle Fort Hotel's delightful central courtyard and swimming pool is overlooked by the wonderful fine dining al fresco restaurant.

The mysteries of the building come alive when the chiaroscuro of the timber is set alight by the splatter of yellow light

of his name have usually done so when visiting Taprobane Island, the extravagant stately house he created nearly a century ago on a tiny islet in Weligama Bay known locally as Witches Island, also famed as the last inhabitable rock between here and Antarctica. Few know he was also an advisor to the Galle Fort elite merchants caste and that he created the greatest architectural illusion of all time for the world famous jewellers, the Macan Markers, crafting a false perspective in the gem merchant's courtyard by using differing spaces between the Palladian columns like a theatre set, doubling the perceived size of the property. You can still see the original shuttered windows, twelve-inch teak floorboards and fifteen-foot lime-washed ceilings, all part of an original design by the Comte de Mauny, if you stay in his Grand Apartment at the Galle Fort Hotel.

So why not live it up Comte style and make your own grand tour. Take a helicopter to the citadel and be greeted at the Galle Fort Hotel with a drink of your choice and a pan-Asian culinary experience second to none while holding court on the panoramic hotel verandah, which overlooks the Grand Apartment (Please note that valet is not included).

"When they were digging up the grounds to make the swimming pool, they found many old VOC wine and spirits bottles, memories of the men who were there before."

The Game Changer

Part-Time
Philosopher
Kumar
Sangakkara
Professional
Cricketer,
76 Leyn Baan
Street
Galle Fort

At the MCC Spirit of Cricket Cowdrey Lecture at Lord's Cricket Ground in July of 2011, Kumar Sangakkara gave a speech in which he explored the nature of Sri Lanka, concluding with a statement that resonated throughout the country: "I am Tamil, Sinhalese, Muslim and Burgher. I am a Buddhist, a Hindu, a follower of Islam and Christianity. I am today, and always, proudly Sri Lankan." It is this rich mix of religions and nationalities that attracted Kumar to Galle Fort, which has been a part of his life for almost as long as cricket has, a place that captured his father just as powerfully as it has entranced him. It was his father who, he says, "told me one day, if you're ever thinking of buying property the Fort is one place you should look at. He had a great appreciation for the Fort and the life of the Fort and the old families living in the Fort and ever since that day it's stayed with me."

Nasser Hussein, a friend from his school Trinity in Kandy and a Fort inhabitant who is a member of the lucky seven Hussein clan, walked the streets of the Fort with Kumar, eventually finding him the house on Leyn Baan Street: "we did happen upon the house that I finally bought in 2010 and it was closed up. Nasser said you know this, out of every property that you've ever seen, this is actually

From taking on causes as disparate as attempting to teach a lesson to cricket's highest echelons of power to preventing suicides, his humbling spirit is felt in the ease with which his presence is immediately accepted in any community

the ideal property for you to buy: this is the one. But it's not for sale!" Luckily for Kumar, fate was on his side as it was quickly established that he had played cricket as a youngster with the owner of the property's son. So, after a brief discussion, the house was sold and Kumar became the proud owner of a little piece of Sri Lankan history: "It was serendipitous really."

Serendipity has played a significant role in Kumar's life made evident as he speaks about the fortuitous events that led to the purchase of his house, a cavernous wonder on one of the Fort's five streets, just preparing itself for a long awaited transformation. You can tell that he has been mesmerised by the magic that surrounds the ancient citadel: "So you know it's all these weird little instances in life that tied up and came together for me to be able to buy this particular house. It's strange, it's funny but also I'm very happy that it happened that way. I think everything happens for a reason. Everyone is attracted to and finally settles on probably the property that they should have bought anyway."

"With changing economic circumstances, with the changing expectations of people there will be some kind of follow on effect so I think like everything it'll change and hopefully keep changing for the better. The greatest shame would be to lose the old families and the people who keep the memories of the Fort and life of the Fort alive."

291

"I don't know whether that's the common perspective because economically we are in a position that we can speak in this manner, where the Fort becomes a getaway. Am I just being romantic because I can enjoy it as a holiday home? The real life of the Fort up until now hasn't shown me anything different, so that's what I wouldn't want to change."

The house's proximity to the Law Courts is significant because, in the time before Kumar's face smiled out from every billboard, he was a humble Colombo law student. He still cannot, however, officially call himself a lawyer as, he tells me with a smile he didn't actually ever complete the course. He still has two exams left to sit! But education, for him, is something that he feels passionately about: "Education is not an end in itself. I think it's a frame that will open up doors for you to seek real knowledge." Kumar and his wife Yehali made the decision to educate their twins, a boy and a girl, at an international school, a decision that was not taken lightly. But ultimately, Kumar says, after much discussion they had to listen to what the children wanted, and that was to stay together. "I think when we really looked at schools the main reason that we ended up at an international school was that my children refused to get separated." He is a man who sticks by his decisions, once carefully made and so he is adamant that, regardless of what anyone says, "you get various pros and cons but at the end of the day you've got to take the risk, bite the bullet and forge ahead," a philosophy that seems to be working.

Kumar is a risk taker, a game changer, busy paving the way for the generations to come. He feels strongly that at the basis of his own children's lives and those of the Sri Lankan generation growing up right now should be strong family values and morals. It is only with these foundations that people will have the means to affect a change in others for the better. "What the children should in the current generation be thinking about is what are the wholesome values that I must always hold constantly dear and as an integral part of my personality? You don't have to change to do that at all because that is who you are. You are a product of your grandparents and your parents: you are a part of that legacy and you have to be able to hold what's good and hold that very closely and dearly and whatever you do, it affects what you do in life. You can go out partying but do you make the right decisions at that party

The man himself with his back to the fourth wall; and the irony is that he has saved the nation when the country was literally with its back against the wall an innumerable number of times by battling on the green path indomitably against insurmountable odds

with what's available, the alcohol, the drugs, what do you say no to? What influences do you let into your life? What influences are there around you that you're impervious to because you have a great moral grounding? You can look at someone, even the best of your friends and understand that some things they do are wrong and you don't have to follow peer pressure or be a part of the in crowd or the cool gang. So it's a case of understanding where everyone comes from and being able to absorb things from that." This moral grounding is what Kumar is striving to highlight as he works closely with various charities, including a suicide support charity called CCC Line whose aim is to raise awareness and expand people's understanding of mental illness. They run a twelve hour constantly manned phone line, enabling instant support to be provided for those most in need, wherever they are

"It is the values that your grandparents had in the century that they lived; the values won't change with the times. They're a constant. You might change your personal life, your outlooks; the moral fabric that makes you wholesome is the same."

293

"I think it was a good thing that I did walk around for eight years because rather than just buying a property at first sight, on a whim, I had a great opportunity to experience what the Fort had to offer, to speak to the locals, a lot of the old Muslim families, some of the Sinhalese families and to understand that the Fort, was actually as they say, a living Fort."

in the country. Kumar believes that behind the shocking statistics lie deeper issues some of which are exclusive to Sri Lanka, to a country and a people that has been battered and bruised over the last thirty years. "People commit suicide under mental stress, from things like relationship pressures, exam failures, could be drugs, the tsunami, the effects of the 30 years of war. Many factors affect them but the real factor is the stigma that comes with mental issues in Sri Lanka. We feel awkward to talk about it, we feel awkward to put it in the public eye so we push it to the back: it's kept in the family."

Whatever social stigma there is surrounding mental health in Sri Lanka, it cannot detract from the statistics that are shocking enough that they speak for themselves. Within Sri Lanka 11 people each day die from suicide, unable to receive the help that they need because of a severe lack of support and resources and that is since the rates of suicide started falling. There is only one psychiatrist per 500,000 people and shockingly only three child psychiatrists in the entire country. These are figures that the CCC Line Foundation is trying to change, harnessing values that Kumar strongly believes in. For him, actions don't have to be or even need to be grand or extravagant: "it can be an evening's conversation that does that, it doesn't have to be on a grand scale. It could be just a little chat that no one else hears about or knows about that affects that change."

Galle Fort one the world's most beautiful historic cities weaves its charms on all that visit the ancient citadel.

Kumar recognises that change is essential to the country as it steadily develops but it is also a reality that has the potential to have both positive and negative effects on Galle Fort. But, he says "I would move in a heartbeat to the Fort and live there. It's just that life gets in the way of what you really want to do. My idea is that it is for friends and family to enjoy and to experience what the Fort has to offer." His house is a special project that combines the ancient history of the Fort with his own present experiences in a blend that he feels is vital to Sri Lanka's future success. He hopes the house will be somewhere that he will never have to sell: "it's a part of the history of Sri Lanka, it's a beautiful piece of history and culture so I hope that there are always partnerships built between the old and the new."

He has watched the Fort slowly develop over the ten years he has been walking its streets but he believes that it has the ability to thrive as a result of its changes, avoiding being damaged by them: "You know you can't isolate yourself from the outside world but the thing is to be able to insulate yourself from all the negativity and the bad effects around you. You need to understand what's going on around you and still make the right choices. In the Fort I hope that that will happen."

For his children, the only change that they are concerned with in the Fort are the various choices of flavour on offer

"I think any decision carries its own risks and that's the beauty of making a decision. You weigh up the risks, the pros and cons and no matter how high or minimal the risk is, if you think that's the right decision, you make it."

"In the Fort, the dream is to fade away into obscurity isn't it? That's what you want to be, just another person, a part of the fabric of life there."

within the ice cream freezer mounted on a blue bicycle, traversing the streets whatever the weather. "My children love the water, they love walking the streets. We had a picnic on the ramparts with them, packed up a picnic basket from Colombo, sat on the ramparts and ate a bit of bread and they loved it." Kumar's entire family have been captivated by the magic of the Fort, from its ancient, weightlifting mango sellers to their favourite restaurant in town, Elita, who, says Kumar, "makes a perfect omelette. It's beautiful." His wife has fallen equally as in love with the old citadel as "she has a sense of belonging and she identifies with that. She gets a lot of peace and comfort from the Fort." The feelings experienced by this little family are such that it seems like they have found their true home, a place where scampering goats still live in back gardens and children dominate the open spaces with their laughter and games.

The Fort has become a haven where Kumar is able to relax with his family and embrace the kindness that is so prevailing within the Fort community. He is striving to create a life for his children that ensures a balance between the old and the new, a balance that the Fort itself is also busy trying to establish. Kumar believes that "We are a product of our past as well, not just our present. The present shapes us." Kumar is certainly a combination of both, a result of his present experiences but also the values instilled in him at a young age. As one of his closest friends Mahela Jayawardene, who has also recently purchased a property on Lighthouse Street, retires from cricket, might Sangakarra be next to embark on a different path? "If you find different callings, different courses, different ambitions that you suddenly discover, I think that's great. Again that's part of evolving and rather than doing it alone you're doing it now with a family. So it's [having a family] really helped me to make better decisions and to change certain parts of my personality. There's lots more that I would like to do, I just need to choose!"

World famous cricketeer Sangakarra's house on Leyn Baan street being restored to its former colonial glory

No doubt whatever choice he makes will be one that will benefit the community who surround him. He is a softly spoken force to be reckoned with whose ideas and beliefs have the power to shake up an entire country's psyche. He recognises that he is in a position to affect a serious change in Sri Lanka and the current developing generation.
His face may be on every billboard in the country, from packaged noodles, which incidentally "I love!" to real gentleman's shirt brands to one of the nation's largest supermarkets. But Kumar's greatest desire is to teach the next generation that it is the way that you conduct yourself in life that will leave the greatest mark.

"Kumar was part of the 20/20 Sri Lankan team who won the World Cup in 2011, firmly putting one of the smallest countries in the world at the top of the game."

"I think it's really important to have more than one dream because I think any child, any person's got amazing potential and talent. To just find your calling. It could be cricket, it could be anything but whatever you do, do it well and never lose sight of the fact that you're interconnected. You're one piece in a larger puzzle where what you do and how you live your life does affect others. So if you live it well and in a wholesome manner, you are guaranteed that you will leave something good behind."

80

AMAZING EXPERIENCES IN GALLE AND GALLE FORT
THE GUIDE SECTION

20 MOUTH WATERING EATERIES WITH LUSH SETTINGS

The Living Room by TPV
50A Lighthouse Street   **Tel: 0912245148**

If you are a merchant of mischief this is the place to be its not just a bar, as it also serves delicious snacks and delightful evening dresses at the entrance, where you can buy a sparkly number to suit the Austin Powers groovey setting. The chicken liver pate is fab.

Galle Fort Hotel Restaurant and Bar
28 Church Street   **0912232870/0912245780**
Web: www.galleforthotel.com

The restaurant is in the stunning central courtyard of the Galle Fort Hotel, that overlooks the lit-up pool, grande apartment and exquisite gardens. The fusion menu is fabulous and it is no suprise that the incredible restoration won a UNESCO award.

SERENDIPITY ARTS CAFÉ
65, Leyn Baan Street, Galle Fort Tel:0776838659

Here you can indulge in fantastic Fort rice and curry dishes. You can book a walk here with the world famous author of Around the Fort in 80 Lives, Juliet Coombe, or do a cooking course and learn how to make hoppers and why spice is so good for you.

DECO ON 44
44, Lighthouse Street   **Tel: 0912225773**
Galle Fort

Deco on 44 is an old Fort family home turned into a luxury boutique hotel. 'We create a second home for our guests' the general manager, Dilshan explains. One of the largest fish platters in the Fort is set against live music giving one the feeling of being in a scene out of the movie the Great Gatsby. It has a garden and inside seating.

Crêpe-ology & Flavours Cafe
53, Leyn Baan Street, Galle Fort Tel: 091 2234 777
Web: www.crepe-ology.com
Time open: everyday 9am-11pm
Location: 1st floor of the Carrousel de Galle

Crêpes – thin pancakes from France are introduced to Sri Lanka by a dynamic duo. A fantastic place for families with the air conditioned playroom and those who fancy something a bit different. The fillings whether sweet or salty are simply delicious and French Kiss is so good you will be going back for more. They serve shisha and so you can sit back read a magazine in this delightful setting.

5

Fort Dew Restaurant – Best view of the ramparts!
22, Sri Sudharmalaya Road
Tel: 091 222 4365/0777526260
Web: www.fortdew.com

An excellent rooftop café, where you can dine during a beautiful sunset over the ramparts having Sri Lankan, Chinese or Western food. As a dessert they advertise curd and treacle with a hit of espresso, coffee or creamy cappuccino. Great spot to watch and take photos of the President landing his helicopters when he comes to visit the Fort, which is often as like everyone he loves the Fort.

Punto Café
42, Pedlar Street, Galle Tel: 091 3923384, 0777599994
Email: nakeebmohamed@ymail.com
Time open: everyday 7am-9pm
Location: opposite All Saints Primary School

The Portuguese used to call this Fort 'Punto Galle' and so Nakeeb thought to keep this name and history alive by calling his restaurant Punto Café. Unique homemade rice and curry is cooked in the open kitchen and fresh fruit juices are sipped in a relaxed atmosphere.

6

7

Peace and Plenty – Restaurant with good karma
59, Church Street, Galle Tel: 0715893340 or 0912242734
Email: gallepeaceandplenty@mail.com
Time open: 7 am - 10 pm

Great spot to chill out, swing in the hammock, sip great juices, play music and chat to Samantha, who is a Buddhist and believes in good karma. For those not familiar with the word it means to collect positive vibes and give them back to the people around you. 'I want to welcome everyone here, I want to fill their bellies with good food!' A place always full of interesting people.

8

Pedlar's Inn Café
92 Pedlar Street   Tel:0912225333
Web: www.pedlarsinn.com
Opening hours: 9am-10pm every day.
Friday closed for prayers 12pm-1pm.

One of the first cafes to open within this citadel's coral walls, Pedlar's Inn has only gone from strength to strength. Having started out as a mere four tables, the current café is one of the more bustling hangouts in the Fort, and over the road you can enjoy the Pedlar's Inn Gelateria.

9

'10

Ameen Hotel - Feast of street level food
Siethey Kadeej, 18 New Lane 1
0777134667

Wrapped in yesterday's aging newspapers giving it the good old fish and chips feel, the rotti comes with chilli and onion sambol or if you don't mind getting into the thick of things it is ideal for dousing in meat gravy and dhal curry.

Nihal's Restaurant - Truly Amazing!
Jetwing Lighthouse Hotel
A2, Galle 80000 Tel: 0912223744
Web: www.jetwinghotels.com

If you want to spice up your life then go on an aromatic journey 15 minutes from the Fort with chef Nihal at his restaurant in the Jetwing Hotel. A true ambassador for Sri Lankan cooking.

'11

'12

The Closenburg Hotel with a Luna View
11 Closenburg Road, Magalle, Galle
0912224313/0912232241
www.closenburghotel.com

Driving up the steep summit to the Closenburg Hotel is well worth it for the incredible view overlooking the Indian Ocean, and beautifully preserved colonial grandeur. Today it is the place to be seen, as a top spot to meet the uber cool Galle and Colombo crowd and enjoy superb food. The Hotel's new Luna pool is wow.

Wijaya Beach
Dalawella, Unawatuna
Tel: 0777 903 431

Wonderful food and the best wood fired pizza in Sri Lanka. The staff are characters and the food whether it's the catch of the day or a Greek salad is the reason people keep going back for more. A very calming place to read, relax, and swim.

'13

Era Beach by Jetwing - Sonnet to the Sun
834 Galle/Matara Rd, Thalpe, Galle
Tel: +94 (0) 91 228 2302 Fax 091 2282 212
Web: www.jetwinghotels.com

An undeniably romantic setting, Era means Dawn and like the sunset, the twin alchemists, fiery and mordant, are engaged like two matadors, enticing one to enjoy the amazing king size breakfast with fresh crab and other wonderful delicacies.

'14

Kahanda Kanda (KK)
Kahanda Kanda, Angulugaha, Galle, Sri Lanka.
Tel: +94 (0) 91 494 3700, Mob: +94 773 429 555
Web: www.kahandakanda.com

This desperately stylish boutique hotel has been on Conde Naste Traveler's Hot List and guests simply love the place: 'such a wonderful home in such a beautiful setting. This must be the most relaxing place in the world.' The villa/hotel overlooks Koggala Lake and is surrounded by the fragrant greenery of a tea estate. Excellent lunch time spot.

15

Sugar Bistro Wine Bar
No – 05 Dutch Hospital Street
Galle Fort
Galle Fort Events/Jazz
Tel: 091 2231799

Nothing beats a legendary Sugar burger and cup of delicious coffee at Sugar Bistro & Wine Bar in the Galle Fort Dutch Hospital. The chalk board is full of delicious dishes to choose from including plenty of stuff for vegetarians and delectable desserts that are impossible to resist ranging from hot apple pie laced with spice to orgasmic home made ice cream.

Mosvold Villa by Jetwing
Ahangama, Galle, Ahangama Beach
Web: www.jetwing.com

16

There is a saying that "the best way to experience a country is by living with a local family" and at Jetwing, this certainly holds true with its new villa series that allows you to experience the country first hand like Mosvold Villa, home of the stilt fisherman.

17

Yathra – Dine and Sail Bentota
Web: www.jetwinghotels.com

For those with a spirit for adventure - Yathra – a drifting, 76 foot uber cool designer boat is an unforgettable fine dining adventure experience that takes in the traditional life of the area. Dinner like breakfast is served on a lovely wooden table with deck chairs on the starboard. They will also show you how to cook.

The Old Railway Café
42 Havelock Place, Galle New Town,
Tel:Catherine +94 (0)778809990
or Rasika +94 (0)776263400,
Web:theoldrailwayshop.com

19

Rasika and Catherine want to share their local knowledge with people who love immersion travel, fashion and all things quirky. Although they charge for their food, it's prepared with so much love and affection, it's as if you were going to their house. Be warned the millionaires short bread is totally addictive and chai tea the perfect accompaniment.

18

Sri Lanka's Garden of Eden - Paddy Tea and Temple
Contact Daniele to make a tea party minimum of 4 that must be booked in advance: +94 (0)773294006
Email: danieletfrancis@gmail.com

20

The paddy fields with reflecting pools of water planted between ancient rock formations in Galle sit like giants watching children flying handmade kites while high tea is served in Sri Lanka's Garden of Eden. One can't fail to fall in love with the hypnotic world of watching the rice grow while sipping a cup of freshly brewed lemongrass tea between wedges of orgasmic cake and perfectly cut cucumber sandwiches.

20 PLACES TO EXPERIENCE

Saskia Fernando Gallery
1 Magistrates Court, Galle Fort
Tel: 0912235422
Web:www.saskiafernandogallery.com

Beautiful paintings hang on the walls, whilst a huge dog made out of wrenches and bolts sits to attention and a rusting horse strides out, frozen in time. The gallery is the perfect size, the art exhibited within it chosen expertly each month, representative of Sri Lanka's best emerging contemporary artists. The pieces focus on the modern with quirky twists.

Idle Bikes Tour
Tel: 0777906156 / 0779855500
Email: alex@idletours.com / lakshman@
idletours.com
Web: www.idletours.com
Prices from 2000-3000 rupees per person ($15-30)

From their base just near Wijaya Beach Bar, the guys at Idle Tours run regular bike rides of varying lengths and interest including the iconic Paddy trail route. This voyage takes you through lush green rice paddies, past wild buffalo, through little villages where old men sit peacefully on their doorsteps and children stop and chat.

Serendipity Arts Café Cooking Class
From $45US upwards depending on the number of dishes
65 Leyn Baan Street, Galle Fort
Tel: 0776838659

In the relaxed atmosphere of the Serendipity Arts Cafe, surrounded by bright photographs and books, walls whitewashed with coral mud ballast that kept a 17th Century trading ship steady, one can enjoy charismatic Juliet Coombe's food tour. Juliet is an award winning author and photographer.

Surfing on the South Coast
Mahatun's Surf Point, Devata Beach, next to
Sahana Restaurant
Tel: 0777650852

The surf school on the beach is run by Mahatun. He will be your personal guide, lending you a board, teaching you the tricks to master the waves' swell.

Galle Fort Walks
Contact Serendipity Arts Café on 0776838659

The only way you can get a true feel of Galle Fort is by walking its streets with one of its own. Juliet Coombe has lived in the Fort for ten years now and so knows a fair bit about life inside the Fort walls and about its history and the people who still live there today. Take a sunset walk and allow Juliet to spook you with tales of ghosts who roam the ramparts or embark on the architectural journey and explore the variety of different and beautiful buildings that make up the five eclectic streets of the Fort.

5

Simplifly Helicopter rides
25 Leyn Baan Street, Galle Fort
Artjom Tel: +94 710 377876
Web: www.simplifly.com
Helicopter rides for 15 minutes from $60.
One-hour whale watching tour from the air $150US dollars per person.
To make a booking email: "galleoffice@simplyfly.com

There is nothing more amazing than hovering atop the gigantic Fort, a tiny atoll with streets worming and intersecting with buildings appearing and vanishing behind the religious buildings that dominate the skyline.

Cricket
Galle Cricket Stadium

Join the Galle Fort community playing cricket on the muddy ground near the Buddhist temple imitating their hero Sangakkara – the famous Sri Lankan cricketer (also a Galle Fort inhabitant) – or take a cheap seat on the ramparts above the Main Gate to watch the professionals fight for a victory on the Galle Cricket Ground. As Hassan from the Dutch Wall Arcade so wisely explains, 'Cricket is a game of unity.'

6

7

Mask Making at Sithuvili
Janaka De Silva
56 Leyn Baan, Galle Fort
Tel: 1177887788
From: 7,800 Rupees. Check online for availability
Web: www.trekurious.com

Masks are crafted by master craftsmen from wet Kaduru wood, which are left to dry, making them easy to carve. The masks are used for the demon dance (Raksha Kolama) when the dancers wear the frightening cobra demon mask (nagaraksha).

8

Queen of temples –
Kataluwa Purvarama Vihara
To arrange a visit call: 0094 (0) 91 228 6289 or 0094 (0) 777 272 772.
To reach this sacred spot head to Koggala Bridge, take the left turning at Kataluwa junction and follow the road for 2-3km before turning right down a small lane.

Reverend Kathaluwe Vajira Sri explains the narrative of the ancient awe inspiring temple friezes. There are paintings of a pipe smoking English gentleman and a portrait of Queen Victoria framed by the lion and the unicorn.

9

10

Blue Sky Travel
The Old Railway, 42 Havelock Pace, Galle
Rasika Amarasena
Tel: +94 77 6263400
Email: rasikaam@yahoo.com

Rasika takes groups of up to 7 from 2 to 20 days. The highlights are the jungles teeming with wildlife, traditional street vendors to comforts in grand colonial era properties.

Whale Watching in Mirissa - December to April
Jetwing Lighthouse Hotel
Tel: +94 0912223744
The chief tuk-tuk driver Azmir on Church Street opposite The Galle Fort Hotel can also organize tours
Tel:0777856601" Tel:0777856601

Get out of bed before dawn to see a migrating pod of 25 blue whales measuring up to 100 feet long each.

11

12

Leopard Safaris - Best in the Business
Noel and Cecile's unique mobile tented safaris in Yala 3/4 hours from Galle Fort
Tel: +94 777314004/+94713314004
Email: noel@leopardsafaris.com, Website: www.leopardsafaris.com.

"It's a pussy cat," says Amzar my cheeky four year old pointing to a tree overhea where we were 'safely camping', not that animals can read signs. Noel and his team are passionate about showing you the wildlife, even taking the kids on wal between safari drives. The food is considered so good and experience so magica that many people repeat book this unique experience.

M.L.P Sugathadasa's Antiques
34 Hospital Street, Galle Fort
Tel: 0770599828
To go diving with his grandson Eranga the treasure hunter

The majority of the products are 100% Sri Lankan. They are as they have been for hundreds of years, a reality that Mr. Sugathadasa is keen to point out.

13

Shipwreck Diving
Maritime Archaeology Unit Central Cultural Fund, Baladaksha Mawatha, Galle Fort
Tel: 0912247677
Email: maritimegalle@yahoo.com
Web: www.mausrilanka.lk
Prices $40 a shallow dive, $75 to go deep

The Galle Harbour, its underwater city, sunken giants, reefs and relics has 26 sites with 12 shipwrecks.

14

Galle Fort Spa - Beauty of Divine Indulgence
63 Pedlar's Street, Galle Fort
Tel: 0777 252502

Calm, tranquility and peace. Chilled lemongrass tea, iced flannel and the idyllic massage experience with complete body and mind relaxation.

For something quirky - Leyn Baan Villa Fish Spa
74 Leyn Baan Street, Galle Fort
Tel: Izzeth 0777901282, Email: leynbaanvilla@placevendome.lk, Price 1,000 rupees ($10) for 15 minutes
Downstairs is the fabulous Mimimango fashion shop by top Galle Fort designer Jo Eden. Truly stunning clothes for a glitzy night out.

15

Virgin White Tea,
Handunugoda Estate
Tittagalla, Ahangama
Malinga Herman Gunaratne
Tel:0773290999

The Virgin White Tea plantation is a mysterious wonder, the closest tea plantation in Sri Lanka to the beach. There are around 200 acres of utilized land on this estate, as well as a fully-fledged tea museum, all of which is managed and lovingly handled by Herman Gunaratne, tea planter by day and world acclaimed author by night. Stay and enjoy his tea restaurant and do buy some white tea it's simply amazing.

Glass-Bottom Boat Tours
Organised by Levanga Hotel, Hikkaduwa
Tel: Anushka 0773061108 or 0770126200
Price: Adult $10 and Child $5 for a 30 minute trip (need a minimum of two people)

16

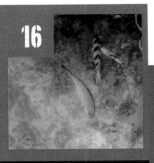

You will see a gorgeous rainbow of fish, the porous coral carpet where sea turtles graze and crabs stand aggressively, pincers raised in mock salute. Afterwards eat at Levanga. The food is superb. Minimum 2 people.

17

Wijaya Vinyasa Yoga
Private classes or find them advertised on the board at Wijaya Beach Bar
Tel: Eva 0773002802
Email: yankawe@gmail.com
Web: www.wijayavinyasayoga.com

Eva Priyanka Wegener mainly teaches the fluid, gentle Hatha vinyasa style, focusing on the physical and mental side of wellbeing. Combines strengthening and toning exercises with the body's connection to breathing.

Pearl Divers Padi Resort and Water Sports Centre
Unawatuna Beach
Tel: 0912242015
Email: info@pearldivers.lk
Web: www.pearldivers.lk
Dive courses from roughly $20 up to $60.
Certifications from $65-$430.
Jet-skiing roughly $35 for 15 minutes.
Water sports and activities from surfing, water-skiing, jet skiing, kayaking to Padi courses.
Snorkel over the reef at the entrance to Unawatuna Bay and see colourful fish and bizarre looking coral like Amzar is doing from a glass bottom boat.

19

18

20

The Dutch Hospital Galle Fort is now one of the most exciting shopping and eating out experiences in Galle with its innovative Sri Lankan Hammock bar on the top floor giving you superb views of the harbour. The shops contain the finest local artisanship and artistry in the country and the island's best gem shops allow every girl to indulge in her jewellery dreams. This wonderful colonial building is at its most beautiful lit up at night and this is when the uber trendy come out to enjoy the wine bars and DJ specials that are finally giving the ancient citadel a spot of nightlife. So go on put on a little black dress and enjoy!

"Artisans of bespoke travel in Sri Lanka"

SriLanka*InStyle* has a great business model. It's all about "amazing the customer"
- Paul Guilfoyle

SriLanka*InStyle*

SriLanka*InStyle* - great hotels, great scenery, great events, great food, great guiding and great organization. Very much look forward to the chance to travel with you again – and will recommend to all our friends!
- Alan Leigh MD, Global Markets & Banking, Bank of America Merrill Lynch, Hong Kong

www.srilankainstyle.com

DUTCH HOSPITAL,
GALLE FORT'S LATEST
ATTRACTION

Heritage of Hospitality

The Dutch Hospital - Hospital Street, Galle Fort

Shops & other outlets

Orchid House
Boutique
Shilpa National
Crafts Council
Sithuvili – for great
art!
Luxury Villas
Lankan
Sifanni
Stone 'N' String
Colombo Jewellery
Zam Gems

There actually hasn't been a Dutch Hospital inside the Galle Fort since the turn of the 19th century, a fact that many people never knew or have subsequently forgotten. The original hospital was built in the 17th century by the Dutch and was in fact three times larger than the building, which now stands on the same site. After the deterioration of this site, when the British took over the occupation of the South coast of Sri Lanka, they developed the structure into a military barracks around 1850 that stretched across both sides of Hospital Street. From there they constructed two more buildings, one of which was a hospital and one, which was the doctor's quarters.

It was in the earlier half of the twentieth century that the three buildings were finally amalgamated and became an administrative office, at one point used by the Galle Heritage Foundation, until the catastrophic tsunami in 2004. For the last few years the grand building has lain empty along Hospital Street, its ghosts rattling around in the empty shell, resembling a sleeping giant that no one quite wants to wake up. But it has seemingly only been in hibernation because it has now been completely rejuvenated by the Urban Development Authority (UDA) and the Sri Lankan Army's Engineering Regiment. Always keeping in mind the architectural importance of such a building and conscious of the heritage of the Fort, the UDA developed a plan that maintained the building's historical importance but also allowed them to create

something a little bit more modern. The Dutch Hospital is now a bustling shopping and eating hub with the likes of the highly popular Colombo restaurant Sugar Bistro, boasting a two-storey experience that includes everything from a hammock café to a gorgeous handmade souvenir and jewellery shop to a villa rental company. The shop owners and restauranteurs who have been lucky enough to secure a coveted space in the Dutch Hospital recognise that it is a strategic move, as more and more visitors will start to come to the Fort to visit this site. Sam who runs the Sri Lankan Hammock Café, who already owns Peace and Plenty in the Fort, chose to set up his new place in the Dutch Hospital because he wanted to create a fun, exciting place for people to go out in the evening, a sentiment that the other bars and restaurants also share.

Yameen at Orchid House, a glamorous souvenir shop, believes that the Dutch Hospital will become a one-stop place where you can get anything you want. With a variety of restaurants and cafes that cater to every taste and shops that sell an incredible range of products, it has become a place to visit within the Fort. It all overlooks the historic rampart coral walls and the glittering Indian Ocean that provides for the perfect backdrop to this impressive site. It has been established as a tourist attraction but, as one shop owner tells me, it will become a landmark in the Fort, firmly establishing it as the destination to visit in Sri Lanka.

Drinks & Food

Tea Breeze
Cannon Bar & Grill
Sri Lankan Hammock Café & Pub
Star Beans – The Dutch Café
Thai Heritage – foodies love it!
A Minute By Tuk Tuk
Tea Spices
Sugar Bistro
The Tuna & The Crab
TAPHOUSE by RnR

20 PLACES TO SHOP

Raux Brothers – Stylish Furnishings
96 Pedlar Street
Tel:0912235201/0912231114
Web: www.rauxbrothers.com

Raux Brothers sell furniture uniquely created using wood salvaged from ancient shipwrecks, bringing Galle Fort's maritime soul to life in your sitting room. This business is spread out over three floors. You can also stay here and test the furniture out.

Casual Edge – Cricket Shirts and Designer T's
7A Rampart Street & Carrousel de Galle,
53 Leyn Baan Street Tel:0914385999
Web: www.casual-edge.com

Suppliers of authentic Sri Lankan cricket shirts within the Fort walls, Casual Edge is in high demand. Its Rampart Street shop has the perfect location just opposite the entrance to the clock tower cricket watching spot. Casual Edge Linen is of the highest quality and much sought after.

Barefoot – Fabulous Fabrics
41 Pedlar Street, Galle Fort   Tel:0912226299
Email: gallefort@barefoot.lk

Looking out from a woven basket a mountain of Barefoot adorable mice welcome you into this exotic fabric shop, that was made famous by Geoffrey Bawa using Barbara Sansoni's fabulous fabrics as part of his many architectural interior designs.

Fashion Jewellery – Out-of-the-box Designs
37 Church Street   Tel:0912234820

The designs you find at Fashion Jewellery are not your typical pieces. They are original and this is what, Devika, the lady of the shop, tells me, makes them successful. They use rough stones in contemporary styles and can make pieces to your designs if given 48 hours notice.

... you don't have to force anyone to buy our goods sell themselves!

Tea Zone – Exotic Flavours
Carrousel de Galle, 52 Leyn Baan Street
0777907878
Email: info@teazonegalle.com
Web: www.teazonegalle.com

The alluring aromas that drift through the air around 53 Leyn Baan Street can only be blamed on one section of this busy building: Tea Zone, the only place to buy exotic flavoured teas in the Fort. Saleem, the knowledgeable shop assistant and tea planter extraordinaire tells me that the shop boasts more than twenty-five different varieties.

5

White Walk
Galle Fort Boutique, 54 Church Street
Tel:0912250133/0777030345
Web: www.whitewalk.com

Hidden away in a small white building just off central Church Street is White Walk, selling beautiful kaftans and rails of flowing fabrics, an explosion of colourful creations that have harnessed the colourful personalities of the Sri Lankan people. Next to the till is a wicker basket with a lovely wooden case of simple beaded jewellery that has been created by a charity called Emerge Lanka Foundation, which supports teenage girls who have been brave enough to speak up against abuse that they have faced.

Shurafa's – Handcrafted Cards
54 Lighthouse Street
Tel:0912234571, 0775111288
Email: shurafaiqbal@gmail.com

Ms. Iqbal is a lady with passion and immense creativity turning her sitting room into a working, one woman factory. Half-finished greeting cards litter the dining room table as glue sticks line up next to glittery pieces of piping, ready to add the sparkly touches to these traditionally handmade cards. The material elephant creations are wow.

6

7

Three by TPV – Designer Chic
43 Leyn Baan Street   Tel:0912231003
Web: www.thethreebytpv.com

The building on the corner of Leyn Baan Street is full of uber cool designer gifts including the handmade Waxed and Wicked collection of candles, which smell of the spice island and are renowned for their creativity. Now it is home to The Three by TPV, a clean, modern and minimalistic mirage inside the ancient Galle Fort. It sells a mixture of interior design, clothing and jewellery, all of which is an exotic blend of the traditions of Sri Lanka and the Scandinavian heritage of the shop's owners. The best item is the armchair book shelf on either side.

8

Mansion Art & Craft – Craft & Clothes
Y.W.C.A Building, 23 Church Street
Tel:0914928484/0912227635
Email: mansion@sltnet.lk

The wonders that make up the incredible Mansion Art and Craft lie housed within a vast, high ceilinged warehouse that sits just back from Church Street. On the veranda a lady makes lace and a grinning gentleman cuts and polishes local rough gems. Great for picking up a glam dress, great book or souvenir.

9

10

Mimimango – Glamour & Glitz
63, Pedlar Street, Galle Fort
Web: www.mimimango.com

A sparkling, glittering, chic haven, the clothes inside
Mimimango, designed by Jo Eden, are beautiful
and original, the patterns ranging from electric blue
snakeskin to rippling waves of orange and white.
Superb men's short-sleeved shirts in Liberty-esque
style, which are perfect for a glam night out.

Hemara – Sparkling Saris, Galle New Town
55 Main Street Tel: 0912224602/0912223003
Email: hemanthaagamage@gmail.com

Hemara is a twinkling empire, a four-storey kingdom
from which you can buy all manner of spangling,
sparkling, magical creations. A small entranceway
conceals the rolls upon rolls. The choice at Hemara is
endless, just remember to haggle.

11

12

Koccoriko – Locally made Souvenirs
66 Pedlar Street   Tel:09177714736
Email: paolabenazzi@libero.it
Rooms: lovingnestgalle@gmail.com)

A two-storey blue and white building that resembles an oversized beach hut is a
magical shop created by Paola Benazzi .She supports countless numbers of
charities and village ladies. Her stuff is quirky, stylish and very special, with all
pieces handpicked by her. She will also gift wrap everything on request.

Thowfeek – Tailor Yourself A Suit
108 & 110, 112 Main Street, Galle
Tel:0912234827

Thowfeek's pale turquoise exterior
perfectly matches the shirt that Mr
Thowfeek is wearing as he stands in the
doorway of his wonderful clothes shop
turned tailor's for excellent linen shirt
finishes and designer saris that sparkle.

13

Yasiru Spice Shack & Garden Shop No.1,
in front of the Historical Green market
Tel: 0788501908
Email: ysunilshantha@yahoo.com

Yasiru's Spice Shack is a far cry from the
norm. Mr. Sunilshantha sells everything from
cinnamon sticks and all home grown and
ground spices produced daily from his home
garden in Galle.

14

D.S.I – Amazing Shoes For Little Devils & Angels
146 Main Street
0912245385

One of the South Coast's largest brands, the D.S.I shoe shop along the Main Street
in Galle is the largest in the area. The shop itself is clean, efficient and gives you
everything you ask for, much like the many smiling staff uniformed in red and blue
who greet you upon your entrance into the store. The ground floor is dedicated to
everything of the shoe variety from sparkling sandals to shiny beetle black school
shoes to the latest in sports shoes just to satisfy your sartorial cravings. The second
floor is home to Mary Poppins' most trusty companion.

Fish Stall – For Getting Fresh Fish
Beachside by the Old Gate
D.Lalith   0771255428

The cries are inescapable but so is the smell as you head out of Galle Fort through the Old Gate, strolling along the beach side road as the sun rises, illuminating the aproned men, giant meat cleavers in hand, who occupy this stretch of land.

House of Hidayath – One-Stop Department Store, Galle Town
83 H.K Edmond Mawatha,
Thanipolgaha Junction
Tel:0917200611
Web: www.houseofhidayath.com

On entering into The House of Hidayath your eyes grow wide as you take in shelves upon shelves of everything you could ever want or need. Downstairs, the food aisles are crammed with never ending delights, a sea of shiny colour. Venture up a floor, up a staircase decorated with green plants and flowers, and it has great value cotton material from $2US a metre.

Sarasavi Bookshop – A Book For A Bus
1st Floor, Central Bus Stand
Tel:0912225221
Opening times: 9am-7pm

Tucked away on the first floor of the hot and noisy bus stand is the Sarasavi Bookshop, that stocks both Sinhala and English books with much of the content focused around English literature, kids books and local writing.

Little Lanka – Cake Creations
For Special Events
22 Gameene Mawatha
Tel: 0770103002

A revolving tiered stand in the window of this narrow shop is where you will find some of Little Lanka's finest creations for special occasions. One kilogram of cake will cost you around 1000 rupees, $8, and Little Lanka will happily design whatever you desire. Easy to find next to the Galle bus stand makes this the ideal place to grab a quick bite to eat before you embark on a bus

Fort Milk Bar – Kids Love It
Baladaksha Mawatha Tel:0771005725

On the beachside of the road as you leave the Fort through the Old Gate surrounded by colourful, wooden fishing boats and shouting fish sellers stands a little, electric blue hexagonal hut. This particular hut is home to the Fort Milk Bar, a stopping point for every thirsty traveller. Within it is sold various types of Highland milk, thick, delicious yogurt and refreshing ice creams. The flavours alter from day to day and except on Poya it is always open and a great spot to meet the locals.

20 FABULOUS HAVENS INSIDE THE WALLS OF GALLE FORT

Fort Dew
22 Sri Sudharmalaya Road, by the Buddhist temple in Galle Fort Tel:0912224365
Web:www.fortdew.com **Rooms from $60-70US**

Fort Dew has some of the best views in the Fort and a gorgeous set of five rooms to suit every requirement as well. Fort Dew will be your haven in this bustling citadel. Water and premium idyllic ocean views, great WiFi and a restaurant open from 8am-11pm daily. Lonely Planet loves it!

Rampart View
37 Rampart Street, Galle Fort
Tel:0914928781
www.gallefortrampartview.com

No 37 Rampart View is a beautiful little house on the corner of Rampart Street, giving it both a view of Flag Rock, where the crazy boys throw themselves off the ramparts in elegant dives, and the guesthouse also has a small garden.

Sea Green
19b Rampart Street, Galle Fort Tel:0912242754
www.seagreen-guesthouse.com
Rooms from $50US

Sea Green guesthouse run by the enigmatic Naman Goonawardena is in a word superb. Naman will make you feel completely at home, so much so that you might never want to leave.

Deco
44 Lighthouse Street, Galle Fort
Tel:0771888829 **Web:www.decoon44.com**
Rooms from $185-325US

Deco on 44 is an experience, not just an overnight stay. True elegance in the heart of the Fort. A great swimming pool at the back and a mix of rooms.

Frangipani Motel
35 Pedlar Street, Galle Fort
Tel:0912222324
www.frangipanigallefort.com
Rooms from 4500-5500 rupees ($35-45US)

Frangipani Motel sits back from bustling Pedlar Street, a dark green towering building with an immaculate garden in the front, cabbages growing happily in the flower beds. There are 15 rooms in total tucked away inside both this house and also the smaller one just across the road, all perfectly made up and beautifully clean. Great value for the central location.

5

Fort Fifty
50 Leyn Baan Street , Galle Fort   Tel:0912248711
www.fortfiftyinn.com
Rooms from $40US (offseason) and $50US (season)

Fort Fifty is situated right in the heart of the action, in the middle of busy, exciting Leyn Baan Street, its restaurant's veranda allowing you to sit and watch as Fort life goes on around you. Step inside and you are greeted with a spacious sitting room, a great range of rooms that companies like Intrepid Travel love. Free WiFi.

Galle Heritage Villa by Jetwing
71 Lighthouse Street, Fort   Tel:0912234384
www.jetwinghotels.com

Colourful drapes hang on the walls giving it the feel of an old merchant house and the white columns that hark back to the colonial period. The four deluxe rooms are individually and beautifully decorated with expansive bathrooms. A beautifully restored house that is fully staffed with a huge kitchen that creates everything from breakfast to a snack at anytime of the day. Jetwing also provides walks and tours of the area.

6

7

Fort Bliss
84 Lighthouse Street
Tel:0912248168   www.fortblissgalle.com
Rooms from $85-120US depending on the high or low season

Fort Bliss is everything its name says it is, its bright yellow exterior not disclosing the cool, simplified interior of this colonial property. The house is long and narrow so it stretches back to Rampart Street, giving a magnificent view of the Indian Ocean and the fortress's powerful walls from the lengthy veranda that wraps around the first floor. The villa has four exquisite rooms.

8

New Old Dutch House
21 Middle Street   Tel:0912232987
www.newolddutchhouse.lk
Rooms from $80US

Situated on the corner of Middle Street, the New Old Dutch House, has excellent rooms and a courtyard restaurant that caters for its in-house guests. Tall rainbow umbrellas shelter you from the sun as you sit in the quiet of this guesthouse and simply just enjoy the silence that is one of the charms in the busy city.

9

'10

Fort Inn & Secret Palace Guest House
31 Pedlar Street & 4/2 New Lane II
Tel:0912248094
Email: rasikafortinn@yahoo.com
Rooms from $60US

Two great places to stay as family run. They are simply furnished and the perfect place to crash after a busy day exploring the Fort.

'11

Lighthouse View Inn
44 Hospital Street   Tel:0912232056
www.lighthouseviewinn.com
Rooms from $30-60US

The Lighthouse View Inn is a superb location as it has the incomparable view of the 1938 British built lighthouse if you book the front room. 4 Rooms air-conditioned and non air-conditioned.

'12

Pedlar 62
62 Pedlar Street   Tel:0773182389
www.pedlar62.com   Rooms from $75US

A large brown house stands proudly in the centre of Pedlar Street, the small white columns of the upstairs balcony glistening in the daylight, green plants wrapping themselves around the walls. It has 4 rooms with all the commodities you will so desire after a long day. The house also has a rooftop area which guests can request for a private meal, looking out over the dusty red rooftops.

Thenu Rest
12 Hospital Street
Tel:0912246608
www.thenurest.com
Great family room (for 5) is $70-75US

Opposite the busy Dutch Hospital is Thenu Rest, the three-storey house has seven rooms one of which can be altered to accommodate a family of five.

'13

51 Pedlar Street
Ring Mandis on 0779878529
Rooms from $100-120US in season

The unassuming exterior of 51 Pedlar Street disguises the extravagance of this building, and of the rooms within it. The entrance hall is open to the elements, a square grassy area providing a splash of vivid colour. Grand four poster-beds and enormous bathrooms.

'14

Fort de 19
19A Rampart Street Tel:0912223728
Email: fortde19@gmail.com
Rooms from 5500-6000 rupees ($40-45US)

Fort de 19 is an old family house that stands tall at the end of Rampart Street, its doorway slightly hidden along this picturesque street. Step inside and you find yourself in a simple sitting room, yellow sofas providing you with a spot to put your feet up and relax. Upstairs there are three rooms but there are plans afoot to convert the rest of the house into a homestay too. The top floor is a small family apartment with a large room, with separate bathroom.

'15

Pedlar's Inn Hostel
62 B Lighthouse Street
0912227443
Email: hostel@pedlarsinn.com
www.pedlarsinn.com
Rooms $12US for a four-bed dorm, $15 three-bed dorm, $60 for a private double room

Pedlar's Inn Hostel is part of the empire run by Abdul Azeez, Galle Fort's busiest man. The hostel markets itself as a youth hostel, a tall pale blue and white building that resembles a little sailing boat, hires bikes out cheaply and an old bicycle sits mounted on the wall, and it is a hub for young travellers.

'16

Mamas
67 Church Street (Small Cross Street)
Tel:0912235214 Rooms from $48-60US
Email: mamasgallefort@ymail.com

Malanee is the brains behind the super brand that is Mamas. Malanee is Mama herself and from this guesthouse she runs a cookery school and successful restaurant: Malanee's curries are legendary.

'17

Beach Haven
65 Lighthouse Street
Tel:0912234663
Rooms from 6000 rupees ($40US)

The Beach Haven is run by the formidable and friendly Mrs Wijenayake and was one of the first of its kind within the Fort. A popular spot for long stay doctors studying in the area and travellers that love their home comforts. Good deals for long stays.

Inn 64
64 Leyn Baan Street Tel:0912235142
Web:www.inn64.com
Rooms from $39-79US.
Whole house $140 per day

'19

Inn 64 sits happily in the middle of lively Leyn Baan Street, a narrow house with an upstairs veranda that affords the watcher unparalleled views of the action occurring below. A roomy sitting room with an open-air centre means that the atmosphere within the house is one of cool calm and you can take your breakfast opposite at the Serendipity Arts Cafe.

Peace & Plenty
59 Church Street   Tel: +94 91 2242734
Email: info@peacenplentyhotel.com
www.peacenplentyhotel.com
Rooms from $25US (breakfast included)

There are three rooms here and the brightly coloured hammock hangs in the corner of the main dining area creating the perfect space to have your afternoon nap in and a sanctuary in which Bob Marley tunes play continuously on the speakers. The café serves delicious snacks.

'20

CHARMING RETREATS

The Jetwing Villa collection seamlessly combines luxurious comfort with a cozy, inviting ambience for the perfect intimate getaway.

We strive to provide the ultimate and most intimate villa experience with each awe inspiring setting.

Jetwing
VILLA COLLECTION

Era Beach by Jetwing • Mosvold Villa By Jetwing
Kurulubedda by Jetwing • Galle Heritage Villa by Jetwing

www.jetwinghotels.com